Hide and Seek

A Dad's Journey from Soulless Addiction to Sole Custody

Paul Summers Jr.

Send permission requests to the publisher at:
admin@thepublishingcircle.com.
Attention: Permissions Coordinator
Regarding Paul Summers

Hide and Seek: *A Dad's Journey From Soulless Addiction to Sole Custody*

FIRST EDITION
ISBN 978-1-955018-97-5 (PAPERBACK)
ISBN 978-1-955018-31-9 (LARGE-PRINT PAPERBACK)
ISBN 978-1-955018-32-6 (HARDCOVER)
ISBN 978-1-955018-34-0 (E-BOOK)

Hide and Seek: A Dad's Journey from Soulless Addiction to Sole Custody

Paul Summers Jr.

Author's Note

The content of this memoir is true to what I believe, based on my recollection of experiences, journaling, and documentation. I have changed some names and identifying characteristics and have compressed some events, the dialogue and sequence of which might be recounted differently by others.

About the Chapter Names

My first concert was Queen in 1977. Watching Freddie Mercury prance around the stage in his checkered tights and hearing gorgeous girls scream to the scorching guitar riffs of Brian May completely seduced me. I knew what I wanted to be when I grew up and never gave up trying. Seeing the importance of reflecting on this and wanting to somehow give back, each chapter of this book is aptly named after a song. Music got me through my darkest hours, humbles me through blinding bright exaggerated moments, consoles me, and energizes me when life beats me down. All things I hope this memoir does for you.

For Lola

Preface

On a crisp October morning, an unsettling dream shook me from a deep sleep. I'd been mourning the loss of my father, who had lost his fight with prostate, lung, and metastatic cancer just thirteen days prior. For all but fourteen of his eight-one years, he smoked the cigarettes without filters. Tears glued my eyelids shut. I smeared the pools onto my pillow to avoid the burn. Contemplating the imagery I dreamed, I stared out the window by my bed.

In my dream, I was visiting a coastal town. A mysterious feeling pulled at me in every shop and on every street. It felt like someone was staring. Each time I looked around, I kept noticing the same person panhandling and rummaging through the trash. I felt a connection but couldn't understand why.

I went to sit on a bench along a boardwalk by the beach. Although the sensation of the sea breeze and seagull aroma were significant, the connection feeling was growing stronger than ever. No one was within sight. As I repositioned my body to sprawl out, my heels butted up against a soft mass.

I couldn't get a good look at whatever it was. I had to stand up first, then turn to see.

"Whoa!" I yelled.

The mass under the bench was a person, the face hidden by a hoodie. Though wrapped in protective bedding, I had a feeling this body was the same person I'd been noticing.

Amped up to blast the mass for scaring me, I stepped back when the person reacted by swiftly gathering up its belongings. The person pulled back its hoodie, exposing a young woman. Her dirty, pock-marked face was not that of just any young woman. Her face was familiar, no matter how aged and disfigured by the elements. This person was my daughter.

The pain in my heart was one of complete parental failure. Through a series of poor life choices—both hers and mine—she'd ended up here.

Upon waking, I felt incomprehensible blame. Destiny had been served. My bad choices led her to believe she wasn't worthy of a functioning, healthy life. My piss-poor, self-centered decisions caused her the same certainty mantra about herself as I had about myself—that of not belonging. Through this dream came a revelation: I *have* to write this story.

This is not just my story; it's the story of hundreds of thousands of addicts, alcoholics—any substance abusers—who are or will at some point become parents and or kids of those parents.

I believe I've been called to help families. Comprehending the disease of addiction, even if you don't agree that addiction is a disease, is a complex process to navigate. Understanding the similarities in how addicts think could prove beneficial to both you and them. The indicative symptoms of substance abuse increase and worsen over time. Whether consequences are set by a parent, judge, or drug dealer, none are stern enough to keep the addict from staying out of their own destruction. None work until the afflicted decide for themselves they are done.

The problem is partially systemic and culturally endemic. Rehabilitation rates are discouraging. I've had friends who couldn't stop after spending thousands on rehab and others who quit cold turkey. Doctors, clinicians, therapists, and psychologists can't relate to an addict or speak the language of recovery if they themselves have not experienced addiction.

I had to write this book because useful information regarding the inner thoughts of addicts is not widely available. The bulk of addiction memoirists recount the downward spiral and the mess. I've also included my sordid past, but only to show the contrast between the monstrous human I was and who I am today. The ugly truth is people die from addiction. It is my intention for this story to give hope to those who contend with this disease.

There are multiple ways to arrest addiction, but there is no known cure. I tried countless methods multiple times before hitting the bottom and finding the path told in this story. The solution that is working for me won't work for everyone.

Before you embark on this recollection, introspection, and message of hope, please join me in a moment of silence for the person who is about to get loaded for the first time.

Table of Contents

"Every great mistake has a halfway moment, a split second when it can be recalled and perhaps remedied."

—Pearl S. Buck

1

New Sensation

It's the first Sunday of August 2003. I'm kicking myself because I'm out of pain pills. I took my last two around midnight but passed out. I never felt them. Now I'm wide awake. The morning sun sends just enough intrusive light through the loose closed slats of our bedroom blinds to prevent a return to sleep. In the stillness, I'm drawn in by how each tiny, floating dust speck moves. Each in its own spontaneous, nonsensical pattern in and out of the rays. I rub my eyes, then turn closer to my wife, who's in a deep sleep.

Why is it so bright this early?

Although tired, I feel relaxed for the first time in months. I've been stressing so much, wondering how on earth I'll ever fill the shoes I need to fill. Anxiety, like a visitor who's become too comfortable to move on, resides.

I've been scrambling ever since the second pinkish-red bar magically appeared. I've been procrastinating most of the last seven months; placing on the back burner my acceptance that soon I'll need to be *that* guy—the one I've never been accused of being: a responsible provider. Jeez, man. I just want to cuddle up and return to a sweet, deep sleep.

Should've saved those pills.

Placing my right arm over my wife, I nuzzle my head into the coolness of our faded black pillowcase. My nostrils flare as I inhale long and deep. My mind drifts. But I can't float away. Each time I do, anticipation of the imminent daily fire drill jolts me.

I need to be ready. Any minute now, she'll make a frantic scurry for the bathroom. Our new normal: her flinging herself from the bed while facing toward the ceiling, gagging back, choking down the rising projectile of hormone-filled vomit. Me beside her for support, holding back her hair from drowning in bile while she defiles the porcelain throne.

With a nudge of my left knee and thigh, I inch closer. Knowing I have only a few weeks of freedom left, I try conversing through telepathy: *Please sleep in late. Just this once, for me?*

The closer I spoon, what with her heaping belly protruding, the more it registers how *not* right our flowery-pink comforter feels. It's not cool; it's wet. Desperate to stock up on sleep, I ignore it. I'd tell myself anything to be able to do nothing.

Curiosity wins. Fuck sleep. I raise my hand up off her side, steady so it won't disturb her. Then I pat the bedding down by where my calf feels moisture, hoping to confirm it's just a night sweat. No. No. The middle of our bed is soaked. I look to the ceiling as if there's an easy answer I can pull from it to solve this. Underneath the comforter, I slide my right hand up to my face.

My fingers are covered in dark, grainy, viscous fluid.

Turning somewhat to check the clock, I then jar upright into an awkward position, so as not to wake her.

Ten-thirty?

It's late. Hard to believe that just months ago this would be the hour I'd roll out of bed. That is, if I had in fact gone to sleep yet. Upon waking, I'd ruminate over anything I had to do, then decide whether or not I'd actually do the thing I had to do or something else I wanted to. Back then, I held the reins to my career. As a professional musician, I found ways to live according to my own terms.

Accustomed to living however the fuck I wanted, having to be gainfully employed with a *real* job wasn't exactly a welcome change. But I have. For the last eight months, I've played the lead part in a strange dream about a man in his thirties who isn't ready to be a grown-up.

Staring with curious intent at my wife's face, I'm again fully present. She should be awake by now. Something's off. Her skin is pale, lips slightly indigo, her breathing shallow.

Restlessness bursts out from each nerve ending with an urgency to do *something*. Stretching my arm out fully, I yank the comforter high above, then away from our bodies. A draught of rotten liver smell punches my nose. Wide-eyed, unable to blink, I gasp.

Blood. So much blood. A three-foot circle saturates the sheet. A still-moist pool excretes from under the middle of her body.

My mind and being seem separated. I shake her slightly to wake her. Physically, my limbs constrict. Mentally, my thoughts are grasping to dispense the missing familiarity and reason.

She should've been awake by now, on her knees, puking. I should be fetching her ice chips and antacids. As much as I've hated that routine, I would much rather that than *this*.

Her eyeballs roll beneath her eyelids, which are not opening. I'm tugging at her shoulder. Gradually she comes to, disoriented. With disdain in her eyes, she whispers, "What's happening?" As I help her sit up, splotchy redness flushes over her skin. She sinks back onto her pillow. I call 911.

The operator instructs me to drive my wife to the hospital immediately, claiming it'll be faster than waiting for an ambulance. I'm scrambling to remember what all we need. I clamber around naked, stuffing full the hospital bag I was supposed to have put together weeks ago.

I grab water and crackers. *Is my baby going to live? Did I somehow cause this?* The obstetrician calls. Dr. Lu asks me to hand the phone to my wife. I only hear her side of their conversation.

"I'm just really dehydrated. No. It looks like blood. Nothing more is coming out. I mean, I'm not bleeding or anything out of anywhere. Not that I can tell."

My wife nods a few times before her eyes enlarge with surprise. I whisper for her to relay what's being said. She waves her index finger to get me to stop pacing.

"You think my placenta was kicked open?"

The drive to the emergency room, the admission process—it's all a blur. During the most important day of my life, I'm unable to fend off a preoccupation with wanting to get loaded. It's like having to pee; urging the feeling to go away just makes it worse. Same as with having thoughts or concerns that I might have a drug problem—I block them out.

I've been intending to quit, especially once we knew for certain we had a kid on the way. Now I'm thinking more along the lines of waiting until after she's born. *Then I'll stop.*

I have every intention of putting my wife and child's well-being first, but I don't know how to. I've never had to care for anyone's needs but my own. Not with any consistency. At least once a day I find myself secretly hoping for a way out. An internal dialogue, spun of half-truths, spirals on and on about how I'm not ready, nor qualified, to be a dad.

I spin until I remember to remind myself I wanted this. I fantasized about how cool it would be to share my unique life experiences and crazy memories with someone who'd always be spellbound by me, by the way I am, and by my stories. I'd be the center of their universe.

I didn't expect I'd have to go through all this crap to get here, though. Birthing and breastfeeding classes, ultrasounds, OB/GYN visits. I made all the "proper" domesticated behavior changes. I cut back on gigs and asked to be full time at work. I opted for health insurance for the first time ever, benefits which, working for a small business, I'm paying dearly for. The good credit I've maintained got us into an affordable rental home. I even agreed, reluctantly, to convert my music studio into a baby room. How was I to know wanting a sidekick would turn into follow-through and responsibility up the yin-yang?

We were supposed to have three more weeks. We haven't purchased baby clothes, or a crib, or a car seat. And now we're at the hospital.

When I see my wife's face, mere minutes after the staff administers an epidural, I get jealous. Not so much of the huge needle, but envious I don't get anything to calm *my* panic of the last hour. The staff asks me to wait in the recovery room while they prepare for childbirth.

The instant the nurse calls me back to the delivery room, my drug cravings go away. I have to be strong for my wife's sake, so I suck in air to fill my diaphragm and straighten my spine to take on a selfless persona.

The doctor determines an emergency C-section is our only choice. A male nurse helps me get scrubs on, then directs me to stand beside my wife, who's covered in a large, propped-up sheet with two openings. The birthing area is dimly lit except for a bright spotlight and the headlamps worn by staff gathered in a horseshoe formation around the table. I tune in to voices speaking words I can't decipher.

I'm speechless as I watch the doctor pull a gray mass from my wife's surgically opened cavity. Then the atmosphere changes entirely. An energy field materializes, as though all present are washed over by a thick, clear gel, making us one organism. It feels like the room is being visited by, and is, in the presence of . . . God. I don't know what other term to use to describe this sense that time is standing still. With no conviction of such things, I can't explain sensing divinity. Being here is ethereal, surreal, dreamlike. Every undertaking, including thought, happens in slow motion.

The nurse nudges me with her elbow, but I don't respond. I'm here, but elsewhere, too. She nudges me again. Light laughter, followed by comments of how wide-eyed I am, breaks me from my trance. She's trying to hand me a pair of scissors. I'm too enthralled to notice. Two nurses are holding my daughter up horizontally, waiting for me to cut the umbilical cord.

I snip once, shaking, but fail to sever the sinewy cord. I snip again, hurriedly, to mask my certain feeling I've already screwed up.

"What's happening?" my wife asks. "I don't feel anything."

Looking over the sterile border at the woman I married to legitimize this improbable family, I confidently clamp down. I look to the nurse for approval. My slice releases a fountain spray of dark, bloody fluids. They splatter my cheeks, neck, chest, and surgical mask with the mother-daughter combination.

"Congratulations! You are a father."

2

Subterranean Homesick Blues

The nurses bring my baby over to a stainless-steel sink. Their movements seem rote, clinical. They hose off the phlegm and blood clot-looking thickness caked on her claylike, alien-looking body. They return to give me a hands-on demonstration about how to support her weight with one hand under her bottom and the other where her perfectly round head meets her neck. Holding my baby in my arms, I go blank. I don't know how long I'm motionless before I extend over the sterile border. I hand Lola to her mother before she's taken to the nursery. A moment of creation to cherish.

The timeless, heavenly daze in the birthing room dissipates like a buzz wearing off, making way for reality. I'm overdue for a wave of cravings to rush through me. Whether from deep in my veins or achy muscles or tired bones, from depression, or with the need to enhance celebration, the cravings always come.

We're shown to our private maternity-ward room. While my heavily sedated wife is recuperating, I sneak in a run to my dealer's shop. *I've earned my right to party, to rejoice in fatherhood. After all, she got to get high. Why can't I?*

Mikey, my dealer, gives me the "you didn't call first" face.

"Did Leann plop out that kid yet?"

"She just did, like an hour ago," I answer.

"And you're here?" he asks, his head askew. "What can I do you for?"

I place my order. He rolls a joint to commemorate—the finest buds he has. I'm not an avid pot smoker, preferring pain pills and speed, but what the hell, I'm a dad. On my return to the hospital, I pull over on a quiet side street. I'm too stoned to face the hospital staff. I space off in my van and listen to music for as long as it takes to maintain. Wow.

I tug at the bracelet around my wrist. It's my all-access pass to the maternity floor where newborns in incubators sleep and mothers, waiting for clearance to depart, rest. I enter our room, anxious about making eye contact with Leann. She's sound asleep. A catheter, two hanging bags, and EKG wires are attached to her. One bag is to replenish the blood she lost, the other, fluids. In stoned appreciation, I acknowledge just how fucking easy I have this parenting thing right now compared to her.

Just as I get comfortable, a nurse recruits me to bring my newborn back to join her mother in bed. It's time to try nursing. She escorts me to the glass-encased room full of infants who share my daughter's birthdate. My eyes are drawn right to the one with the pink-striped beany whose incubator has Summers on it.

The nurse shows me how to hold my baby properly for transporting to our room. My wife is awakened by tiny cooing sounds. I outstretch my arms to hand over our daughter.

"Hi, Lola Jaybird. I'm your mother."

Seven serendipitous words spoken in a tone I'll never forget. Tender, sweet, maternal. More so than any ever expressed by her, whether being on ecstasy experiencing nirvana, or taking repeated bong rips. I initiate eye contact, smiling while my eyes well up. I don't know what to do with this joy. It's uncomfortable.

Leann's gurney is tilted upright so the nurse can assist in teaching Lola to latch. She does her best but isn't nursing properly. I move out of the way, behind Leann. She's getting frustrated.

While they try to get Lola to feed, I pop two pills. I crush them between my teeth to get the narcotic into the bloodstream faster. The crunching is a dead giveaway. Leann's young ears tune in. She turns to give me the look, the one that says, "busted."

As the nurse picks up Lola to return her to the nursery, Leann asks if she can have anything for pain. The nurse, pointing at a chart on the wall, asks what her pain level is on a scale of one to ten. Knowing to respond by saying eight or higher to ensure being prescribed something strong immediately, she answers, "Nine, maybe ten."

"I'll be right back."

After the nurse documents medicating Leann, we're left alone. We share our different pills with each other. Soon the two of us are floating in the warm, liquid, gravity-less mist of opiate inebriation. It's the way we manage best, anymore. We don't fight, argue, or disagree when we're on pills.

~~~

One day in, and Leann is ready to go home, worn thin by the monitoring, interrupted sleep, and the nurses' suspicion of her pain level.
~~~

But the hospital can't discharge us because Lola still will not latch. The specialists (other staff call them "nipple Nazis") see to it our stay is lengthened.

Two days into complaining, a compromise is reached. Our release becomes predicated upon our purchase of a breast pump. *Let the healthcare fleecing begin.* We can't wait to be together as a family and celebrate the way *we* prefer.

Three days into fatherhood, work calls, begging me to come in. I should be flattered. I've made myself irreplaceable there due to my work ethic. I'm reluctant. I love being home with my baby. However, with ten grand in birthing bills to cover, I go in.

Fourteen straight days of prescribed opiates is enough for the physical addiction to become entrenched. When those run out, I buy up the last of my dealer's supply. Leann pleads, successfully, with the doctor to write another refill.

Twenty-one days into being parents of a newborn, we're off—running and gunning. Parenting a newborn is hard enough. Getting in the parenting groove with a monkey on your back is not making anything easier.

Before Lola is a one month old, I start ordering pills online. I'm not sure if it's legal, but I'm more afraid to risk getting busted while visiting my dealer. When a package containing a "nonnarcotic" medication from Mexico arrives, I thank the postal carrier. Leann and I wait until Lola is asleep to crush up the pills and snort them. The high is more instant and intense this way. Tonight we're letting ourselves have fun, getting our old lives back for a minute.

Many pills later, I notice the international symbol of a woman breastfeeding with a red circle and a diagonal slash through it printed on the carton. Leann sees it too, then asks, "Do you think this means not to take while breastfeeding?" She is breastfeeding. I don't answer. We both know what it means.

We're still partying when the sun is coming up the next morning. I get up to pee. From the bathroom I hear Lola make a crying sound I've never heard before.

"Is everything okay?"

No reply. The din is too weird to ignore. I stop midstream to hear more clearly. I zip up while returning to the living room. Leann is on the floor, her torso convulsing. I don't see Lola. Bubbles of foam dribble out of Leann's mouth. Her eyes are bobbling back into her head. Lola's cries are muffled. She's being crushed. I pull Leann off, then move Lola away to the safety of her fold-up day crib.

I call 911.

The operator instructs me to lift Leann up onto the couch, then set her upright on my lap. She has me talk to Leann until she comes to. After a few minutes, it works. Her body stops convulsing with as much intensity. Right as Leann opens her eyes and appears conscious, the paramedics enter. She digs her nails into my arm and looks at me as if to ask why they are in our house.

After some testing, color returns to Leann's skin. The EMT's deduce that Leann had a seizure, perhaps drug-induced. The paramedics note the mirror, straw, and lines of white powder lying in plain sight on the coffee table. At their suggestion, we to go to the hospital for further testing. There we are told the same thing. This is it. We are done with drugs.

3

Hey Nineteen

Leann and I met as coworkers at the portrait studio—a job my ex-fiancé Candy got me while we were still together.

I never took my engagement to Candy serious. One morning, on a whim, I got on my knee to propose, no ring. Later that night, I hooked up with a stranger after my out-of-town gig. Ultimatums, scruples, and commitment being toxic concepts in my world, I later had a change of heart and called it off. Though she had cheated on me too, she ended our relationship, citing my inability to commit because I wouldn't marry her.

This left me single again. I was also going through a midlife crisis. I started having recurring paternal dreams, coupled with noticing images of fatherhood, which seemed to pop up everywhere. Known for proclaiming with certainty that I'd never have children, I suddenly felt an overwhelming desire to. I could picture it.

My dad once scoffed, "Son, you're not a man until you have kids." He meant for such ludicrous comments to piss me off, as if to say he was more of a man. He likely knew I wouldn't listen any other way.

This permeating need for paternal fulfillment mystified me. I confided these unwelcome thought-hacks of nature with Lisa, a coworker my age. I admitted feeling loneliness, worried I'd never find someone to parent my own child with. She suggested I find someone younger. By telling me what a phenomenal father I'd be, she instigated enough hope to keep my parental dream from passing by.

~

I've been plotting a last-ditch effort to make it in the music business. I have the necessary tools; I just never got my big break. Virtuosity on the guitar, two self-produced CDs that sold thousands of copies, years of performing experience, pro gear, a decent singing voice—but I'd yet to try moving to a music center. Determined to etch out a name and go for it while I had nothing to lose, I made arrangements to live on a musician friend's couch in Los Angeles.

Meanwhile, Lisa was playing matchmaker. She informed me that our co-worker, Leann, who was half my age, expressed an interest. Not that I'm a magnet for young women, but I am, by trade, youthful and mature *enough* in my thinking and attitude to relate to them.

Lisa set it up for us to hang out at her house party one night. Things went better than expected, and a relationship began. Weeks afterward, Lisa threw a work party. Leann invited her parents so they could meet me in a public setting. We intentionally left out our dating status as well as lied about my age.

Why would someone so young choose me? I didn't have money, or privilege, or even a great body. She had a job, a car, and was taking college courses. I hadn't come on strong, nor manipulated my way into her heart—other than being myself.

I guess she thought me a beautiful, broken bird. She was the ever-curious coworker I could be transparent with. I held the keys to a world her naïve eyes had yet to see. I possessed special ingredients, feeding her frivolous need to be swept away.

She was the next newer, better drug for me to try. She came without baggage; no tainted history of bad men whom she failed to domesticate. I could mold her into the woman I wanted. *If only I knew what I wanted.*

Our long talks at work became a friendship, a foreign place I'd never started a relationship from. She listened when I complained passionately about being let down by everyone and everything, especially the dreams I pined for.

Then there was my drug problem.

She wanted to save me. I was good with that.

Candy continued working for the portrait studio, but at a different location. When she found out I was seeing Leann, she was furious—in part because Leann is just three years older than her daughter, whom I'd helped parent during the years we lived together. It sucked, hearing she was upset. I'd found a long-sought way out of her "couldn't be with her unless I married her" trap: Leann. Consequences are a dumb reason for not doing whatever you want. Candy soon moved away, leaving me a wiped-clean slate to soil.

In a whirlwind, Leann and I dated, moved in together, then discovered we were pregnant. Ensuring the child we were bringing into this world arrived as part of an intact family seemed a good enough reason to tie the knot. We didn't do it to please any religious or familial expectation.

Learning I'd become a dad changed me. The future suddenly mattered. Getting married was my idea, but I was afraid. Questions loomed. Would marriage mean getting a taste of the chaos and disorder I'd served others my entire life? How the hell was I going to afford to bring a kid into this world on musician's wages?

I'd been playing music for twenty years. At no point had I earned enough to set aside for a rainy day. I barely managed living paycheck to paycheck. I often worked part-time jobs to afford rent. Having a music career as my dream-come-true-someday gig, I didn't dare learn other skills to help me later in life. Doing so would show a lack of faith. In such a competitive, cutthroat biz, you either go all in or don't bother.

But I didn't want to expose my baby to this lifestyle. I was getting so burned out on living the musician life. Late nights at bars, powerfully sexy, loose women enticing me, clothes reeking of smoke or booze. Drug use. Not the future I wanted for my child. I didn't even like it for myself.

We chose to get married in Las Vegas since my family lives there. It rained on our wedding day. I didn't know if I should take that as an omen or a signal to run while I still could. Although I was scared to death, the brief sense of pride I felt in doing the right thing for once won out.

I wanted our wedding night to be special, but I knew of no way to do so without getting high on something, anything. Leann told me she wouldn't mind if I did. But she was pregnant with my child. The very least I could do was respect that.

We were in bed by ten o'clock. *Seriously?* I lay still, gazing at the blue light of the smoke detector above. My ears perked up when I overheard twentysomethings in the hallway on their way out for the evening. My thoughts swam like crazed sperm for the ovum. *Is this what married life is going to be like? Joyless? Pretending to be happy? Am I good enough to do this? I already don't like having to be responsible and accountable. This woman, this unborn child, this life of having to do, or be . . . ah, who am I kidding? I wanna get high.*

There's no preparation for the impending reality of fatherhood. More questions joined the race upstream into the effluent waters of my psyche. *Do all men go through this? Why are some more prepared to handle this? Prepared! What does that even mean? I'm not prepared for anything, let alone raising a child. I don't have a real job, I don't have a home, I don't have this, I don't have that, I don't have . . .* The boxes of life were still mostly blank.

This woman is pregnant with my child. Check. I put a ring on her finger to testify to whatever it is I believe in, and to my family, the promise I will raise this legitimate child. Check.

That was it.

Anxiety and fear reared their ugly heads like monsters poking up from the bottomless cesspool of my mental contemplations. Against my efforts to do the right thing, they stood at the sidelines yelling out defensive plays to feed my fears until I gave in, as I always do. Ever resigned to the notion I would not be good at, nor was I cut out for this life, my lies win out by looping into endless, unbreakable knots of restraint, designed to hold me back from growing up, committing, and fully understanding how often I'm behind my own demise.

The only dispensation I've ever allowed to be effective for this level of mental rape was a good bag of dope. With nothing to numb the internal dialogue, nothing to slur its discouraging banter, I was hopelessly drowning in my own reflections, seeing clearly for the first time how slim my chances were of building on the foundation of my shitty, self-serving life.

I didn't sleep on my wedding night. I could not shut off my mind-hell long enough to do so. It knocked me on my ass. I was a sleep-deprived jerk the next day, short-tempered, witless. Growing pains, I guessed. A married man.

Starting a family felt a bit defeating, like a new beginning where nothing I've acquired in all my years is of any value.

~

As Lola's first birthday approaches, the boredom of repetitive living sets in. My 11:00 am to 7:00 pm shift facilitates my staying up late searching the internet for good paying, solid positions with benefits. Money is stretched thin, even with both of us working. The path to do drugs at night opens up . . . you know, to help me focus on securing a better future. I promise Leann I'll stop if it gets out of hand.

I get a job with the Transportation Security Administration. They offer part-time hours only, but with good pay, plus government benefits—the best around. Their preemployment drug screen turns up trace amounts of opiates in my system, but they hire me anyway. Under oath, I tell them I've been prescribed opiates for restless leg syndrome.

At Lola's first birthday party and knowing I am about to embark on a new career, we celebrate extra heartily. Smack dab in the middle of hosting over twenty guests, my dealer calls. He has procured the party favors I ordered days earlier. If I want them, I have to come immediately since he is going camping. With as vague of an explanation as will work, I excuse myself from the gathering.

I eat two pills on the drive home, then set aside a couple for Leann. With artificially induced giddy excitement stemming from opiate levels rising in our bloodstreams, we light the sole candle and sing *Happy Birthday* to our one-year-old. We let Lola tear open the cake with her bare hands and mow it down unrestrained, like a wild animal.

I can't wait for everyone to leave so I can stop pretending I'm not higher than a kite. We put Lola to bed, certain she'll stay down from the sugar crash. I keep taking pills, never quite hitting that sweet spot where one rides the crest of the opiate high like an hours-long climax. I find myself chasing some fleeting apex—an imaginary, constant moving bullseye. The high I desperately want to feel again ends up becoming more like a mirage. It exists somewhere beyond the tipping point, that place where my body overdoses, rejecting each careless attempt.

4

Burning Down the House

Because I'm working two jobs, I can qualify for my first mortgage. The only way we can get preapproved for a loan we can't afford is by declaring my new employer, plus the present one, as well as padding my income earned playing music. It helps that Leann has been with the studio for five years.

House hunting is a bitch. During one of multiple house showings, we find a bottle of codeine cough syrup in the bathroom medicine cabinet and take swigs from it. We see it as a sign to make an offer. We've found our home. Once approved, I put in my notice at the photo studio.

Home becomes an area in Southeast Portland nicknamed Felony Flats—neighborhoods full of ex-convicts, drug dealers, prostitutes, an abnormally high percentage of registered sex offenders, and at least one house with two dope-fiend parents. We move in on Halloween.

Upon unpacking our final load, Leann discovered the gram of speed I'd already dipped into. I didn't ask in advance because I knew she'd say no. *It's easier to ask forgiveness than permission.* Snorting speed means being distant for days, inevitably watching porn, getting around to doing nothing planned or promised, and devouring junk food just before crashing for sixteen-plus hours. No room to be loving, tender, intimate, nurturing, or present. I might as well have christened our family abode by snorting dry ice.

Months after settling in with a new address, new employer, and an early onset of terrible twos, I book a weekend gig at Lloyds of Bandon—a hotspot nightclub on the Southern Oregon coast. I count on the long-awaited return to playing guitar as a way to rescue the massive ego I call my soul.

A reputation from past shows precedes me. Extreme drug and alcohol consumption, spontaneous nudity on stage, and uninhibited after-parties in our hotel hot tub, each incited by yours truly. *Will I be letting fans down by showing up with my wife? And my kid?*

~

Prior to crossing the Coquille River bridge on the outskirts of town, my cravings kick in, causing my drug radar to circulate. The smell of fresh fish riding the whipping winds off the wharf, greets us upon arrival. My opened lungs are assaulted by stale cigarette smoke the moment I enter the saloon door to load my gear into the club.

I approach the bar where a familiar patron, a drug dealer, sits hunched over. Tapping his shoulder, I recall the last time he sold me pills. Neither of us knew what they were. I took them anyway. Doing so left me unable to function for two days.

He's not holding. Before checking us into our room, I drive another fifty-eight miles round trip to Coos Bay to buy some pills from my reliable friend there. By the end of the night, we've already taken all the pills even though we bought enough for two days.

I'd brought some speed, but I never liked tweaking while performing. Meth flattens my personality. In a social setting, my mind races too fast to hold a conversation, relax, be funny, or focused. I always feel strangled by feeling too self-conscious.

The next night, I get paid at 2:00 am, load my gear, then go to our room to pack and leave. Leann pleads to stay, opting to leave first thing in the morning.

"And deal with Sunday drivers?" I snap. "Hell, no. If we leave now, we can be home, chillin' in our own bed. Lola's asleep anyway. What does it matter if she's in her child seat or crib?"

Sold it.

About halfway home, in predawn pitch black, I start yawning, rubbing my eyes, sloughing off sleepiness by shaking my head. Crossing the double yellow line of the winding Jason Boa Corridor Highway one too many times wakes up Leann. It's a most unsettling feeling, being pulled from REM sleep by imagined terror. That's why I always drive, even when I'm high.

"Look, I don't know if I can make it all the way back. Would it be okay if I did a little bump?"

"Ah, come on man, really? You brought that shit with you?

"Yeah. Just in case. Can I? Please, please, please?"

"Fine. But I don't want you up all day. You've gotta work tonight."

"Okay, boss."

I pull over, bopping and bouncing in place, instantly reinvigorated, ready to drive a thousand miles. Yet I hadn't even started chopping up a line. I empty half the baggie onto a CD case.

"You gonna do that much?" she asks. "Please don't."

"I'll be fine. This'll be enough." I force my words to sound calm. I grimace once the powder hits my nasal passage and slithers down the back of my throat. Seconds later, an expression of pleasure kidnaps my face.

I get back on the highway. In order to avoid an interaction with the law, I'm driving at exactly the speed limit. We stop for gas.

"How bad off do you think I'd be if I swallowed just a little of that?" Leann asks. Her voice sounds rushed with worry; her hands are fidgeting.

"Ugh. I don't know."

I don't want to share, but it might get her off my back. She'll be a hypocrite now if she gives me any crap.

"You'll be fine. Worst that can happen is you'll talk the whole ride home."

"I'm tired of being tired all the time. Okay, let's do it."

As I shake a small amount onto a torn-out section of tissue paper, a seared memory drops in on my racing brain.

~

Fifteen years ago, a different girlfriend, Bella, and I were out late. We went for a drive in the desert. She held out a mirror, straw, and finely chopped line before me. Being drunk most of the time, I tolerated her meth use. It made her horny.

I gave in to spontaneity. Snorting that first line, my eyes watered shut. It burned so bad, I had to pull over. She couldn't stop laughing. The initial burn melted the mucous membrane, sending a horrible taste incrementally down my throat. By force of will, I dipped down to whiff the rest of the small stripe up the other nostril.

We—mostly I—talked. We explored two-lane desert roads until the sun rose eight hours later, me still yakety-yakking. I felt I had discovered Ponce de León's unattainable Fountain of Youth, or at least my holy grail of self-absorption.

"I hope I don't regret turning you on to this," she said.

"Why would you?" I moved back slightly. I couldn't understand her concern.

Fast forward a year. Not after the many times friends and cops had to separate us from physical altercations. Not after smashing the mirrors and shower doors in our apartment, then taking the shards and carving her name and *fucked for good* into my chest. Not after losing two jobs due to poor attendance. Not after I put the barrel of a .22 rifle into my mouth but couldn't reach the trigger, so defiantly aimed it toward a high-rise of condos and emptied the magazine because, "If I'm going out, I'm taking out those motherfuckers who made me hate myself first." Not after totaling my pickup truck by rear-ending a parked car. Not after losing forty of my entire 150 pounds. Not even after having to move back in with my parents at age twenty-six did her words resonate.

I ran into Bella eighteen months later at a bar. Looking at me with sad, desperate eyes, she confessed, "One of my biggest regrets is turning you on to speed, seeing how much you loved it right off the bat. I'll take the guilt to my grave."

~~~
~~~

Here I am, offering the same miserable future to my wife. Twenty minutes after placing the wrapped tissue at the back of her mouth and washing it down, Leann asks for more. Twenty minutes later, more. My knuckles turn white as I grip the steering wheel, listening to her rant on and on with conversations that longed to be unlocked from her brain. *She's hooked, just like me.*

Only now does Bella's concern make sense.

We score a bag on the way home. I'm still awake by the time I start my airport security shift. Halfway through, I begin to sweat profusely. Paranoia is getting the best of me, coming in swells of chills and heartbeats speeding out of control. I run off the floor to the bathroom and vomit a gallon of thick, yellow liquid—the nutritious microwaveable mac and cheese I'd forced down to have something in my stomach because I hadn't eaten since dinner in Bandon. Out of sick time, I am forced to wallow in self-inflicted misery.

~~~

Like a weed, a disdain for my marriage and job grows, overtaking the deep gratitude of being a dad. Being present and interactive daily is exhausting. I'm handling house maintenance and laundry. I'm scouring up juice box spills and magic-erasing crayoned walls. My days are filled with potty training, baths together, naptime stories, feeding, and walks to the playground with Lola in the stroller.

I haven't been putting much effort into being a good husband. Because of the gap in our age and responsibilities, I feel I should get to skate for a while. I feel entitled to my choices and methods of escape, for I have lived. Been here, done this. Your turn.

I'm stuffing down resentments over Leann's carelessness with our finances. How many times can you overdraw a bank account buying
~~~

cigarettes or fancy coffee? The final straw drops the day she quits working to be a "stay at home mom", which really means full-time pothead.

Yet, who am I to judge? I'm a functioning dope fiend who chooses to avoid setting boundaries lest some be set on me. When I told myself her daily marijuana use was not that big of a deal, I was being fake. Pretending to be open-minded instead of open and honest is easier than confrontation.

Now I begrudge her. I carry guilt. She's become a reflection, hooked on my drugs of choice. I have to share.

Our dependency on pills is growing as fast as our debt. I need pain relief to ward off the withdrawals that come when I run out of pain relief. My solution is breaking me, yet I can't stop. I keep telling myself I'll find a way out . . . just one more pill to help me figure it out.

~

Loading travel bags and suitcases into an X-ray machine takes a toll on limbs. But it's costly to keep re-upping via the dope man. In a heated discussion over dinner, we conclude, "After this bottle of pills, we're done."

The entire bottle is empty by 8:00 pm.

Vomiting for the next seven hours, I seek relief. Hair of the dog. Unable to find anyone holding, I blame my wife in the most unkind ways imaginable, then sleep through the next day. Every few hours I'm awakened briefly to fits of anger mixed with fears of withdrawals. Every cell of my being aches.

Studies have shown how the human brain is capable of manufacturing pain. Pain that is not, in reality, being experienced. A culmination of stressors like anxiety, depression, and emotional duress can cause physical or cognitive symptoms. The brain releases cortisol, which can cause inflammation in areas of the body not requiring it. I don't know which thoughts to trust.

By afternoon, my stomach churns. I get diarrhea, a sign I'll be going through a premature onset of horrible withdrawals. Around 11:00 pm, moaning with aggravation, I beg Leann to accompany me to the hospital. This means we have to wake up Lola from her crib, dress her, carry her out to the car and strap her into her car seat. We take two cars so the ER staff will think I have a ride. All for Daddy's little drug fix.

Even with two consistent drug dealers, I don't mind "doctor shopping" to get more. Dignity is a thing of the past. I've faked accidents and pretended to have fallen or twisted an appendage. Anything to get "relief."

For this visit, I cover every imaginable base to get the hookup I crave to counteract being dope sick. I've even brought a stool sample to "prove" a stomach malaise. My feces looked unnatural earlier, so I shit into a baggie at home. I brought it to show the doctor, hoping to add validity to my unexplainable cramps needing to be pain managed.

"That's gross," he says.

He asks what I believe is causing problems. I concoct a story of how it might be work related.

"I'm enduring a dull, persistent pain from repetitive motion," I bullshit, smiling inside at how my creative brain never fails to come up with greatness on the fly.

"Great! We'll start a workman's comp claim." He sounds relieved.

Because I'm a government employee, this would entail a mountain of paperwork. I adapt my story that instant, outright refusing the option to file a claim. I know damn well workman's comp will ask for a specific incident to move forward.

His gaze cuts into me. He's onto me—this junkie's trying to work a script. With an unwavering tone and ridged demeanor, he directs me to wait on a cot in the examination area while his team discusses my triage plan. I lay there for over five hours. I refuse to be released until they prescribe something strong for the "intense" pain.

This becomes a battle of wills. My wily, drug-seeking mind thinks long term. If I give up on acquiring pain relief, it will prove I'm faking an illness. Once proven fraudulent, future chances of getting narcotics could be compromised.

At 6:00 am, I'm discharged with two sample packets of a nonnarcotic pain reliever and a prescription for six Tylenol with Codeine #3s. What an insult. My tolerance being what it is, this is barely enough for a buzz.

While waiting for the pharmacy to open, I have regrets. Not for dragging my family through these exhaustive drug searches, but for having to share my hard-earned loot. For as long as Leann and I are using together, I'll only get to enjoy half of what's available. Likewise, if I keep purchasing more, we'll go broke. I don't like the idea of either. Plots to hoard, sneak, and lie cross my mind.

5

Please, Please, Please, Let Me Get What I Want

The difference between a rat on a wheel and a working-class adult is that the rat doesn't know when it's fallen behind.

For the second month in a row, I have to make our mortgage payment with a credit card so we don't lose our home. Any hope of being caught up financially long enough to think straight is depleting. I used to laugh when someone said, "I'm so broke I can't even pay attention." Not anymore.

I've been putting out feelers for better-paying employment, but responses are taking forever. Ever resourceful, I beg the photo studio manager to hire me back part time. She offers a few hours a week.

It's not long before I show up late after being up all night. Still tweaking, I'm antisocial, unwilling to put on the mask of professionalism. During a mad rush of customers, my coworker calls me up front.

Instead of helping, I hide in the bathroom and succumb to lizard brain—obsessing about sexual fantasies, paranoid delusions, and a relentless hankering for more drugs. It infiltrates my hazy efforts to be a decent human being. Without saying a word, I walk out.

Somehow I reclaim enough wherewithal to stop at my dealer's. Then home to the solitude of my bed. I continue getting loaded while Lola plays with her mom, who intermittently runs upstairs to take bong hits.

The feelers I put out months ago finally pay off, landing me a job as an academic advisor for an online university. No more TSA. No more rifling through bags for drugs—er, I mean, threats to our nation's security. No more military hierarchy—ranks I'll never rise within anyway, given my civilian background. No more physical exertion.

With our bank account empty and a mortgage payment due, I cash out my TSA retirement, taking a substantial taxable hit. We spend my distribution on pills.

I soon discover the university advisor position is a boiler room sales job, cutthroat, dog-eat-dog, swim or die. My first month's sales are top-ten stellar, which turns out to be beginner's luck. Soon, the pressure of seeing my name hover around the bottom producers month after month proves unbearable.

One gray morning, I'm sitting at my cubicle making endless cold calls to reach quota. I've been hung up on a hundred times before noon. Then, out of unknown depths, a determined sadness emerges. My surroundings feel colorless, my thoughts deadpan. I'm despondent. Tears pool on my eyelashes before escaping onto my cheeks.

I speed-walk out the door, circle the parking lot twice on foot, then get in my van and drive around. Keeping in close proximity to the office building, I fear spinning out of orbit if I venture too far off. I return to the lot, but am unable to get out of my van and go in. Some force field of apathy immobilizes me.

My boss calls to see if I am okay. I try explaining what I am going through, but without understanding it myself, I jumble words. He keeps repeating, "Just come in and we'll talk about it. Everything will be okay."

I accept, trusting he might understand.

Walking through those doors, feelings flood over me like those a demon might confront entering a church. Everyone is staring. A hissing in my ears deafens me as I wind through the cubicle maze to his office.

He shuts the door behind me, then closes the blinds.

I wilt the second my butt hits the chair in front of his desk. Through unrestrained sobbing, I relay how terrible my life is: a failing marriage, floundering finances, the insane drowning feeling and gripping fear of rejection I get by having to make one more cold call.

"Is there anything positive you can think of?" he asks.

"My daughter, Lola."

"What would your daughter think if she saw you right now? Do it for her, man. Take the rest of the day off. Come back tomorrow refreshed."

As I'm driving home, squinting to see through dried-out eyeballs, I have an epiphany. Grateful for having a brain that excels at solving problems, I ask myself: *When times get tough, what keeps me grounded? Duh. Pills. If I get them more regularly and don't share them equally, I won't have to worry about falling apart totally.*

I call around. No one local is carrying. My reliable friend in Coos Bay returns my call, so off the three of us go. The excitement of knowing we are promised pills makes the drive bearable. The same enthusiasm is not shared coming back. Eight hours on the road to split just four Vicodin.

On the way back, we stop at the Coos County Fair to give Lola a break from her car seat. I win her a poster—the first time I've ever won anything anywhere. On one hour of sleep, I return to work, momentarily cured. *It's settled. My problem isn't pills, running out of them is.*

Desperate for a conveyor belt of pills to feed my insatiable cravings, I sign up for a sleep study after hearing about a doctor prescribing opiates as a panacea for sleeplessness. They deny my participation in the study but prescribe Ambien, which I try after a weeklong bout with insomnia.

Leann informs me the next morning I sleepwalked in the middle of the night. With bugged-out eyes, she said, I made a bowl of cereal, turned the tv on, and lay down on the floor to eat. Minutes later, my head dropped into the bowl. I started asphyxiating, blowing bubbles in the milk.

Other doctor-shopping visits turn up psychotropic meds, muscle relaxers, and benzodiazepines. None offer what I'm after—the warm, orgasmic bliss I get from opioids. I don't want to get numb. I want to "feel" life. I'm raising a kid. For God's sake, why would I not want to feel?

I spend hours searching websites for any swindle known to help score dope. Claiming to have severe, chronic, debilitating restless leg syndrome, I see a new doctor. Presuming I'll help her make an informed decision by providing documented proof, I bring in printed out research by a clinician who is having measurable success curing RLS with opiates.

Instead of being persuaded, the doc sends me home with Neurontin, a medication for Parkinson's. It gives me violent thoughts. My medicine cabinet is a micro-pharmacy; Xanax, Valium, Soma, Flexeril, Norflex, Topomax, etodolac, Torodol, 'azepams, and 'azepines. Everything but opiates for pain—or, in my case, pleasure.

Infuriated by not getting what I want, I punch a fist-sized hole into the plaster wall of our 1920s bungalow. Of course, with a freshly bruised hand and sharp wrist pain, I am able to get a script filled.

~

I'm pushing against the walls closing in. Blaming my unemployed wife for not staying busy or my stressful job for not paying enough doesn't let off enough steam. I ponder going back to drinking again. Not once, in over a decade of illicit drug use, have I returned to my original vice of choice: alcohol. Doing so would mean dumping eleven years of abstinence down the drain. Leann is dead set against it. She has never seen me drunk. My drunken war stories scare the shit out of her. She prefers I keep my sobriety streak going. I couldn't care less. With booze, at least there's no withdrawal.

One cold, rain-blasted winter night, I sit in on a gig at a bar with my party buddy, Danny Boy. I'm playing okay, considering I'm a few days into being out of pills. Performing helps keep my mind off withdrawing.

A receptive crowd hangs out past midnight. A fan sends the cute waitress up onstage with a round of shots of my favorite whiskey. She's irresistible.

"Fuck it."

Decision made. To my lips she goes. *I got this.* Like a toilet flushing, the stinky whiskey swirls south for my bloodstream, emptying into it a warm longed-for familiar embrace.

"I thought you didn't drink, PSJ?" DB asks.

"I do now."

I hear the defiance in my response. Spoken by an old, familiar craving clawing up from depths nearly forgotten. Fear grips me. What if I can't ignore my insistent internal dialogue of "have another, and another?"

I resist taking sides in the arguments in my head that defend the sides I take.

I am not getting drunk! I'm doing this to get level. I swallow, hoping to shut off the voices. *That's it. Just one.* My brainwaves resemble a steely ball tossed in sideways on a Newton's cradle—snarled, misplaced momentum. They ricochet in all directions.

The bar is closing down. *Just one more.* I wobble toward the bathroom. DB is in the stall with his buddy Shawn. I hear them snort something, so ask to indulge.

"These are OxyContins, PSJ. I don't think you wanna get started down this path."

When I hear the word *don't,* I take it as an invitation. I finagle my way into trying some.

If speed is God, this drug is Mother Nature, courted to be Mrs. God. At forty bucks a pill, I scoff at buying one. Twenty minutes later, I hand DB the forty bucks I earned from the gig. I bring the pill home to split with Leann. Misery loves enlightenment. *Welcome to a higher class of drug abuse.*

~

Danny Boy's steady prescription refill provides us a trifecta of reliable dope sources, locking us further into a whirlwind drug frenzy. There's a catch: figuring out how to maintain when wells run dry. We manage that monkey with speed. It's always available. Until we hit an extended dry patch.

On the second day, I decide we're all going out for dinner. Impulsivity helps take my mind off the withdrawals. I'm driving without deciding first where to eat. In an innocent tone I say, "Oh, look, we're right by DB's, we might as well stop in and say hi real quick."

Leann smiles. She's been trying DB's phone. It's disconnected. We knock on the garage door. The aroma of stale piss greets us as it rolls up. There's a foam pad, blanket, candle, and a few books on the concrete floor where he stays. DB looks pale, sweaty, and sullen. He's jonesing, too. He is out of Oxys but can get heroin. We need to decide now, since he has to use his landlord's landline to call his cartel connections before they get here.

It would save us money to go for the black tar. Leann and I get in the van to discuss it. Neither of us have tried heroin. We labor in indecision. We're double-parked with a hungry kid kicking in her car seat while DB paces and stares.

Heroin?

You can't deny you're a junkie once you start shooting heroin or meth, or smoking crack. Lola's kicking expedites our decision. I drive away before we give in. Empty-handed. We choose, for now, to keep putting on the face of good parents, managing to just say no to going down heroin's dark road, even though it leads in the same direction our lives are heading.

Hours pass. The unfulfilled need grates on my nerves. Dejected. I'm strangled by my obsession to use. I've held my head down since we got home. I wish I could quit. I just want to die.

An hour later, my other dealer calls. He scored some pills from a client who traded them for meth. Eureka! Life is wonderful. *Just this last score, then I'll figure out how to get off drugs.*

For months on end, a consistent supply becomes available, including my new qualifier, OxyContin. It's the perfect drug for titrating down after being up for days. If only the jones wasn't so intense. *Why is it when I'm dying to get high, I feel like shit until I do? But when I'm feeling like shit for how much I get high, the only way to not feel like shit is to do more?*

I have no choice. I keep giving in. No matter how much dope I do, there's never enough to bury the awful fear that this glorious run will one day end. So I do as much as I can.

They say the things we fear the most we attract. My sources dry up. I'm unable to score and unable to quit. In a panic, I burn through the last of our stash. Fuck stretching it out or making it last. After being up for days, I crash for twenty straight hours. When you've just watched the sun rise and set three times in a blink, you tend to dread its return.

It hurts to get out of bed. Instead of greeting the day, I get up only to satisfy a need to move in *some* direction. In loud, clunky steps, I lurch toward the kitchen to pour a bowl of cereal, then go right back to my room. I'm unable to sleep and unable to stay awake. If the house were burning down, I'd see myself going down with it as a merciful gift.

I never wanted to live the way I'm living. Since I can't be someone else, suicide, I conclude, is the most appealing option. If only I had the courage to follow through with it. When I look in the mirror, I see a carcass—a worthless strung out nothing.

No powerful infatuation or desire, no compliment or words of motivation or aspiration, not even drug-scoring excitement—nothing can convince me my life is worth prolonging. Not that anyone's going to bother trying.

I'm steeped in contemplation, sunk in this sullen stew, when Lola comes to the doorway of my room, peeking in to check on me. I fake a smile, knowing damn well it won't cover what I'm plotting.

However, kids *feel* things. I was born with an oversensitivity about and insight into this, though I can't provide tangible evidence to support my perceptions. Since toddlers cannot yet communicate like adults do, they rely on a variety of impressions (beyond identifying postures and gestures) to comprehend what's happening around them. Because two-year-old Lola and I have such a strong bond, I believe she *feels* my dire state. I discern how her empathy is affecting her. She's feeling, then internalizing, *my* inner pain and melancholy. Unable to show indifference to it, she blames herself for it. She does this to protect *me*.

I sense unnatural fears growing inside her—mine. This prods me to dig deep. Pull together every fiber of strength I think I don't have.

For two-and-a-half hours, I'm paralyzed. Lying flat on my stomach, deliberating over every single movement, including breaths, I contemplate. Then, in one numb burst of physical fury, I throw off my covers. I sling myself off the bed, then yank my queen-size mattress off its frame. I must do this action without thinking, or else I won't.

Pores break into a cold sweat as I push, tug, and drag the bed through the house to our living room. Relocating the mattress among our other mismatched furniture, my pasty, limp limbs flop over on top of it. My eyesight fades.

Hours later, I slide out of deep slumber to find Lola playing next to me, happy as ever. Daddy is okay. Though my muscles feel crippled, my blood drunk with depression's lethargy, I can feign happy play-time long enough for her to stop worrying.

At bedtime, Leann brings Lola to her crib, then joins me. I revert to advertising how much I hate my life. This goes on for three days.

6

My Prerogative

"Suicide Hotline, this is Mandy. Can I get your first name?"

"Sure," I answer, ready to hang up. *Maybe I'll use a fake name. This is stupid. Fuck it.* "Paul."

"Hi, Paul. Tell me a little about what's going on."

Since the day I had a nervous breakdown in front of my boss, this is the first—and only—time I recall anyone showing genuine concern for my well-being. *She's paid to.* Mandy's question should be simple to answer. But it releases a flood of relived disturbing thoughts and counter-thoughts; baited hooks fishing for an awareness of how I got to where I am now. *What does she expect me to admit?*

"I feel like everything I do is for someone else."

"Is it hard for you to tell people no?" Set boundaries?" she asks.

Boundaries? Not how I'm hard-wired. I'm a people pleaser. Give you what I think you want first, so you'll feel obligated to be kind. In return, you'll give me what I really want from you—which, by the way, is never clearly stated.

Nondisclosure, ambiguousness. These have served as my safety net from having to be direct. My personal style of hostage taking. *My flair.*

Convinced you'll discard me once you get to know me, I find ways to charm you into submission first. As ransom, all I ask is that you stick by my side, accept me more than I do myself, and tolerate my unpredictable, rebellious dissension, no matter what. Knowing I'm fallible, I expect you to meet my expectations. I'm not even sure why.

Enter stage left my rebellious side. It despises the people pleaser. I never know which side is the *real* me. The entire spectrum is never revealed all at once. Yet, because I do have a conscience, I suppress or disguise the rebel side.

My rebel side is unapologetic. It comes out after a boundary no one knew existed is crossed, in some cases for the second or third time. Unpredictable. The rebel is cruel, owns no concept of accountability, is deceptive, and is diligent at undermining everyone around. The rebel is an opposite, a stark contrast from the personality I display daily. When it surfaces, it is adept at pointing blame and creating problems without any desire whatsoever to see solutions. The rebel wants to rub your nose in dog shit so aggressively you'll never be comfortable shitting again.

Internal conflict arises when the people pleaser, seeking acceptance, tells the rebel how tempestuous its behavior is and that it must stop. The rebel responds by making matters worse. It's a cycle of viciousness and devotion, provocative passion, and emotional erosion. Stuck in this conundrum, unable to find resolve, I engage the hotline counselor.

"Well, Mandy. Honestly, I . . . I don't want to go on living. The only reason I feel any need to stay alive is because I don't want my little girl to grow up without her daddy."

"Go on."

"Lately, I've been praying for God to take my life. No one cares about how I'm doing—I mean, how I'm *really* doing. Everyone wants me to be something I'm not. I put on fake faces for my wife, my parents, my boss, even my kid. The sacrifices I'm making. The anguish of living . . . no one knows or even wants to know who I really am or how I truly feel."

"Why do you suppose that is?"

"Because. Why bother telling someone the truth who doesn't want to hear it? It's too much for them to handle."

I'm feeling only drab, colorless emotions. I don't want to speak the truth, not even my own.

"There's something wrong with everything I do, something bad about everything that matters. I shouldn't be alive," I say.

"Let me ask you a question. Are there any issues with drugs or alcohol?" she asks.

My hesitation to respond probably answers her question. More energy has been spent hiding the extent to which drugs have taken over than on anything else. I can't function without getting high. For as long as the desire has been there, I've been dumbfounded as to why I can't just stop. My inability to come up with a way to do so on my own baffles me. I use even when I tell myself I won't, which has led me to believe I can't trust myself with anything. Still, I'm afraid to let Mandy know too much.

"Can I read you parts of something from my journal I wrote a few weeks ago?"

"Of course."

~

Valentine's Day. 3:05 am

I feel so stifled by the thought just before I begin to write that I must come up with something profound or sublime—NOT GOING TO HAPPEN! This is just one of those things that absolutely must come out.

I'D SAY I'M DEPRESSED BUT I'M PAST THAT. MAYBE SUICIDAL. BUT THAT'S NOT A POSSIBLE REALITY EITHER. INSTEAD OF DEFINING IT, I'LL DESCRIBE IT!

I'm wanting to be high all the time on anything, really, just don't want to be straight, don't want to take on any challenge, don't feel positive results have any necessity, don't feel positive gains have any longevity, don't feel positive goals have any chance.

It's like, why work out, why diet, why learn computer programs, why fix the house, why be romantic, why try for a better job, why be straight at work, why be respectful of myself, why get excited about my marriage's future?

AND THEN THE OFF-CENTER WHYS . . .

Why bother writing this out, why am I still playing music, why BELIEVE in anything, why pray, why be patient, why not continue to take drugs, why not go totally broke and lose the house and job doing so, why trust Leann to be a savior, why fantasize that I'll just come to my senses one day because of my duty to family (Lola), why did I ever think I was going to be important, rich, famous, respected, why do the behaviors that have gotten me in this position become more attractive the deeper in debt I become?

I COULD GO ON MUCH, MUCH LONGER.

It's like my past haunts me as much as my flushing present. All those years of knowing how bad drugs were for me, but I NEVER QUIT. I always went/fell back. How the fuck did I quit drinking? Wouldn't it be smarter to just do that? What about the times I quit for a substantial period of time? Those haunt me too. Like, what good did it do to quit?

What did I gain/progress? NOTHING.

What about the SELF-HELP BOOKS?

What about the DAYDREAMS of being an author?

What about wanting to help OTHERS through books?

What about the intense love I once felt?

What about being so excited about this house?

What about being so excited about this job?

What about planning for the future for our child?

What about planning for the future for our family?

What about planning for the future for our JOY?

So much work went into making all these ducks line up pretty and neat in their little row called the American Dream. And WE DID IT. We achieved the unthinkable. Two people who barely surpass $30K and we're able to have a baby, buy a $140K house, and have an abundance of things.

ALL OF THIS

All of this and I feel life leave me with every breath I take. Pills are the only thing that makes me feel good enough to get through the day.

ALL OF THIS

And I feel I'm choking on a house payment. I feel like everyone is out to fuck me—or putting it less paranoid sounding, I feel like as obvious as this hardship is for me, NOBODY (except my parents and bro) can be counted on to lift a finger, or to make me feel better.

ALL OF THIS

I pay for all of this. I'm covering all the bills, and as we slide recklessly into deep debt, Leann overdraws our checking account.

But when I confront her and steal from the deepest compassionate bones I have left in myself, she flirts. She puts on this teary-eyed, red-faced "I'm sorry" that means something for about ten hours, maybe days, but is sure to happen again.

ALL OF THIS.

But I plod on, thinking it's gonna get better in time, but time is proving that it's getting worse. And getting high is the only way I can tolerate that I work five nights a week, and single-handedly watch Lola three days a week, and clean up after Leann six days a week, and pay all the bills and deal with all the outside world, and pay the medical insurance she misses appointments for, and the stress gets to be sooo much, but she's asleep when I get home from work so I can't get any attention, and usually she sleeps through Lola waking in the a.m. So, I'm just generally dissatisfied.

I really thought I married a sensitive, affectionate, progressive being. But I now believe I have a resentful, immature, wanna-be rebellious, self-centered young woman who has declined so far below her potential, while I may seriously destroy myself trying to become something at forty-two.

I HATE BEING ALIVE.

IF NOT FOR LOLA

4:00 am. I'm going to go pay late bills now. I hope I don't wake my wife.

~

"To answer your question, yes. I take a lot of drugs."

I exhale, relieved to speak words of transparency without fear of being persecuted or reprimanded or worse. I want to get better. I've never tried being honest.

"Paul, I think you should seek help in the form of inpatient rehab."

"That won't work. I can't be away from my daughter. There's got to be something else."

"Sounds like you could really use some time away to get well. Rehab will provide the space and bandwidth to deal with your outlook healthily. Wouldn't you agree getting well is the best thing you could do for your family, for your daughter? I strongly suggest you take this opportunity, Paul. I see here you have insurance coverage. What do you think?"

No, no. No! my brain screams. My internal lie factory spits out an overrun of product: *I made it sound worse than it is. I'm fine. I'll figure out how to manage. I was just being melodramatic. I'm better now. I don't really have a problem. Besides, if I go to rehab, my family will fall apart. Lola will miss me. Let me take another shot at getting this under control.*

Ever defiant, I refuse her recommendation for inpatient rehab. I do, however, check myself into an outpatient program the next day. This is my way of committing to rehab on my terms . . . which is to do the minimal.

My first task at the clinic is to fill out a lengthy drug history questionnaire. I turn it into a fun assignment, recalling the times and ways I used. Having the best intentions, I believe my honesty will help them help me.

I describe my dope history in glorified detail. It feels good, like my past is worth bragging about. Exulting in my tarnished suit of armor, I hand my form over to the receptionist.

Rehab isn't run according to my terms. Through their intake process, I naïvely offered up a firsthand account of two drug addicts raising a toddler together. I'm assigned a counselor. A rough-on-the-edges guy who gets belligerent when I try downplaying the safety risks of my behaviors. He "forces" me to notify Child Protective Services. He dials their number, then hands me the phone so I will self-report in front of him. *Total guilt trip.*

CPS doesn't seem too concerned. A truly negligent parent wouldn't own up to it, especially from a rehab clinic. One thing comes from making that call: I lose trust in the state-run commercial rehab process and seek only to protect myself from engaging with the system.

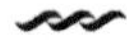

During group therapy, my rehab counselor, Andy, suggests everyone attend twelve-step meetings. I pick the program that focuses on narcotics. He hands me a meeting schedule and a slip. I'll need to get it signed each time I attend.

I'm driving to my first meeting ever when I remember the time I called their anonymous hotline number. I suspected having a problem with opiates. I must've been somewhere along the slope of being desperate enough to do something about it.

The hotline volunteer had strongly recommended I get my ass to a meeting.

"But I'm not a drug addict," I had insisted, adding, "Can't you just tell me how to stop popping pills?"

He laughed, then repeated his recommendation.

"Look. I don't belong in a room with a bunch of derelict junkies," I said before hanging up. At the time, I thought, *I can see right through this pitch.*

This time is different. I've admitted wanting help. I pass through the doors of my first meeting feeling skeptical, hardly willing nor open-minded, yet anxious for assistance. I sit in the front with my arms folded.

The person chairing asks, "Is anyone here for their first, second, or third meeting?"

I won't succeed at this staying clean thing unless I push myself to take part. With a mix of enthusiasm and reservation, I raise my hand. He signals me to come up in front of everyone to welcome me. He asks for my first name, then hands me a little white key tag, followed by a firm, warm hug. Everyone applauds. I sit back down, perplexed. Why are they rewarding me for being a loser, a fuckup, a leach to society?

This kind of acknowledgment feels good. A departure from my brokenness. As often as I lined my dealers' pockets with money, I don't recall any of them being so happy to see me that they clapped.

I'm surprised at how diverse the members are. Each person who shares their recovery story speaks in a plain truth language I feel I've spoken my entire life. For the first time—maybe ever—without substances, I feel at ease. My head isn't somewhere else. I have finally found people like me.

At the second meeting, I introduce myself confidently.

"Hi. I'm Paul. I'm an addict alcoholic."

Making this declaration aloud triggers an epiphany. I don't have to go on thinking I'm predestined for solitary confinement anymore. I've always felt uniquely different, as if from another planet. I can feel alone in a crowded room. By attending meetings, I'm connecting with humanity, getting plugged in.

~

My parents' fiftieth wedding anniversary celebration in Las Vegas occurs as I near thirty days clean. Andy advises against going, but I go anyway. There is no way I would miss my parents' milestone. My family already thinks low enough of me.

Andy, it turns out, is right. Being around family at such a fragile point proves too difficult. Because I made it there, I want to boast, "You can trust me now. I've changed. I won't be doing anything stupid tonight that I'll need to apologize for tomorrow." But I know they'd shake their heads in disbelief. They've heard my half-truths and best intentions play infinitely, like a lame song stuck in your head.

All it takes is a few inquiries from my family about my "plans," asked in the usual derogatory you'll-never-be-good-enough tone, and I'm floundering. I end up at the bar, sucking down whiskey and sodas. Sissy drinks, according to my dad.

I'm determined to bury my self-loathing alongside my guilt. Earlier in the evening, I promised my Uncle John I'd be his sober buddy. Alcoholics Anonymous saved his life. He has forty years of sobriety and an unbreakable bond with his daughter to show for it. My change of heart leaves him as the only adult there not buzzed. When he sees the drink in my hand, he doesn't express disappointment. I interpret his graciousness as some mental trick to get me to feel like crap; I'm that self-centered. Amidst loving family celebrating a truly remarkable anniversary, I can't wait to be home.

~

Staying the drug-free course brings a semblance of normalcy into our home. Lola wants to play more and talk again. I believe she's okay because I'm okay. My kid *feels* my energy. She's picking up on the vibe I'm putting off. She understands down to her marrow that I'm substance-free. I know this by making a comparison.

Some months ago, I was up all night on a cocaine bender. The next day, I was home alone with Lola. I had run so far off the rails from bingeing, I was unable to vibe with her emotionally or spiritually. She *felt* my distance. From her crib, she kept holding out her arms and she wouldn't stop crying. When I picked her up to hold her, I must've felt like a clay dad. It frightened her.

Remembering that day and her reaction to my being in that mindless, *non compos mentis* madness, I'm having a gut feeling. I must prove our connection isn't severed, so her mind will be at ease. She doesn't know the difference between me being distant because I'm loaded or because I'm depressed. Since most toddlers don't possess the ability to explain their deep feelings using adult words, they express themselves through other means. An adult would need to be extremely attentive to pick up on these expressions. Let's just say, as an overly sensitive person whose awareness is often heightened by illicit stimulants, I pay a *lot* of attention.

One morning, Lola and I play this made-up game. We start out about ten feet apart, crouched down on all fours like animals. We're not allowed to blink. Glaring wide into each other's eyes, we crawl toward one another. I stop when our foreheads bump, but she continues pushing hers into mine.

"I see you, Daddy," she says.

"I see you," I reply.

In the lightest of moments, there's something heavy about her glaring. I feel her searching the vitreous depths of my eyes for validation. For reassurance that I'm here, that I'm me. It is satisfying to know that, because I'm drug free, she'll find clarity. If only I could relieve her psyche of the burden, permanently fix the past by promising accountability in the future. Our still-held eye-to-eye contact unveils an opening into each other's soul.

"I see you."

We repeat until we fall over laughing.

~

I still attend meetings, claiming continuous sobriety as if I hadn't relapsed at my parents' anniversary. "Alcohol's not my drug of choice," I reason. I take my sixty-days-clean key tag, knowing I'm not being truthful. The ease at which I'm able to pretend and vault away my dishonesty weighs on my mind.

I string together enough time clean to pass a random drug test for rehab. I can't wait for the results to come back so I can quit going. The minute the lab results come back, I give notice—my voluntary departure from the program I voluntarily signed up for. Whatever is broken inside me wastes no time reminding me how adept I am at denying, rationalizing, and blaming all my problems away.

Free to use again.

Not so fast. I want to stay clean; I really do. I like meetings.

One afternoon I bring Lola along. No daycare person is available. Lola is in a rambunctious mood, competing for my attention. I can't focus on each person's message. The noise in my head splinters it in too many directions.

Whenever I'm this overwhelmed, it's like an open invitation for self-will to corral and control my thoughts. A switch flicks off. God doesn't want me in recovery. *If I've been able to quit this long, maybe I don't have a problem.*

A phone call to my dealer from the bathroom seals the deal. I walk out mid-meeting, then drive straight over to score. My streak of sixty-four days without drugs (aside from alcohol) ends.

~

Instead of starting the summer poised to enjoy outdoor functions, my world is comprised of indoor isolation, infinite drug combinations to cop a sustainable high, and inconsistent attendance at the online university job. Courtesy of my stint in rehab, I have a disability pass at my disposal. Sick leave can't be disputed.

Eventually I lose interest in showing up altogether. I resign, blaming it on stress and pressure. Burned out by the rat race, I step off the hamster wheel without a plan in place.

We decide to put our house up for sale. It's either that or lose it to imminent foreclosure. There are no certainties when in a daily drug haze, not even to commitments of security, safety, and shelter.

A sneaky suspicion that we're making a bad decision stays with me. We've distanced ourselves from family and friends. No one is left to ask us what the hell we are thinking.

The months of waiting in limbo for the house to sell leads to drastic measures. To make ends meet, aka feed our habit, I sell most of my music gear, including studio master recordings on two-inch reels. I shrug my shoulders at making such a final decision to fix a temporary financial problem. I tell myself the disposing of old relics will provide a clean-slate opportunity to start over. I believe myself so invincible that I'm entitled to an endless supply of do-overs. You know, because my head *never* lies to me.

A below-asking-price offer is made on the house. We can't refuse. The amount we will receive in equity at closing will be substantial. We have less than two weeks to find a place to move.

By lying about how much I make playing music, we're approved for an apartment without either of us being employed—a continued benefit from all the years I laboriously kept a stellar credit rating, even throughout the poverty of being a starving artist.

On Halloween day, exactly two years after moving in, we're out of our first home. Putting our dreamed-up life behind us, emptied of hope, filled with ghosts, and haunted by recurring nightmares of addiction. Instead of staying put to look at why we keep damaging the things that matter most, moving is our way of fixing them.

I have a lot of experience moving. I pack everything but our washing machine into the moving van in one load. It gets left out front. When we return a few hours later, the copper water connection has been hacksawed off.

"Fucking tweakers. If I ever get this desperate for drug money, kill me," I tell Leann.

"I won't have to. You'll already be dead," she answers.

We choose an apartment close to Leann's family in Beaverton. Closer to our most reliable babysitters, Grandma Carol and Aunt Darcy. No more long drives across town. Since Lola was born, I've made that eighteen-mile drive so many times I could do it in my sleep.

~

Last year, I had to take a knowledge test for TSA. It was being given outside my usual shift hours, so I needed Grandma Carol to watch Lola. I had snorted too many Oxys the night before and was nodding off while driving. I slapped my face to stay coherent.

The bumps in the road woke me. Driving by braille. Just as my minivan scraped the concrete median, a car honked to warn me I was drifting. The honking startled me back to a state of consciousness. I flipped him off.

I checked myself in the mirror. My pupils were tiny dots surrounded by red webs. A bluish tint had replaced the pink in my thin, dehydrated lips. By the time I got back across town to take the test, I was throwing up from overdosing. I failed the exam. Instead of being upset about my results, I was upset that my high had been interrupted. I went home and snorted another pill.

7

Three Little Birds

Another All Hallows Eve has passed. At dawn, I'm still awake, unpacking. Sifting through boxed belongings, I unearth forgotten nuggets—legal pads and folders of time-faded rantings. Finding them renews an interest in reading and writing.

Tucked between weathered pages of a long-lost journal, I discover a letter I'd written. It's an inspirational piece intended to be an affirmation of self-worth. I got it from a prompt in a personal development workbook. The assignment was to write to my future self from the perspective of myself as a child. It seemed silly at the time, but now I'm that future self.

Rereading the letter, I see how I've failed to live up to the dreams of my inner child. Without ever meaning to, I drifted off course from my idealized path. This realization awakens me from the mental deadness of being up for days. Tears create puddles in the decade-old ink.

The only antidote I know to ease the restless pain pressing on me from the inside out is to sprinkle a few more shards onto a mirror. Then repeat.

~

Our check from the house sale arrives. It's a valid reason to celebrate. Deep down, however, it serves as a poignant reminder of where our lives are headed. With fifty-eight grand deposited in the bank, a lower-middle-class person could breathe easy. But what about the thirty-one grand we owe on credit cards, plus rent, food, and the cost of raising a child?

It's sad to think this check represents the culmination of a lifetime of work. How is it that giving my all has only earned me a crown of financial insecurity and endless fear? Acting like everything is okay feels forced. Meanwhile, one hit of dope at a time, I'm succumbing to the pleasures severing my connection to the only pure joy I've ever known—being a dad.

This bleak outlook lingers throughout the holidays. Leann and I put on the facade of active parents. We take Lola to the library, the park, the mall, or gymnastics, but each outing feels less engaging than the last. Always just the three of us.

Enslaved by the obligations of continuous using, we neglect to buy Lola Christmas presents. We don't even have a tree. On a cold Christmas Eve, the only place open is a convenience store. I pick up a card for Lola of a Christmas tree in a wintery scene. The bulbs sparkle, illuminating when the button inside the card is pushed.

Lola thinks it's the coolest thing. She presses the button over and over. Her giggles don't alleviate my guilt. I strain to feel anything else. Allowing feelings means opening the door for pain. My dying spirit is reflected in the dark and bitter cold of winter. In chilling whispers, it tells me I am nowhere near the victim my baby is.

January brings gloominess the likes of which I've never known. I try setting limits. Limits on how much we spend, limits on how much we use, limits on Lola's increasing defiant behaviors, limits on days cooped up inside. I get only more conflict in return.

Up again for three days and nights, I write a poem called "The Terrible Threes." It is written in stream-of-conscious prose; a four-part in-the-moment excavation of my malfunctioning mind. The poem covers my visceral world like Allen Ginsberg's *Howl* covers the mindset of 1950s American subculture. Parenting, drug abuse, marital demise, loss of control, and ineffectiveness are explored.

Weeks go by without visitors, phone calls, texts, or emails. I stop looking for gigs. No recording or practicing scales. Three lives collecting dust. I have a hunch that I've isolated us to make sure no one comes around to question our inhumane condition. The only time we turn on our cell phones is when we're contacting our dealer. Lola's outbursts and rejections of rules endorse my cause—driving across town for more dope. Our only interactions are with our dealer and fast-food or supermarket cashiers. Okay by me. Not good for Lola.

Leann and I blame our problems on speed. We vow to be done with it.

~

In the post-dinner quiet of our apartment, Leann and I startle at an ear-piercing bell that hasn't rung in months: our landline. We look at each other like, *What the fuck?*

Leann's Uncle Phil is on the line. He sounds more buzzed than usual. I'm given an interrogation about our recent whereabouts.

Believing his concerns are disingenuous, I react, saying, "What business is it of yours?"

I'm certain he's spying on us and tell him so. In an angry, passive-aggressive outburst he hurls out, in no uncertain terms, how I'm too difficult to deal with.

As if I didn't know.

"Most of the time you're fun, you know? But now and then, you're really, really not. It's like dealing with Dr. Jekyll and Mr. Hyde. Not to be rude, but if you weren't family, I'd have nothing to do with you."

Oh no, that's not rude at all.

A dam inside me breaks. Phil gets read the riot act. Anything and everything I'm angry about is taken out on him. He gets a last word in and hangs up, which only intensifies my rage. I start to call back but stop myself. I can't let him think he won. I stomp around in circles, trying to put my foot through the floor of our upstairs apartment. I'm nearly frothing from the mouth as I spew obscenities.

Lola knows to cuddle her mom for safety. Seeing the fear in their eyes no longer gets me to chill. I'm numb to my own improper conduct, ignorant of clues that *should* make a parent recoil; out of control with no internal message indicating when it's time to back the fuck off.

My tantrum continues uninterrupted for forty-five minutes—until the in-laws stop by. They've come for a surprise visit. They assure us it's for no reason other than not having seen us in a while. *This is a wellness check.* After some small talk, they casually hint at being suspicious we might be using drugs around their granddaughter. They've "heard" things. They don't flat-out accuse us of getting high, but it's implied. I'd tell them to leave if they did.

They list reasons for concern such as our weight loss, not calling, and not coming around as much as we used to. I put on my best "all is well" face as if my life depends on it. I'm not saying the grandparents fall for it, but I give a Golden Globes-level performance. An improv skit is enacted. A ruse I call "perpetrating a guise to preserve a disguise." Because I perceive their visit as a threat to my intoxication, I become a chameleon. Whether I've been up on speed for days or coming down off opiates, I can perk up to pull off this act. No matter how bad off, enraged, or dope sick I am, I'm able to flip my personality like a light switch to deflect the unwanted attention.

The grandparents' obligatory walking on eggshells around me brings out my inner ire. Instead of being grateful for their concerns, I'm resentful. I'd rather be less interactive or stop seeing anyone altogether. Once they're somewhat satisfied we're safe and sound, they leave. I blame Uncle Phil for the surprise visit and make a mental note not to trust him. Even if I get the fleeting sense he cares for our family, he has no right to judge my ability to parent.

The next evening, Leann's childhood friends, Corrine and Jocko, show up unannounced with their two toddlers. A snowstorm has canceled their flight back to the Midwest. I'm resistant to their stayover because they never approved of our marriage. I'm going through withdrawals and have no strength to argue. They stay on our living room floor.

In the middle of the night, on my way to the kitchen, I observe how close Jocko keeps his two daughters while Corrine sleeps by herself on the couch. Corrine was molested as a child by a drug addict who her mom, a drug counselor, was "rescuing" by taking into their home. I draw insomnia-stricken conclusions that something is not right about Jocko. I fall asleep on Lola's floor instead of in my bed.

An hour later, I overhear Leann and Corrine talking in our bedroom. Corrine's not staying with family again tonight because there's a horrible stomach flu going around.

Late the next morning, I awaken to Lola throwing up. As I clean her up and go to put her sheets in the washing machine, I notice our guests have left. Leann gets the flu next, then me.

Losing bodily fluids during withdrawals is a new low. No relief.

I have got to get high on something. Between diarrhea and dry heaves, I dial my dealer until his girlfriend tells me to "stop fucking calling." Fueled by adrenaline, I scream back how I have every right to call because of how much I've lined their pockets. She hangs up.

I'm accosted by body temperature shifts—icy-cold sweat followed by boiling hot, noxious rushes of blood. Wearing only a long-sleeved shirt and sweatpants, I walk barefoot outside into the snow and sub-freezing air. I need to feel. I stand in misery until my body shakes, then run back inside. I repeat this three times. Then Mikey calls.

Just before dawn, I haul ass over roads covered in patches of black ice to purchase as much speed as my dealer will part with. My fingers, nose, and ears are blue from having the windows down. Mikey expects me to apologize to his girlfriend before he lets me in. After I do, he accepts my money and kicks me a free line.

I need to be alone, so I stop at the porn store. I'm so gacked out on meth, my concept of time gets dizzy from the second hand's spin. I ogle the front and back cover of nearly every DVD on the shelves. This painstaking yet satisfying escape is interrupted by the cashier.

"You've been here a long time, pal, and it's making me uncomfortable. I'm gonna have to ask you to leave."

It's noon. Going to another porn store would prove to be undeniable dereliction. I return home empty-handed.

Another month of the same passes. The only difference is I'm drinking again. Whisky helps get me through opiate withdrawals. When it doesn't make the symptoms go away, I have to get more pills.

One night I find the perfect mix, the sweet spot combination of being up, down, and sideways. I wake up the next day with a smile. I've finally perfected dragon chasing.

Leann discovers me sitting up in bed, happy.

"Fuck you, asshole," she shouts.

"What? What's this about?"

"You really have no idea what an asshole you are, do you?"

"What did I do?"

"Don't give me that 'you don't remember' shit."

Her face is bright red; her hands shake. She leaves the room. My posture collapses.

"I'm not playing stupid," I yell.

She returns to explain.

"You turned into a mean, cruel drunk."

I have no recollection of calling her names, spitting on her, threatening to fuck other women, or raising my fist at her. No button was spared. I've never been a blackout drunk. I used to be proud of how well I maintained my alcohol consumption . . . until this.

I take the three of us on an impromptu trip to the Oregon Coast town of Seaside to make it up to her. The ocean air doesn't clear my brutal hangover, so I stop at a liquor store. Leann's eyes go wide when I come out with a brown bag. I take a huge swig beside the minivan. My hand is halfway down in the trash receptacle to dump the bottle. Then I retrieve it just in case my swig doesn't fend off the tremors.

"After this pint, I'm done," I promise as I get back in the van.

~

The weekend party nights we used to look forward to are daily now. I use so often, I'm not getting high anymore, no matter how much I take. Our bank account finds its way down to zero. I manage to gain employment through a temp agency. It's the best news in quite a while.

I'd like to be hopeful or plan out a future, but I've found solace in accepting there's no way I'll ever get clean. Whatever place I get to from where I'm wanting to run from, I'm just going to want to run from it when I get there. What's the point?

With rent due in seven days, we withdraw our last two-hundred bucks to buy speed and pills. This is it. I know I've said it before, but this time I'll have the backing of bankruptcy to stop my cravings. After being up all weekend, I call in sick.

At sunrise we take a long walk to talk, leaving Lola in the apartment alone, sleeping. This talk takes priority. On the last fumes of conviction my spirit holds, I profess to Leann how I'm entirely ready to either die or get off drugs.

"That's not fair! You got to do drugs for years. I'm just getting started. I'm not ready to stop."

Clenching my fists, I take her response as a blatant disregard of my plea. Using never dismantled my life as much as while she's been a part of it. I'm tired of fighting. But giving up makes me feel like my will to live is slipping away. I can see the end nearing. My dying wish is to make sure Lola is forever free to be anything she wants. But I've got to set Leann on the right path before my last rites can be read. If I rescue Leann from addiction first, motivate her to carry on, maybe I can plot my demise without guilt.

Taking this new approach, I ask her what she would do with her life if she could do anything. She looks frustrated by my question. I grab her hand. It is ice cold. She probably sees the entire talk as a ploy.

Back in the apartment, I pass out from being up too long. Leann is still awake when I get up for work. I ask how she feels about our talk, if she has put more thought into a dream she'd like to pursue. She looks down when she answers.

"Yeah."

It dawns on me when I pull in to work. Something changed in her sometime between last night and this morning. A switch went off.

8

The Last Time (I Mean It This Time)

After loading my work truck, I call Leann to have her and Lola meet me along my route. I ask her to bring our last pill, with an emphasis on how much I need it to get through my shift. No response. She must've nodded off mid-conversation. I yell to wake her. Silence. I hang up to try again.

For an hour, I try to reach her. Busy signal. My tires go over the divider rumble strips of the road. Busy signal. Is she able to take care of Lola? I leave a message with Aunt Darcy, pleading for her to check on them. I don't know what else to do. I'm across town.

Leann calls back a little while later. She's wide awake and upset that I involved her aunt. I, in turn, respond nastily.

"Don't be a fuckin' idiot. You can't be nodding off when you're watching Lola, bitch. Now bring me my pill!"

Click.

I can't blame her for hanging up. I've spun out of control. Seeking more, always more, has brought me less and less. The only way to sustain the energy levels I need to live like this is to use more drugs. I call back to really let her have it so many times that I lose track.

"She'll call back," I scoff, bitter yet cocksure. My head bobs in short, bouncy nods.

I make it through my shift without getting high, though not by choice. I'm anticipating snorting that pill. I have been since I left for work at 5:30 am.

Home at last. The first thing I do, after unlocking the door and slamming it behind me to make a scene, is look through our usual stash places for my hit. The disorder ruling over me is transfixed by an insatiable desire to find dope.

"We must have something, anything, left over somewhere," I say out loud, expecting Leann to answer.

Withdrawals are bad enough, but when you're expecting to get high and you don't get to, it brings about a whole new level of anger and despair. In this state of mind, I come to realize neither my wife nor daughter are home. Incensed not only by their absence but also because I can't find anything to get high on, I pull out my phone. Setting pride aside, I call her. It's been nine hours since we last spoke.

This time she answers.

Instead of saying hello, Leann is silent.

"Hello?" I ask, leaning into the earpiece to hear better. She screams, "Don't you ever fucking talk to me like that again! Asshole! You *do not* talk like that to me!"

"I'll talk to you any fucking way I want." Adrenaline tingling, I scream louder than her scream to cut her off, drown her out. Our commingled screaming causes crackled distortion over the earpiece.

"If you don't bring my daughter and drugs here right now, I'll come find you and kick your ass!" It's an idle threat. I've never kicked anyone's ass, nor ever will, especially not the mother of my child. This is the level of toxicity to which our relationship has escalated.

"You *do not* talk to me like that!" she reiterates.

Her tone is unfamiliar. We've had lots of fights, some bad, but never once has she come off this insistent. Not that she's weak. She just gets overwhelmed and then shuts down. I think she means business this time. Her tone is consistent with someone drawing a line in the sand. We scream synchronous indecipherable things. She pauses, then starts in again.

I'm silent only for the amount of time it takes to inhale a deep breath. To rest my seared throat, I wait for her to stop yelling long enough that I can get in the last word or two. My blood burns; muscles tense with rage and withdrawal-fueled agitation.

The next eight words gushing from her venomous mouth might as well be tattooed on my drug-riddled heart.

"You will never fucking see your daughter again!"

Click.

My eyelids do a single slow-motion blink in unison. Numbness expands between my lungs. From there, dulled to a whisper by tearful backwashed saliva, a single spoken word frees itself.

"Great."

There's no dial tone like there used to be to add dramatic injury, just silence. I hold the cell phone away from my face to scowl at it, then bark a single laugh. My mind replays Leann's avowal, the finality in her words, repeating them again and again as if there's some way to change them.

My head tips back, loose on my sweaty neck. A lone syllable, toneless, wrapped in a thickening voice, is released.

"Fuck."

It bounces off the four empty walls I've come home to. My proclamation dwarfs me like an echo returned to its orator who's standing at the bottom of a narrow, sheer-walled canyon. If only I were able to shout it out meanly or sarcastically, or at somebody. Aside from me.

I can't pretend anymore. It's not like I'm giving in by choice. Bargaining time has passed. I stand dazed and directionless at the entry to our bedroom. Nothing will ever be the same. My posture sags. Anger, which I rely on to feed me strength, would be pointless. If only the past twelve hours were just some bad dream I could shake off by waking up.

No longer present are the sounds of my daughter's baby-girl voice saturating her room, making up conversations with her secondhand dolls while dressing them up. No longer present are the naptimes together, plopping her down to watch DVDs of cartoons, or *Baby Einstein* on infinite repeat.

I look around for something to take; anything to snuff down my guilt. *Why the fuck was I too high to spend time with my only child?* In a way, I'm being relieved of guilt's stranglehold now that she's gone. But I never asked for this.

Gone also is my baby's mom. Sometime during the afternoon, she must've grabbed and packed as many necessities as could fit into our minivan. It's gone, too. I'm doubly insulted that Leann stooped to this level while I was at work, trying to keep us above water, making deliveries for a temp agency who foolishly hired me without first doing a drug screen.

"No wonder she didn't answer her phone all day," I say in a softer tone. Remembering our fight earlier this morning, I realize I could've taken her more seriously.

My leg muscles give way. The hallway drywall catches me as I fall. My body slides down to a knees-bent upright sitting position on the carpeted floor. My well-worn crutches of pride and anger won't hold me up anymore.

~

Soundless and stillness. I haven't felt this in four years. Not since my wife discovered she was pregnant. The absence of sound is peaceful, yet I'm devising a plan to get high enough to silence the quiet. Defile it with noise. I know what comes next: pain. Four empty walls. Buried emotions. Ruminating.

Is this the first time I've suffered loss because of addictions? No. But this loss is much more than just some piece of property smashed during a drug-fueled rage or a relationship broken by neglect. This is my *child* I've lost. By bottle, baggie, pill, or pipe—what does it matter how?

My fear is that I won't face this reality until the uncertainty of it passes, as have so many bottoms I've hit before. Same as when I tell myself I have the ability to stop, but then don't. *When does it end?* I'm consuming drugs all day long, yet never getting high. I don't want to; I have to keep the cravings and illness at bay. The best "solution" I can come up with is also my worst problem. But it's not just *my* problem.

I know I've said this to myself before, but tonight is different.

My wife of five years has left. She has taken our baby. There have been countless situations I've sabotaged in ways only I could repair. Not this. Instead of laboring over what I can do to remedy the situation, the question rattling around in my brain is: *How can I circumvent this reality without drugs?*

My ego is bruised. It's swelling up to battle my conscience. It tricks my brain into allowing itself to be fed rationalizations. Succulent lies are concocted, laced with the never-to-be-underestimated power of denial. Momentum parasites. Things like:

I'm not strong enough to be her dad.

I'm too weak to beat this addiction thing.

My little girl is better off without me.

She's someplace where she'll be happier and safer.

I wasn't cut out for this anyway.

Dial the dope man.

Why am I so quick to forget? I've ended up *here* as a result of believing lies. Tricks played by both my ego and my brain to barricade my heart. Neglected far too long, releasing itself from forlorn depths, my heart cries out, *Lola means more to me than anything in this world!*

My ego attempts to crown self-hatred victorious. It tells me I'm the problem. Here's additional proof of my inadequacy and that I will never amount to anything. Usually, I take the easy way out, but a bout of worthiness ensues. Just before the second knot on this tug-o-war rope crosses the center line, my conscience heaves, wrenching out a high-powered assertion.

"Liar!"

I gasp to breathe. Tears stream down my face. I slap them away.

"Enough!"

My hands, wrists, and forearms shake in an erratic effort to make these feelings go away. I'm outside my body. I get chilly bumps.

"No. More. Lies!"

I've seen enough over the years to forecast my daughter's future. The conclusion reads like an obituary: innocent little girl, abandoned by father, raised by mom or whoever mom is seeing, then raised by one pseudo-parent after another until, based on allegations of abuse or worse, she becomes a ward of the state, which then gives her away to a foster home. Her adulthood spent seeking male approval while battling addiction and codependency.

This swirl of premonitions and likelihoods become a dark, twisted, tree-root-clogged rabbit hole my imagination races down, cutting, scraping, and staining my spirit along the way. I can't let this happen. If I don't do something, my little girl is going to end up like all other broken, lovelorn, inherent daddy-issue women who bad guys have their way with and then discard.

I just used "bad" to describe guys like me. Guys who have fun with, then leave broken women like the type I'm fearful my daughter will become. This outcome feels certain if I don't reclaim my yet-to-be-earned place as her rock. Or die trying.

I bend my knees to get up. Shattered and alone in my abandonment, I make a vow. Although I've let myself down more times than I can count. Although I've proven to myself over and over that my word means nothing. Although I know deep down I can't trust myself even to keep a promise to myself, I make one anyway. I mean it, so I say it.

"There's no fucking way I'm gonna be to blame for my little girl's fractured spirit. No fucking way!"

Contemptuous ego laughs.

9

With or Without You

Winded, I free-fall onto our peach-colored recliner in the living room. The weight of all this misery occurring simultaneously causes me to struggle to draw in air. Years of insufflation have irritated each nasal passage to where they scab into blood boogers daily.

I've abandoned social mores and neglected my appearance. All given up for the sole purpose of milking the utmost out of every inebriation. Hygiene is an interruption, not a necessity. I haven't brushed my teeth in months. I shower once or twice a week.

Having not taken any drug for eighteen hours, my senses are muffled. My mind sorts through clogged filters for meaning. Nothing? Using, not using—none of this is by choice. *Will I ever change? Or will I just replace what matters?*

Instead of wallowing in self-pity, I get up to eat. My fridge is bare. To quiet the pangs of my starved belly, I head out into the warm evening for food. Walking helps clear my mind. My debit card is declined. One slice of pizza is all I have enough cash for. It's too late to resolve this tonight, so I eat, then go to bed.

The instant my heavy eyelids shut, my legs start wiggling back and forth. Each thigh muscle convulses involuntarily, as if succumbing to electroshock therapy. I'm having an acute attack of restless legs syndrome. This ailment worsens when I'm not high, causing insomnia. The only remedy I've ever known to minimize its symptoms is copious opiates.

"Don't be afraid," I tell myself. Matching my insides, my words come out cracked, broken. Desperate for a courageous headspace, I try to will a paradigm shift. I don't know where I'll find strength enough to stave off past methods of calming myself.

Out of options, I ask for God's help. The God I turned my back on. The One I believed in, conditionally. I ask God to watch over me. I don't know *how* to pray. I only know how to petition, or, when I've really screwed up, beg. I'm not even sure how to be humble. So, with tattered sincerity, I do my best.

"Great Creator, Higher Power, Good Orderly Direction, whatever I should call you," I pray. Pausing for a second, I allow my words to flow unchecked. "I pray that you stop me from adding one more time to my 'one too many times' list. One too many times I've done what I said I wouldn't do. One too many times I've put off what I said I would do until it was too late, then wouldn't do it at all. One too many times I've preferred lies over truth or blamed others for the things I chose to do. One too many times I've sacrificed values for wants by indulging in pleasure, then telling myself it was more important than anything I needed to do. In fact, I've put my wants before everything and everyone else. One too many times I've let family down and myself down. Please God, watch over Lola tonight. Keep her safe. Amen."

~

From under my sweat-saturated comforter, I jerk up vertically. Daylight sifts in through slits in the blinds. It dawns on me how they've never been drawn.

"Aw, shit!" I grumble, afraid I've overslept.

My pulse races until I stabilize the erratic breathing. I twist and turn in search of my alarm clock. This is the first real, deep, non-drug-enhanced sleep I've had in years. One minute at a time, I've now accumulated twenty-four hours without drugs. One day won.

It's 5:25 am. I forgot to set my alarm. Since I'm early for work, I step into my single-person shower stall.

The lukewarm water is annoying. I turn the heat up to where it's too hot to handle, melting away the ever-present toxins oozing through my pores. I rest half my body against the cool fiberglass wall. This sensation provides my reddening skin a contrast that's borderline sensual. My body's either remembering what it's like to feel or sidetracking me from feeling the imminent withdrawals.

Withdrawals are more wicked than the worst flu symptoms—the ultimate mindfuck. For multiple hours, sometimes days, nothing feels good. Applying something moist and cool keeps the skin temperature down, yet also feels gross. Any pleasure or comfort is short-lived. Sensitivity is diminished by the sticky, icky film of rejected chemical microbes covering every pore with a glue-stick-like paste.

Vomiting, diarrhea, fever, chills, repeat. The replenishing of solids or liquids feels repulsive. The addicted brain holds firm its conviction that nothing will help; any suggestion is futile. Only taking the next hit will end the malaise.

Right now, I can't let those impulses in. They would break me. I think about work instead.

The only food left in our pantry is a box of stale cereal, weeks beyond its expiration date. The milk is also expired. I pull the cereal bag out of its box so I can eat it dry while driving. I tear away a piece of the cardboard and scribble out a note in case Leann stops by to remove more things while I work.

Please don't take my daughter from me!

I promise I won't hurt you. Just please come back home.

I cross out *my* and write *our*. Setting the note conspicuously at the front entry, I lock the door behind me. The sun is coming up, same as it always does, yet it appears to illuminate the world in a way I've never noticed.

As I drive to work, *Hello, It's Me* by Todd Rundgren plays over the AM radio. His lyrics bring me to tears. Music used to be my blood and livelihood. When did it lose its ability to move me like this?

Leann calls, but immediately hangs up. Each time I call back, she hangs up. My hopes are raised, my tears discontinue, my hopes are destroyed, and my tears return—all in less than two minutes. I bet she's checking to see if I've left the apartment. This is so unlike her.

Throughout the morning deliveries, I grapple with an angry, urgent hankering to drive across town to apprehend and confront Leann. But work is keeping me grounded. Feeling immobilized, I pull over onto a quiet road to take a break. An ad for a law firm offering free advice comes on over the radio, so I call. The receptionist connects me with Monika, a new hire. She's curt and gets right to the point.

"Were you served a restraining order yet?"

"What's a restraining order? Oh, wait. Yeah, I think I know what it is. No! She wouldn't do something like that."

"Expect it. Trust me, one's coming."

I stare off over the rims of my glasses while she's talking. My past comes up like a clogged toilet—all the crap I've gotten away with—how many times I've beaten the odds, slithering in and out of situations most can't; how lawlessness never caught up to me; how rarely I gave a damn, yet somehow always managed to land on my feet.

I imagine hearing my dad's voice. "Son, the house always wins."

"No, Dad, the house does not always win," I respond, disobedient, as if he's with me.

Monika lays out the writing on the wall. Without Lola, I'm at a disadvantage.

I'll need to quit being so certain of my specialness and become pliant. Why, at this juncture, am I having to admit Dad was right, or worse, that I've had it all wrong?

Is it because of Lola that any of this matters?

Yeah, this is for her.

Who the hell am I kidding?

10

Shake the Disease (In Situations Like These)

Speaking with a lawyer is empowering. A cargo net of plans and ideas. Having a river of to-dos temporarily unfettered by the usual virulent craving to score is a welcome reprieve. I end up working twelve hours, then stop to grab fast food with my last twenty dollars.

While ordering, I'm adrift through each motion, paying little or no attention to detail, including human interaction. My thoughts are absorbed in "what-if" scenarios. Floating along my swift stream of consciousness, I'm already back in the box truck. One hand feeds my mouth. The other is scribbling notes, churning out as many observations as I can recall, leading up to today.

I try to make sense of quitting. Immediately, I'm having thoughts that would be better to snuff out. *Staying clean is impossible for me. Climbing back on the wagon only offers a short-lived euphoria.* Like a voyeur of my own life, I observe my thoughts manifesting a return to using. They're already telling me it's imminent. Before long, I'll be damming the energy flow, drowning the muse all over again. Ill-prepared to resist hearing my own prophetic voices, I drive home.

Once inside the door, my shoulders and head droop. The apartment is emptier. All the worst-case scenarios I envisioned are happening. It seems fitting.

This is what I've deserved all along. I haven't been a good man. The recompense I'm left with feels . . . right. Familiar. I welcome it. Like the revelry around a soldier returning home with PTSD, the celebration is a brief interlude, putting something sinister off until later.

The serenity I was hoping to feel by accepting my role in this tragic outcome gets sidestepped. I can't tell if it's from my ego or conscience. Something intervenes, channeling thoughts of vindictiveness. A wild-hair belief tickles my better judgment into submission. *I can leverage this somehow.* Thoughts then feed themselves. My Leannf, honorable, best thinking denigrates into impulsive self-righteousness.

"Nine one one. What's your emergency?"

"Hi. I want to report my wife has disappeared with our daughter and has stolen my minivan."

"Sir, do you believe she's been kidnapped? Is she in danger? Is this a missing person report you'd like to file?"

"No. I'm pretty sure I know where she is. She's taken my minivan and kidnapped my daughter."

"This sounds like a civil matter. You'll need to work this out through the court system."

"I don't think you understand. She's high on drugs, driving around recklessly in my minivan, endangering our daughter's life."

Even though the nonemergency operator reaffirms her position, I adamantly refuse, based on what I consider her insufficient handling of the situation. Citing the endangerment of my child at the hands of her intoxicated mother, I demand an officer perform a welfare check.

"If something were to happen to my kid, it would be on you. Are you prepared for those kinds of lawsuits, media attention, and the like?"

Hours later, an Officer Hamilton contacts me. Retelling what led up to this situation, I provide added details to make Leann look dangerous and unfit. He promises to do a wellness check. After spending ninety minutes on the phone satisfying my need to do "something", my nerves are calmed.

I try calling my severed other half. The call goes to voicemail, so I leave a message.

"Please let Lola hear my voice, or at the very least put the phone to her ear and let me sing to her. This really isn't fair. She doesn't deserve this. Come on, please! Let her hear my voice. I'm worried she'll be sad."

I sing *You Are My Sunshine* as I've done every night just before kissing her good night and tucking her in. This was *our* routine. Hijacked. I hope Leann feels sorry for me and plays my message for Lola. After saying, "Good night, honey. Daddy loves you," I get a throbbing pain in my chest.

I want to sling the cell phone at the wall, but it's my only means of reconnecting. A warm feeling comes over me, coupled with the sense that a presence in the room stares down from the popcorn-textured ceiling. I don't see anything or anyone, but I speak to "it" as if there is someone there.

"Please, God, watch over Lola. Please kiss her good night and whisper in her ear *your daddy loves you* for me."

I let a half smile slip, knowing when I wake up I'll have accumulated forty-eight continuous hours clean. Half of my lips aren't smiling, though. The worst is yet to come. Every junkie knows the wickedest withdrawals are on the third day.

I miss Lola. I miss watching her eyelids get puffy and heavy before closing. I miss being needed. I have to keep my eyes shut tight so they don't burn when I open them. This way I'm able to fall into a deep, tranquil sleep.

11

Miracles

A jerking motion—my own—pulls me out of a rich dream state. Another morning up before the alarm, eyes peeled wide, comforter saturated in absorbed sweat. I kick it to the bottom of my bed, then lie back to stare off. *Is this how I'm going to wake up every day?*

My brain acclimates to a tired body. Rolling onto my stomach, I reach for the clock. I'm up an hour early.

The extra hour provides an opportunity. I snap to. A secret plan's been formulating in my head since last night—how to pull off retribution. Constant scheming is a norm for me. I'm going to steal my daughter back from her mother. I think I know where Leann's holed up.

I rush in to shower, enjoying the baptismal effect on my skin and spirit. To execute this plan, I'm skipping breakfast. Food will only slow me down. My cavorting continues as I head down the concrete stairs of my second-floor apartment. I leap over every other step. Same as when my dealer calls.

As I near Aunt Darcy suburban home in Murray Hill, doubts propagate like fungus, peppering my overinflated will. Idling at a traffic light, my resolve weakens. A gut feeling is telling me to reconsider.

I'd like to do the right thing here. But even my healthiest thoughts are deviated from, especially if there's no payoff in sight. *You've come all this way. Don't be a little scaredy-cat.*

With help from its allies, rationalization and sheer determination, my will resumes control. *This has got to work.* With my face out the window, emotionally charged, I yell, "Daddy's on his way, honey!"

The first traces of sunshine peek over the horizon, sending pinkish landing strips of colored heat rays through the baby blue and pastel purple sky. I continue up the two-lane road, looking for a spot to pull over. The truck is too big for traffic to easily get by.

Miracles by Jefferson Starship comes on the oldies station. In an instant, I'm carried back to a purer, more innocent time when my brother took me along on a spontaneous sunset drive from our Las Vegas home to Mt. Charleston. Nevada Highway 157, the Kyle Canyon cutoff, leads away from the barren desert up to the lush ponderosa pine, white fir, and aspen groves of Humboldt-Toiyabe National Forest. A nearly six-thousand-foot elevation change covered in less than thirty minutes. Gary had just purchased a 1970 Ford Boss 302 Mustang. He wanted to see how it handled over mountainous terrain.

He blasted the song over the Sanyo car stereo he bought at Montgomery Ward. I held on for dear life as he went through the gears, bobbing the tachometer needle up and down as we wound around mountain turns at seventy, eighty, even ninety miles an hour. Scared as I was, the blaring song set me free to fantasize. I felt invincible.

If only you believed in miracles, so would I.

The refrain solicited fear to subside and dissolve. I was beckoned by Grace Slick and Paul Kantner's harmonies and how the layers aid Marty Balin's sincere lead-vocal testimony. By surrendering, placing trust in my brother's driving skills, I could embrace the danger and excitement. Oh, to be that free again!

I'm heavier on the gas pedal because this particular song comes on at this particular moment. *This proves it!* I latch on to the tune as my battle hymn. *This is my sign!* For six minutes, their ballad of faith reinforces my scheme.

"Thank you, Lord!" I shout over the low gear whirring of the transmission churning its way up the steep hill.

Aunt Darcy house can only be reached by a long driveway off the main road. I can't pull into it and there's no turnaround. Besides, it would be too obvious. To enable a quick exit, I park half on the road, half on the dirt shoulder, blocking the driveway entrance. I put the flashers on, exhale out my nose, and hustle by foot up her driveway.

The driveway extends out from the road about 100 feet down a hill, takes a ninety-degree turn, then heads back uphill fifty feet to her garage. Because of a neighbors' eight-foot cedar fence, you can't see the road or the long part of the driveway from the house.

As I come around the blind turn to head uphill, I nearly walk smack dab into their Border Collie. Seeing me, Sam rolls around on the dew-sprinkled grass, wagging his tail with extreme joy. He wants to play. I came prepared.

"Go get your ball, boy. Getcher ball."

I throw a tennis ball I brought a few feet away to instigate play. Sam goes running around until he picks up its scent. He quickly returns, letting it roll out from between his teeth, then runs off to get his favorite ball instead. He brings it over, but growling playfully, refuses to drop it for me. With a forceful tug, I snatch the ball from his jaws. It's covered in slime and saliva and the fuzzy hairs on it are matted. I pump my arm back a couple times, faking the throw with the ball hidden to see if he'll go after it. Sam spins into position, all fours crouched.

My throwing arm is decent. I take aim toward a verdant gully down a steep hill in the opposite direction. At its bottom is plenty of foliage to hide the ball. I release, throwing with all my might. We take off running full speed, him for the ball, me for the house.

"Get your ball, boy," I whisper-shout, looking back, throwing my voice.

Hastily, I search around the outside of the house, casing for a way in. Through a bedroom window with open curtains, I locate Lola's belongings. Next, I spot Leann's purse in the kitchen. The garage has a slightly ajar window with a small fan propped up in it. *Bingo!*

I push the window open as far as it will go. While plopping the screen off its track, the fan falls onto a workbench inside, making a solid thud. I sprint to the bottom of the hill, stop, then reassess. Sam's still trying to find the ball. *Remember why you're here.* I run right back.

My heart thumps like a kick drum in a speed metal band, forcing me off balance. If only I could stop time, pause right here, right now. If only.

I'm seeing this through to completion. No reasoning. I make a bold leap inside the window, ignoring the strain in my body. Pure adrenaline motivates me onward. My movements are swift through the garage. As I open the door to peer inside, I'm slower, methodical. No one's awake.

Two gently placed steps and I'm in. The door squeaks as it closes behind me. My spine snaps straight. Reaching back, I jam my fingers, trying to halt the door from shutting. One sharp breath to pause and listen for any movement. *Coast is clear.*

I tiptoe past Lola's kid-safe utensils and favorite bowl left out on the kitchen table. A direct stride reflects my arrogance as I bounce along until I reach the living room. My bones lock up my muscles. Someone's on the couch under a blanket, facing away.

I hear my heart. The low rumble of each beat bounces up, into, and around my skull. It ripples my eyeballs like a camera repeatedly shaken out of focus to simulate an explosion or earthquake. I'm overcome by an ominous feeling. My lungs switch to short survival-mode gasps. Suddenly, this doesn't feel right. *Why now?* The person on the couch coughs, then turns over.

I spring backward, repelling behind a plaster wall that divides the living room and kitchen. This spry movement bears a dizzying reminder. I haven't eaten. Trying not to overcompensate, I fling myself off balance into the microwave oven stand. I attempt to keep my footing by not falling forward, but, arms flapping wildly, I fall backward into the dining room table. My shoulder takes the brunt of the fall. The clang of dirty dishes and rattling silverware sends sirens louder than a server's tray dropped in a restaurant.

"Hello? Is someone in my kitchen?"

Crap! It's Aunt Darcy. If I make a run for it, she'll hear me for sure. She can identify me.

Like an energetic puppy hyper for a treat, I leap off the linoleum floor. I tiptoe backward, out the same way I came, with composed panic. I hear a strange flapping sound coming from the direction I'm headed, getting closer.

"Who's here?"

Aunt Darcy daunting, half-awake voice cracks. The fear and protectiveness in her timbre is unmistakable. Looking forward, afraid I messed with mama bear, I back into something. Frozen in place, I practically come out of my skin. Something furry sideswipes the inside of my shins, nearly knocking me off my feet. I blindly reach behind for clarity, afraid to turn and look. I then hear the flat bobble of Sam's grass-and-saliva-matted tennis ball drop out of the side of his mouth.

A welcome culprit, Sam zips past, then entirely around to face me. He's come to claim the attention he deserves for finding his ball. His swinging tail stings as it slaps against the bottom of my shorts and thighs. I've got to deal with Sam if I want to make a safe exit.

His ball continues bouncing toward the living room.

To keep Sam from barking, I make a sweeping motion with my arm. Starting from my chest, I extend it outward, ending with a pointed finger. I make this motion over and over. Sam just stares. He spins in circles, awaiting a verbal command. I'm frantic because I can't see whether Aunt T's still on the couch or on her way toward the kitchen.

"Get your ball, boy," I mouth in a faint whisper, again pointing with outstretched arm motions. His favorite toy might just be a Hail Mary prayer answered. Perhaps a divine decoy. Sam runs for his ball, I for the garage. Aunt Darcy calls out behind me.

"Damn it, Sam! I thought you were an intruder."

My green light to get out couldn't be any greener. I close the kitchen door behind me, slowly turning the handle to make sure the dead latch doesn't clang against the strike plate as they meet. I'm not home free and clear by any measure. I still have to climb up and out the garage window, a feat much easier accomplished coming in. As I lunge upward, my shorts catch a corner of a vise on the workbench. I stumble sideways, falling onto the bench. A screwdriver cuts an open gouge into my thigh, but I don't feel it. I'm laser focused on the freedom of getting away with . . . nothing.

Right as I'm about to hit the ground running, right as I force my legs to be flexible enough to fit through the windowsill, a preemptive thought causes me to hesitate. With one foot on the ground and one stretched into the house, a liberated feeling comes over me. It's like I'm being freed of my lifelong skepticism. I'm coming to believe. Sensing the presence of God, I'm certain He is with me. His grace is why I'm getting through this. Although I denied Him by doing what *I* thought best, He still shows His love. My head tilts skyward to apologize.

Time bends to the stillness.

I pull my leg through and refocus on what I'm doing. As both feet meet the concrete, I hear Sam push through his doggy door into the garage. I poke my face back through the window. Sam barks at me like I'm an intruder. I slide the window back to the slightly open position. My hands are too shaky to set the screen back in place. I run off, forgetting to replace the fan in the window.

After zigzagging behind bushes and trees to avoid being seen, I run full speed down the hill. I'm short of breath, swinging my arms to help me walk uphill to the work truck. I come around to the driver's side, mouthing "Sorry" at a line of cars waiting to pass around it to avoid oncoming traffic. I jump in, start it up, and go.

My leg muscles vibrate beneath my skin. I'm shivering with anxiety, fear, and adrenaline. I will not be arrested, charged with trespassing or child abduction. *Not today.* No court in America would rule in my favor for what I just did. Father or not, this wasn't a practical decision.

Now I'm late for work.

12

Smooth Criminal

I text my work to let them know I'm running behind. At 6:00 am, the traffic isn't bottlenecking yet. The sun saturates the atmosphere with warmth, illuminating the unequaled lushness of the Pacific Northwest. If only I weren't feeling so numb. I just dodged a bullet. I'm either extremely lucky, or I'm being given more of God's grace than I truly deserve. Throughout years of lawless living, I've been fortunate. Interaction with the police has never been part of my story.

The forty-minute drive allows time for contemplation. I could've ruined everything with the stunt I just pulled. Instead of giving myself a browbeating for letting my will take over, I reflect on how and why I did so.

"It was the song, maannnn," I say aloud in my best Charles Manson impersonation. I misinterpreted hearing that song as a sign I should believe in the "miracles" of *my* doing. In actuality, I should've seen this as God's doing.

"Thank you, God of my limited understanding. I pray you teach me how to trust you. Not so much that you teach me, because I'm beginning to see you've been trying all along, but to open my mind so I'm able to listen and learn!"

I pull into the warehouse parking lot where I load my truck with the day's deliveries. As I'm backing into my loading bay, I notice movement in the driver's side rearview mirror. A motorcyclist advances in my direction with obvious intent. I know what this is, which is odd because I've never had anything like this happen. I just know. My left hand rolls the window down as the motorcyclist reaches inside his vest. I outstretch my right arm, holding my palm upward, wide open.

"Paul Summers?"

"That's me."

"You've been served."

He slaps an official-looking manila envelope in my hand. My name is written with Sharpie across it. A part of me is satisfied this is happening. It feels like closure. I no longer have to wonder if Leann's going to have me served.

He looks perplexed by my wide smile. Finally! A legitimate legal battle. It may serve as a chance to see Lola again. After years of drug-induced hibernation, I'm assimilating into the modern world. The exhilaration takes about ten minutes to wear off.

I load my truck, then start along the day's route. Every few minutes, I glance over at the envelope. *Is it really a restraining order?* I pledge to wait. I'm not going to open it until I'm done working, otherwise my thoughts will be hijacked the rest of the day.

Come quitting time, I pat myself on the back for having the discipline to hold off. In the safety of my apartment, I tear the thick envelope open. Inside is an officially photocopied Restraining Order To Prevent Abuse from the State of Oregon.

I read, then reread Leann's handwritten statement. A long-winded testimonial. It's chockful of one false accusation after another, some serious. I'm mortified. Not in an outburst sort of way, but I'm angered by how believable her telling of events sounds. This unpredictable, explosive bully depicted on these pages isn't me. Is it?

By putting myself in her shoes, it's easier to see how she has interpreted the events. Integration of her point of view, however, doesn't come without the suspicion that one—or both—of us is a fraud. Either way, this feels like I've prematurely been proven guilty—until a large retainer, manipulation of facts, or "proof" deem me innocent. My entire being wants to fight this bullshit today. Since I can't, I start cleaning the apartment to temporarily take my mind off things. She left it a mess.

I bounce from room to room, boxing up what's left of her things. This way, if she returns to grab more stuff while I'm at work, it'll show her who has the upper hand. I want her to think I'm over us already. Although a restraining order is considered a de facto divorce in some legal circles, my pretending I'm over her might get her to reconsider filing it. If I can break her self-confidence, she'll come to realize she needs me. Tried and true guerrilla tactics of my past.

Is this still who I want to be? How many times have I sought to prove the actions and thoughts inside me were right by making everything outside me wrong? Should I continue to do the things I've always done? My ego screams a resounding, "Hell, yes!" But another part of me whispers, "Why bother? These head games never change the outcome."

I'm reminded of a saying: "If you always do what you've always done, you'll always get what you've always got." Competing in my head with my ego's need to win is a conscientious desire to grow. My personality is split, but I can't stand being idle. I box up Leann's belongings—a gentle gesture of kindness . . . maybe a smidge of bartering.

I start by taking down framed images of a relationship I assume is done. Stubborn nails in the wall require removal with the aid of a claw hammer. I see its use as a metaphor for our undoing. Blindsided by all of this and what it truly means, my eyes tear up. The thought crosses my mind of how I'd be better off to own my part in the dissolution of our family. Not my usual thoughts after a breakup.

It helps.

Just as I settle into this reflective moment, my reflexes are shaken. There's an aggressive banging on the outer metal frame of my wide-open front door. I hurry to the entryway thinking Leann's come back home with Lola.

There, filling the doorframe, stands a Washington County Sheriff's Deputy. He doesn't bother to wait for my greeting. He asks my name. Before I finish introducing myself, he tells me to put the hammer down. I barely have it lowered to the carpet when he asks to come inside. I don't mean to escalate, but I ask him why.

"For your safety and mine. That's why! I've come to serve you a restraining order. I'm here to make sure wife beaters like you understand the consequences of failing to recognize the law."

"Again?"

"I said, I need to make sure wife beaters like you understand—"

"No, sir, what I meant is, I'm getting served *again*?"

"What do you mean?" His stern jaw suggests he thinks I'm playing a game.

"I just got served today by some guy on a motorcycle. Is this different?"

"I don't know. Do you mind if I take a look inside?" He points in, having already taken a step inside.

In *my* living room he commands, "Have a seat."

Then, like Muhammed Ali hovering over Sonny Liston's knocked-out body during their rematch of 1965, Officer Steroid (not his real name) pokes his finger into my chest in a chastising way.

"Let me just tell you what this order means. Are you listening?"

"Yes."

"Good! Because you really need to pay attention. First of all, you will *not* try to contact Leann. If you do, you're going to jail. You will *not* have your friends try to contact her. If they do, *you're going to jail*. If your friends contact her friends on your behalf, *you'll go to jail*. You will *not* come within one hundred yards of her. If you do, *you'll go to jail*. If you leave a message on her phone, I'll take *you to jail*. In fact, I'm looking for any excuse to take abusers like *you to jail* where you belong. Do you understand?"

My rib cage aches like someone has punched it in. I nod in acknowledgement.

"What about my daughter, sir? When will I be able to see her?"

"That's for the courts to decide. But until you speak to a judge, you come anywhere near your wife or kid and—"

"I know. I'm going to jail."

"You wanna get smart with me, mister?"

"No." I smile, relieved he might be done.

"Is this a laughing matter to you? From what I read in this, you're not cute nor are you a funny person. Guys like you, guys who beat women, are not men. You're a boy in my book. It would give me great pleasure to take you in right now. So, if you wanna get smart, just give me a reason."

Not knowing how to respond, I glance up at him, then down to the carpet. What else is there to do or say? Standing up for myself could make this worse.

"One's all I need," he adds.

Telling this protector of the people my side of the truth would be a waste of breath. I'm deflated enough. I'm not an abusive husband or father.

He sees himself out, prolonging his intimidation by slowly stomping down each step. After the clomping stops, I try cleaning again but end up back against the same hallway wall I was at the other night. Unable to hold myself up, I slither down, my head between my palms. Overcome with pain, humiliation, and the hopeless sense I'll never be allowed in Lola's life ever again, I wail.

It's uncomfortable feeling this vulnerable. I'm terrified of what Officer Steroid will do if he comes back. I run out to my balcony, double-checking to make sure he's left.

I know what I have to do next. I've procrastinated far too long. I drive the company truck to one of those anonymous meetings I attended during outpatient rehab. By sharing my restraining order story there, I make new friends. Some people really don't like cops or any form of authority. Some with good reason, some because law enforcement limits their ability to do whatever they want. I'm somewhere in between.

A handful of recovering addicts invite me out for coffee. They call it the meeting after the meeting. At first I'm hesitant. Sensing this, they ask me how I can be helped if I don't let people get to know me.

Under dim LED lighting and the ambience of lo-fi Spanish guitar music, we find a seat. I'm leaning in to hear them talk about how we have a disease. One that will take how a person treasures solitude and distorts it into a craving for isolation. A lesbian Native American woman at our table named Makela asks me how much clean time I have.

"Today makes three days."

The group claps as if we are still at a meeting.

Makela, however, doesn't smile or clap. She stares at me with concern in her eyes.

"And how are you doing with this?"

"Fine!" I respond automatically.

Her expressive eyes peer deep into me. I try looking around at the others, but my eyes are guided back to hers as if by tractor beam. My vision becomes blurry, except around her face. She communicates something spiritually. In a coffee shop full of conversing voices, I only hear the one in my head.

"Three days," it whispers.

Oh yeah!

This is the day I was supposed to be an absolute wreck. The day I've been afraid of. The day I'm normally too sick to function. I'm not feeling any withdrawal symptoms whatsoever; not even close. *When's the last time I had a thought about how much I miss getting high?*

What changed? Is it because I miss Lola so profoundly that I'm done willingly handing my life over to the slavery of addiction?

"You can do this, Paul. Recovery is possible."

What's happening to me? For what seems like an endless succession of years, I've been making one bad choice to cover the last. I can't recall the last time I had positive dialogue within my skull. Could this be a tipping point, the one where the saying *one day at a time* comes from? One thing is for certain: tonight I'll go to bed with three days clean. Tomorrow is up to tomorrow.

13

It's Been A While

Eighty-four hours without using. Not that I'm counting.

I have personal errands to take care of after a long day at work. There's a meeting I want to attend called Spiritual Journeys, but it's across town. SJ is the meeting I walked out of ten months ago before relapsing. How I'll get there forces me to make some hard choices.

The drive from my Beaverton apartment to Southeast Portland is seventeen miles through some of the worst traffic in Oregon. Ironically, this is along the same route I took three, four, maybe five times a week, every week, to my dealer's house. It's been said that because we addicts will go to great lengths to serve our addiction, we should be willing to go to just as great lengths to recover. The clichés are like breadcrumb-littered paths ingrained in my psyche. Funny how I never thought of them until after I relapsed.

Would taking the company vehicle across town be worth losing my job? Come to think of it, my employer neither approved—nor denied—my use of their box van as transportation. What could be more important than the daily reprieve from wanting to get loaded that I get by being around addicts sharing recovery? I also need groceries.

If I can't eat, I can't work, right? I decide to risk my job instead of my recovery, based on which one I'll have a better chance of getting away with.

~

Because the company logo is embossed all over the work truck, I park off the main road, away from the church where the meeting is held. Some addicts are already gathered. A set of creaky wooden steps lead into the dank basement.

Standing at the edge of the entryway, I'm gnawing at my fingernails; pulling at each cuticle. I'm pinned in place by spinning thoughts. *Will anyone remember me? Do I have to raise my hand as a newcomer, admitting relapse?*

My brain's jammed. I wanted to come to this particular meeting. But, now that I'm here, I don't want to be here. I can't follow through. This is such a divergence of thoughts from when I was using. Back when no counter-thought was ever shaming or stammering enough to keep me from going to get drugs—regardless of where, how, or who I got them from—once my mind was made up.

Why, then, is potential embarrassment powerful enough to keep me from going inside?

It's seventy-five degrees. Summertime in Portland. Yet, my arms are trembling. I'm unable to process this other than wanting to run off. Like a diabetic suffering from low blood sugar instinctually knows to drink juice or eat glucose tabs to keep from getting severe hypoglycemia, I retreat to the work truck. Acuity returns, but not until after I'm in; slamming the heavy door and inhaling the odor of acrid perspiration and cigarette smoke embedded in the bench seat.

The instant I drive away, my mindset changes. I've never had this kind of physical reaction to mental stress. I'm not yet ready to face the weight, real or imagined, of being at this meeting. I go get food instead, scarfing it down while driving. A strong urge to head home sets in. I tell myself no. *No, I will not give in.*

What is this bullshit? What am I *really* considering? Is this a sneaky persuasion to get me to stop taking part in a program of recovery? After only three days? What about Lola? We've never gone this long without at least speaking to each other. She's somewhere, missing her daddy right about now.

Still, my head keeps searching for excuses to drive straight home. *Then what?* Wouldn't that be turning my back on her? These meetings offer the only hope I've found to stay clean, maybe long enough to come to her rescue. Not that meetings are a panacea for all uneasiness, but they offer an antidote: the calmer headspace and reassurance I feel when I'm among people who have found a way to stay clean. If I go home, I re-embrace insanity. It would be like choosing dope.

I am not cured. I need this recovery thing—the constant reminders and motivation. The regular *atta-boys* offer a much needed assurance I'm doing something right.

I need these people. I cannot do this on my own. I've tried.

I check my attitude by comparing where I'm at right now with the last time I wanted to get clean.

Back then, I didn't let myself get close to anyone at meetings. I just showed up. I figured all I had to do was stay off the dope; recovery would come through osmosis. I didn't call any men's numbers from the list they gave me. What would I say? I honestly thought I could do fellowship without one-on-one interaction. But by not comprehending how much my disease had control over what and how I thought, I kept getting sicker.

I flash back to a placard pinned on a corkboard in an old church. It read: The only thing we have to change is EVERYTHING.

Back then, those words were too intimidating. I wasn't ready to do whatever it takes to get clean. Now I'm curious. And willing. *I'm going to the meeting.*

~

As I pull up, I tell myself I'll just listen. No one said I have to open my mouth, although it *is* suggested.

Right when I walk in, I'm handed a laminated placard with this meeting's format. I'm asked to chair, or lead. This means that I choose the topic, share my story about it, then call on people. Although it's a reasonable request, I don't know if I'm qualified. While thinking about what I'll say, my legs keep crossing and uncrossing. If only I could fast-forward to the end of the meeting.

Once my mouth opens to speak, I realize something. My Higher Power wanted me to end up here all along. Words flow as I share about the indecisiveness and debilitating fear I was just feeling; about being too ashamed to admit I was starting over, and about the events which preceded my recent relapse. I candidly detail my discovery.

"Things aren't any better out there," I say. "I've done the research. I still cannot use drugs successfully. The fact that I made it back is telling. If God saw me fit to save, maybe I should believe that, too."

I stick around to help clean up afterward. I'm approached by a young woman with two days clean. She thanks me. She was planning on using tonight. Then something about what I shared changed her mind.

My story laid out the most likely outcome if she does. Even though she's holding back tears as she describes how humiliating just having her kids taken away is, the glow around her face exudes hope. I hug her to let her know she is not alone.

"Thank you," she whispers.

She pulls away with hesitation at first, then with certainty. Off she goes into the night. Recovery is beautiful, human, raw, and incalculable.

Despite my impulsive addict brain, I came here anyway. I used to believe I didn't possess inner strength. I've made it through my first Friday night in nearly a decade without wanting to use. I thank God for a fourth day clean, praying for Him to continue watching over my little Lola.

14

The Payback

After food shopping, I get home very late. I'm filling the barrenness of my fridge when my phone rings. It's Uncle Phil checking in. He's asking a lot of personal questions. I'm hesitant to offer any information until I first find out what he might let slip about Lola's whereabouts. A little *quid pro quo*.

They say we train people how to treat us. Phil knows me. His avoidance of my inquiry is fluid, smooth. I try changing the subject. As I'm telling him how I'm actively taking steps toward becoming a changed man, I realize I'm still trying to manipulate him. By tooting my own horn, I'm secretly hoping I'll convince him to drop his guard and divulge where his side of the family is keeping my kid. It isn't until after I give up prying for information that he assures me Lola is okay.

"Can I talk to her?"

"Well . . . I don't think that's a good idea right now."

Hearing this feels like someone holding a lighter to my nerve endings. I hold back a "Who the fuck are you to tell me what's a good idea right now, Mr. Kidnapper?" retort. It's important for me to be on good terms with Phil, as well as practice some spontaneous discipline. I only have control over two things: *my attitude and actions*. This feels like a test of both. I try changing the subject.

My withheld irritation distills down to bitter melancholy. Then, a distinct laugh overheard in the background whisks it away. Lola giggling. Peace fills my heart; tears fill my eyes. My exoskeleton turns to Jell-O. Phil is talking, but I'm trying to hear Lola.

"Dude, this is really wrong. She misses you so much. She asks about you constantly," he confesses, then continues. "What I want . . . I mean, if I had my way, I'd drive her down right now to see you. I really mean that. All of this is so frickin' wrong."

"It *is* wrong!"

My words spill out with too much emphasis. I tell my head to stop pushing Phil away, to be on his good side. *Speak through the heart, not the mouth*. Seeing Lola again is more important than righteous pride. I can either be humble or be humiliated. I open my mouth, this time using a voice I don't believe is my own.

"That's nice of you, Phil. I appreciate your concern. But keep in mind it's crucial we all observe the restraining order. I wouldn't want you or anyone else to get in trouble for violating it."

"Yeah. About that . . ."

"Yes?" I perk up.

"Man, I just wish . . . I wish I knew you'd be . . . umm—"

"Just say it."

"If you'd be cool. I mean, you wouldn't get violent or anything, right? Would you?"

"Of course not! I didn't do those things alleged in the restraining order."

I hear how my combative persona is getting defensive. Aware of this, I put myself in his shoes to predict, from his point of view, what's best to say next. In a way, it's laughable that anyone would be afraid of me.

Distorted interpretation is a symptom of this disease. Life is a never-ending game of chess for addicts. To win, we give our pieces heterodox moves. I'm not saying we're all cheaters, but because we perceive our adversaries as such, we respond with prejudice. We have an arrogant propensity to avoid being limited by rules steeped in societal expectations.

A normal person can more easily adjust to the etiquette game. To us, it's a rigged scheme. When our opponent figures out our unconventional moves, then adjusts, we tend to run all the pieces off the gameboard. Or, as retaliation, we break off interest from the game and its outcome. How does a normal person adjust to that?

Realizing this, I gain empathy and decide to be honest about the person Phil is dealing with—me.

"But of course I'd say that now, right? I haven't been a good husband. I don't deny that. But a wife beater? Come on. Yes, I lose control of my temper. Yes, I fight with harsh, demeaning words, which I know can cross a line, too. Maybe I'm not the best father, but you said it yourself—Lola misses me. I just don't understand why she has to be taken away from *me* while this gets sorted out."

"Well, it's not that she's taken, Paul. It's just . . . we're worried that if you get Lola back, none of us will ever see her again."

If only he knew how badly that's exactly what I want to do. I've never had to quell so much antagonism, rage, resentment, and thoughts of vengeance. Although often pigeonholed as a horrible person, I've never felt like such a monster, never been treated so inhumanely. Never has my nose been held to such a disfiguring grindstone. *Do I really deserve all of this?*

"However, if you'll give me your word you won't cut and run, I might be able to work something out."

I forget to exhale, which causes a floating sensation. I will say or do anything to hold Lola's hand again. Being a father himself, Phil knows. He shouldn't dangle a carrot he can't deliver. I'm guarded. Controlling my tone, I answer flatly. Like keeping a secret, I'm containing excitement building within. I won't let him take that away, too.

A compliant, "Yes. You have my word," is given, but not without a slow release of venom. In an even flatter tone, I add, "I will not steal her away like she was stolen from me."

Phil's response is immediate. "Whoa! Those are pretty harsh words. No one *stole* her from anyone."

"Okay, okay. I'm sorry. This is really hard for me." Pulling the phone away from my face doesn't minimize how loud I'm sniveling.

Hearing my unimpeded sobbing, Phil asks if I'm okay. He promises to call back after verifying plans with Aunt Darcy.

Later, as I lay in bed, my eyes puffy, I smile so wide my cheeks hurt. I tell myself I've won this round. Because God wants me to see Lola. Because I'm doing everything right. Because I deserve to have her back.

Minutes later when Phil calls back, I answer the phone casually, not wanting it known how the prospect of seeing Lola has me beside myself with excitement.

"Hey, man. Darcy said she'll work it out with the grandparents. You should be able to see Lola around noon tomorrow at their house. Will that work?"

Choked up, I practice showing gratitude—a principle I swore I'd never allow myself to express. I always thought that if you show gratitude for people's assistance, you'll be expected to return their favors. Instead, I always acted like people owed me. Thankfulness, I'm learning, is key to recovery—whether or not things go my way.

"Yes. Thank you, Phil."

I reach back to the headboard to grab an item I kept out while going through boxes earlier. It's the card I got for Lola. The one with a Christmas tree and wintery scene that lights up. I can't believe the battery hasn't died. Now it holds a special bittersweet significance.

I hug it close to my chest and sing, "You Are My Sunshine" as if Lola is winding down her day beside me, readied for bed, as she has on countless evenings. I imagine her drifting off to sleep, listening to the sound of my voice. Observing her eyelids change color from mauve to orchid as they sink into slumber. The scent of baby shampoo in her freshly washed, golden-brown hair. Touchstones of perhaps the sweetest innocence I'll ever witness. My fingers lift the card up above my breastbone. I depress the button, giving it power to illuminate the darkness surrounding my spirit. Darkness I once invited to live inside me.

"Good night, honey. Daddy loves you. I'll see you tomorrow."

~

I wake up with a gleam in my eye. A new morning. I have five days clean under my belt. Something feels different.

As I'm eating breakfast, a reminder pops into my head of how many times I've accomplished five days. Too many. My self-dialogue switches to such generous negativity, it spills over the brim.

I've sworn on my life, on my soul, to God, to whatever or to whomever, that I was over drugs and booze. Then, mere hours later, I've dug through trash to retrieve pills I'd just tossed out or taken apart a picture frame to scrape drug residue off the glass.

Following one particularly irresponsible four-day bender, I felt reprehensible, begging for divine intervention as I came down. I used again the very next day. Afterwards, I told myself God's trust was lost and could never be restored. As if His choices were up to me. These types of self-dialogue twists remain prevalent. Maybe forever.

Yet, something *is* different.

Instead of ignoring my negative, skeptical, deprecating thoughts, I'm letting them be. It's a sunny July day. Birds are chirping ecstatically outside. For the first time since moving here, the blinds get drawn and windows opened. Alone with fresh air filtering in, I start to sing while cleaning up after breakfast.

Looking online, I see that our checking and savings are cleaned out. Today's paycheck isn't enough to cover rent, which is past due. Despite facing possible eviction and homelessness, I'm full of an unnatural calm feeling of optimism. I whistle along the walk to the office, where I explain my situation to the landlord. She promises to work with me, accepting my offer to pay half for now. Yes, something is indeed weird and different. The world I've been battling since active addiction took over is willing to work with me.

Back upstairs, I'm again singing, checking the clock, counting down the minutes to when I get to see Lola. I'd like to sustain this attitude until we reunite, to show her everything's going to be okay. I just know she's hurting, being stripped away from her daddy without knowing the whole story. Imagine how many hateful words and undesirable remarks she's overheard. This is not the time to throw gasoline on a fire spreading on its own. That day will come.

By 11:30 that morning, I've cleaned my apartment twice over. I go clothes shopping at a resell store for something to bring Lola. While walking, I discover my minivan parked in the strip mall lot. Leann must've abandoned it here, left unlocked for who knows how long. The keys are on the front seat in plain sight. My belongings are scattered about, loose change in the console missing.

A stranger helps jumpstart it. No more worrisome driving around in the company truck. I return to my apartment with bags of gifts. My landline rings.

"Top of the morning, Phil. I'm ready to go when you are," I say. I expect my ample enthusiasm to be contagious.

"Hey."

Uh oh, his tone.

"We just want you to know something changed. Really sorry, bro, but you'll have to see Lola another time."

My heart stops, drops, splits, then shatters as it falls away from my chest cavity onto the cheap, durable linoleum.

"What?" Emotionally, I'm as anxious as a wild animal who just realized it's stuffed in a cage.

Silence.

I know who's behind this. Bring it. I won't back down from a fight, even when I know I'll lose.

"Put Darcy on the phone. Please?"

Aunt Darcy is right beside him, listening. She comes on.

"Darcy, what do you mean, it'll have to be another time?"

"Yeah. Don't hate me. We did our best. Somethin' about the grandparents feeling uncomfortable with the arrangement goin' down at their house. But, hey, I tried. I really tried." Her tone seems too snappy to be genuine. This feels intentional. It reeks of spiteful reprisal. I'd prefer a hatchet in the back.

"Why are the grandparents making custody decisions? Where's Leann in all this?" I ask.

"I did what I could, okay? It's just not going to happen. I'm so soowwwry."

"Can you hold on just a moment?" I ask. *Do something now!* I think. I turn one direction and then the other, then back again, while cupping the mouthpiece in my hands.

Without an action plan, I'm fighting inertia. I succumb to survivalist, tactical plotting, speculating about where they have Lola. *Maybe she's still at the grandparents' house and they don't want me to see her. If I go over there, I can force the issue. Now's my chance. Every second counts.*

I tell Darcy to hold on again, then set the phone down but don't hang it up. I'm hoping the empty airspace will buy some time. I run out my door to get there quickly, leaving my apartment open.

Within ten minutes, I'm knocking on the grandparents' door. Grandpa Patrick answers in sweatpants and a food-stained long-sleeve shirt. He's mumbling into a phone nestled between his shoulder and his beard.

"Where's my daughter?"

"She ain't here."

"I am her biological father. Where is she? Why have you guys abducted my child?"

"We didn't abduct anyone." His brows furrow.

"Then why won't you tell me where she is? She's my daughter, and she's missing her father. She's not some ball for you to play keep-away with."

"I don't know what to tell you."

My emotions dart in every which direction. Indecipherable thoughts run amok. Then, an atypical idea overrides it all, breaking through like an Amber Alert notification. But it's not coming from me. Not exactly.

An inner voice suggests I sit down on the front stoop this instant. At some intrinsic level, I understand. Sitting down is nonviolent, non-confrontational. My knees bend to sit, as advised.

Just as my butt cheeks smack against the concrete stoop, I hear engines revving. Two police cars come speeding in from opposite sides of the street. The closer one skids to a screeching stop. As the bluish smoke of burned rubber lifts, the officer bolts out toward me. His left hand unbuckles the snap holding his gun in its holster. His pacing slows slightly once he notices my cross-legged sitting position.

"Sir, is this guy bothering you?" he yells, pointing at me, while making eye contact with Patrick.

"Naw, he's not bothering me."

"You! Hey. You! Step away from the front door. Go stand at the bumper of my car."

"I'm just trying to see my daughter, your honor."

This is probably the wrong time to test my theory that cops don't like being called "your honor." He reaches back to pull out handcuffs.

"Shut up and do as you're told, or I will arrest you for resisting."

Having never been in this predicament, I don't take this a tiny bit lightly. To do what the officer tells me is how I was raised. Again, there's too much at stake to be self-righteous. I wait where I'm told as the first responder speaks with my in-laws. I overhear T's name. She must've called the cops. *Set up like a bowling pin.*

If a case can be built to make me appear violent, aggressive, or noncompliant, I will surely lose custody of my baby. *Why am I unwilling to trust in how the truth's going to come out eventually?*

There isn't a single shred of evidence to prove I'm a threat to anyone's safety. The restraining order is hearsay, conjecture. Until I get a hearing, it's purely postulation without proof. Pulling stunts like this just helps to confirm their accusations.

I am the only chance Lola has of having a father in her life.

The officer speaks something about being all clear into his shoulder microphone while approaching me. If I look stupid, at least I look remorsefully stupid. I don't know how the laws work exactly. If I violated the restraining order by trying to see my daughter, there must be some way to convince a judge of my intentions. But if it comes down to my word against theirs, I may have blown this. A huge mistake I'd have to live with. But could Lola?

"Do you have an Aunt Darcy who was trying to work out an arrangement for you to see your daughter?"

"Yes, sir.

"But you have no business being over here. You know that, right?"

My brain spins. What possible outcomes or reactions could be had to what I should, shouldn't, will, or won't say?

"I'm just trying to see my daughter, sir."

"But *you know* you have no business being here, right?"

"I do now, yes sir."

The officer widens his stance like Wonder Woman, minus the hands on hips and bright red lipstick. He glares at me, evaluating my demeanor. Making eye contact briefly, I then lower my gaze toward the street. I am not defiant. I'm compliant. Because I'm scared, I'm not conveying it very well. He won't need to test my will or use force to extract any hidden, sullen desire to escalate.

"You got two minutes to leave the premises."

"Thank you, officer."

I gratefully hold out my hand to shake his. He grimaces at my gesture.

"I don't do that. You got less than two minutes."

On the drive home, my foot shakes in fits over the pedals. Two cop cars make themselves apparent in my side and rearview mirrors. One eventually peels off. The other continues tailing me, mirroring my lane changes and speed.

While five days clean is something to be proud of, everything else is spiraling downward. Knowing I'm growing isn't enough. Right now, it doesn't seem like recovery is *ever* going to be worth it. If I didn't have such a bitter taste in my mouth about being set up, I'd probably go use. I can't believe I haven't yet. My resolve is being reinforced by fantasies of retribution instead of positive principles. It's still morning. I've got a long way to go to call this another day won.

Then it hits me. This is my bottom, the result of consistent poor choices, and even poorer excuses. *How did I get here?*

Systematically, I isolated myself. Recklessly, I took my family hostage, forcing them into my well-shrouded world of darkness, deceit, and drug-fueled madness. Obstinately, I got so adept at hearing only what I wanted for so long that I believed my own lies. How else could I allow this to happen? The man I've been is not who I was meant to become.

Throughout the tense drive home to lick my wounds, I curse myself for having hope earlier. I'm not replenished by some "when the going gets tough" type of cliché. This is not my "aha" moment. Nor is it a motivational "pull yourself up by the bootstraps and dust yourself off" epiphany. I'm withering inside, too disheveled at my core to cry.

Returning to my open apartment, I plop down onto the crayon-marked-up chair at my faux office desk. I pull paper from the ream in the tray. With Lola's baby blue Sharpie, I write:

HONESTY

OPEN-MINDEDNESS

WILLINGNESS

Using a pair of rounded-tip kid scissors, I cut out the words into a small rectangle. Three spiritual principles to take wherever I go. I gently slide the paper into the see-through identification compartment of my wallet.

A quick glance around the desk brings a grim realization. I had once spent hours building this home studio, my head giddy with grand possibilities of writing and recording new songs. I dreamed of selling them online, generating followers, landing a record deal. A last-ditch effort to obtain the notoriety I'd devoted my life to. That was eight months ago.

I look down at the digital eight-track equipment's knobs and faders. They're covered in built-up dust. Best intentions cooked up in a meth pipe. Instead of being a DAW (digital audio workstation) where I'd hone my craft, this space ended up being where I'd surf the internet for days on end. Instead of learning or influencing, I indulged in pornographic stories, images, and videos for self-gratification. Instead of engaging with Lola as she came running out of her room to play with me, I'd have to hide my computer screen, each time infuriated with her mom for not corralling her.

I don't have a way to turn from the shame. So, instead of further debasing myself, I try out an alternative perspective. This painful awakening is a blessing. I don't have to—I *get* to—feel it.

This is my bottom. Here, in this moment.

For in this moment, after multiple attempts at going up against the forces of the universe, my will *has no other choice* but to allow itself to admit defeat. Up until this moment, I've harbored the notion that if I can appear presentable enough to get through societal hoops and preserve my facade, I can go right back to who, how, where, and what I was without any repercussions. Up until this moment, my idea of compromise meant vowing to never, ever give up or give in to anyone or anything—except in the buying, using, or finding of more drugs. Up until this moment, my way of getting what I wanted was to slither my way in, through indirectness, passive-aggressiveness, betrayal, coldness, bullying, divisiveness, treachery, and charismatic self-centeredness. Up until this moment, my well-managed, best-conceived plans were just brilliant and strategic enough to bring me here, to my bottom.

In this moment, I'm brought to my knees before God. Not knowing whether I'm begging to be forgiven or baiting to be further broken.

Life as I know it is not going to simply go my way. My way is not working, nor was it ever, really. I cannot continue lying to myself. I cannot continue manipulating everyone and everything around me, controlling outcomes, testing boundaries—not if I want anything to turn out different than it has thus far.

At this bottom, I discover the only way my powerfully selfish ego would ever *surrender*.

When I'm ready to believe in a Higher Power that's not some whimsical self-serving god of planetary pleasures, I'll equally need to learn how to set aside my will long enough to hear Its plan for me. And then to practice it. It will require my all-out effort to alter how I think and do life.

Rather than react or try to control going into a tailspin, I lean into it. Allow myself permission to feel it. Be in the moment.

I bring the Lola's bag of gifts to my room and set them down beside me on the bed. I want to lie here and forget. The adrenaline of interacting with the police is still splashing against my veins, so I sit up. In doing so, my attention is diverted to the Christmas card. I hold it to my heart.

In a motherly whisper, a voice tells me we will be reunited. The tender faith I'm opening up to helps me keep going. Blind trust that a power greater than myself can move me toward the direction in which I will earn my worth to be a part of Lola's life. I can't work my games and trickery to force it. It's out of my hands. Broken by a trivial convenience store card, bought as an afterthought, I recite my unconditional surrender.

"God. Please, if you are real, please help me. I can't do this alone."

An overdue clearing-out of emotion takes place. Tears stream down my cheeks for fifteen minutes straight. Stuff I've clung to for years empties away. The unexpected joy of evanescent lucidity is like a high. It has me craving more. A man from my phone list suggests a Saturday night podium meeting. It's across town, but now I have my van back. I leave early, stopping at a park to take a regenerating walk in nature. While meditating beneath an old spruce tree, my complete surrender gets confirmation.

"God, I pray to you. I will do whatever you ask. Please show me how to stay clean so one day my little girl will be proud to call me her father. Please? I will do anything!"

15

Gone Daddy Gone

As I near the church where the meeting will be held, I drive up on an all-too-familiar scene. Scanning ahead, off to my right, I count four squad cars. One in front, three behind a rusted-out white mini truck. I know a drug bust when I see one.

Slowing to a crawl, I'm eyewitness to a series of images. Three cops stand tense around the person being arrested, an unkempt man on his knees, slightly younger than I am. They've restrained him in handcuffs. His head hung low, the distraught man looks up sideways at the officers, deceitful desperation in his eyes. His body language tells me he's pleading his case, denying accountability. I brake to about five miles per hour. My eyes pan quickly back and forth between where he's standing and where his truck is pulled over.

The doors, held wide open by an officer, are missing their side panels. The officer's drug-sniffing dog is barking like crazy. With a wave of his arm, he commands the canine to jump up onto the bench seat. The man's posture slumps. The canine paws at the glove box. Reasonable suspicion just increased to probable charges, thanks to the olfactory senses of a lawfully trained German shepherd.

Some thirty yards farther down, a female officer kneels alongside a two-foot cinderblock wall. There on the wall, kicking her dangling legs up and down as if on a playground swing, sits a little girl. She's roughly the same age as my little girl. She's dressed in the same trendy, inexpensive clothes from the same big-box store I buy from.

The concerned expression on the face of the female cop isn't having the desired effect. She's doing her best to tactfully ease the severity of the situation the little girl may be facing. The child doesn't seem to hear a word the cop is saying. Her eyes, wide and wistful, stare off in her dad's direction. Her forward-leaning elongation suggests a yearning to return to the "safety" of her father.

I have a unique vantage point. My focus shifts between what I see out my side window and my side-view mirror. Wearing a Kevlar vest and body cam to accentuate her armor, the female cop modifies her stance. She shifts left and right to protect the child from witnessing images with the potential to be tragic. She is unsuccessful. As the three officers sternly force the resistant man into one of the squad cars, the little girl freefalls to her knees, then teeters onto her stomach, pounding her fists on the grass. Her screaming cries drown out my stereo. The hard female cop, a total stranger, is now her only source of comfort. A gulp in my throat puts pressure on my eardrums.

"Was that for me to see, God?" I ask. I know the answer.

Examining just how undeservedly blessed I am, I reflect on the life I've lived. I've never been incarcerated for my unlawful misdeeds. For whatever reason, my Higher Power didn't make the justice system part of my story. I believe He knew a criminal life would've been as much, if not more, attractive to me as using. For had I headed down that road of criminality, I would've been hooked on getting good at it, stubbornly embracing and defending it. If I needed a sign of verification God exists, here it is on the side of the road.

A stinging in my nose tickles my tear glands. Continuing toward my destination becomes difficult, yet more necessary than getting anywhere, ever. It may be uncomfortable or embarrassing to share about tonight, but I must. I am humbled and broken by the scene I just passed. God offered me a peek. An opportunity to preview a predisposition my own brain disguised as fiction. This lifestyle, of which I can be masterfully oblivious, nearly killed me. But not *just* me.

~

What's Really Going On is a popular Saturday night meeting. I stand at the entrance, waiting for my turn to hug the male greeter. My anonymity feels more secure here. Not only is there strength in numbers, but there is camouflage in them as well.

I find a place to sit at a table next to two guys mandated by the state to attend. They're part of a group driven here on a small bus with a chaperone. Also at my table is a woman with her infant boy, a well-groomed man in business attire, and a teenager with earbuds who never looks up from her phone.

During fellowship time before the meeting begins, I take a furtive scan of the room. I wonder how many folks come in and out of recovery and if I should bother introducing myself. Arms folded, I remain glued to my seat—because of who I am, not where I am.

A woman gets up to speak. She has chosen Building Upon the Foundation of Recovery as her topic.

"By renewing our commitment daily, and maintaining it as a top priority, it's easier to stay in the middle of the program. If you hang out on the edges, you're more likely to fall off. Complacency is the enemy. We have a disease. One which is not only patient and progressive but also incurable."

I feel like she is speaking directly to me. I'm hearing extra meaning within each word. I'm able to listen without distraction. Every nuance of being here feels brand new.

The woman opens the podium up to whoever wishes to share. I position myself to go first by speaking out well before I reach the kiosk. I introduce myself as an addict.

Standing still, I face the room. My palms ooze sweat as my grip on each side of the wooden stand increases. So does my sense of vertigo. Gazing out at over a hundred recovering addicts and alcoholics, I clear my dry throat. My stare shifts out to the multitude of tall windows lining two sides of the hall, then to the outside.

The somewhat typical gray of the Pacific Northwest's natural mood light filters in. That, coupled with the story I must tell, helps notch down my nervousness. Before speaking, my attention goes skyward, asking in silent prayer for openness.

The room is brimming with movement, tension, and agitation. The pause I take to ground myself is an unintentional attention grabber. I look up, out over the group. There are no empty seats.

From the singed, rotting, and worn woven fabric of society, they have come. Cracked souls, broken professionals, rehabilitating criminals, workaholics, predators, artists, spouses, derelicts, non-workers, prominent community leaders, adulterers, corporate executives, gamblers, betrayed bad boys, and fractured femme fatales—the gamut.

Addicts. Alcoholics.

My people. My peers.

I share about losing. About how I let my addiction back in to take me back out. Taking me far away from here, in these meetings, the only place I ever felt a welcome part of anything. How I lost my house, my marriage, my dignity, but most of all, my daughter. How I found my way back, thanks to providence. How the drug bust scene I just witnessed on my way here was no coincidence. I saw my future.

"Some say, if you're not sure you've hit your bottom yet, then you haven't. Now I know. I have. Today is my fifth day clean. Today, I'm starving for more recovery."

After the meeting, fellowshipping continues. A few people give hugs, telling me my story really touched them. Even though I wonder what was so special about it, I thank them. Their feedback reinforces this notion that I just might have some worth.

I've always been a pretty damn good storyteller. I'm also a damn good liar and improvisational truth stretcher. Tonight, though, I got real—like, in the mirror real—which people can relate to. Exchanging numbers, making new acquaintances, I'm a part of, not apart from, the solution. If recovery's going to be like this, I just might be okay. I'm the only person who can screw things up, which scares me, because I could fuck up a free lunch.

~

A full moon peeks above clouds in the east. Its illuminating rays redirect me back to a time when I held different beliefs. I'd been reading books about Native American tribes and the sacred power of the full moon. One night I thought I'd try channeling its energy, believing the missing ingredient to my getting clean was its healing power.

"With the aid of the next full moon," I vowed, "I'll quit using."

Twenty-eight days later came my first test. Leaving Portland that afternoon, I was driving to Reno to kick off a three-week tour. By the time I reached the Trinity National Forest around Mt. Shasta, a full moon brightened my way.

I pulled down a Bureau of Land Management forest service road and found the perfect place to cleanse and quiet myself before invoking the full moon energy. Being in such a remote wilderness made it magical. The entire cosmos seemed to be aligned. The animals became motionless, the insects silenced, pine trees gave off visible dancing waves of frenetic energy.

Through prayer, I sequestered the full moon spirit's power to help me attain purity. Touched by the stillness and filled with cosmic vibrations, I felt invincible. My soul opened up to the unknown. But the good vibe didn't last. The possibilities got scary. Perhaps prematurely, I climbed back in my van and hauled off.

I arrived in Reno around 1:00 am. I met my friend, a fellow musician, at a bar. He invited me onstage for an impromptu set.

Swaying in front of me, a drunken patron made herself more than noticeable, her flirting irresistible. Afterward, she summoned me to follow her outside. Assured the coast was clear, she then pulled a spoonful of white powder from a vial and held it up to my nose.

I could have refused. I could've considered the toll. I could've considered my girlfriend back home. I could've been thinking about how much I wanted to stay clean. The usual automatic behavior, based on my "get it while you can" mentality, came next. With just one sniff of a nostril, I crossed the moon's electromagnetic virtue off my ally list.

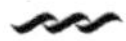

Gazing up at tonight's full moon, I wrestle with a voice that mutters convincingly, "This time won't be any different, so why try?" My lips bend into the type of smile a family member smiles for a loved one dying in the hospital. I return inside for continued fellowship.

16

Whisper to a Scream

Melancholy awaits my waking brain. Better to feel down than feel my own powerlessness over whatever pain reality offers. Assumptions arise around yesterday's exchange with the police. Thanks to my actions, it seems apparent I'll never be in Lola's life again. The only thing I ever cared about more than myself—which is debatable—is slipping from my grasp.

Of my blood relatives, the closest are a thousand miles away. They'd have all disowned me by now if I wasn't family. Any support within driving distance is done with me or worn thin. The lucky ones are those who figured out early on to create distance. Nothing they could do would save me. Convinced I'd burn them anyway, somewhere along the way I stopped building bridges.

My overthinking holds me back from reaching out. When it comes to asking for help, I either feel I don't deserve it, it won't be good enough, I'll owe too great a debt for it, or I'll thanklessly bite the hand of the helper. Chains of my past show up to restrain me whenever I'm willing to move forward.

Spinning thoughts and I are longtime friends. To sit in them is like slumping down into an old, broken-in recliner with the footrest extended. There, complacency is its own reward in that, by avoiding difficult decisions, ultimately they get made. These automatic tendencies need to stop. If I keep letting history predict my choices, I won't rise from this. My sober Uncle John would say, "Turn lemons into lemonade."

A call from my parents snaps me out of daydreaming. They're vacationing in Oregon. They want to see their granddaughter. Instead of an elaborate story concocted to cover my ass, I hear a recovery slogan: "First thought wrong."

"That's not going to be possible right now," I say, using my deepest, most sincere voice. One I rarely use.

"What? Why not, son?" asks my mom.

"What did you do?" My dad sums me up in his usual disappointed tone.

"Thanks, Dad," I answer. I'm shaking my bowed head. Normally, I take their criticism personally. But I'm not as offended as usual. In fact, my sarcastic reply carries a bit of lightheartedness.

"All right. Do you want to tell us what you're talking about?" Mom asks.

Letting them know the extent to which I'm responsible for what's happened is risky, but it gives birth to an opportunity to practice humility. Without letting the fear of feeling shame limit me, I fill them in with details, this time from the perspective of what I made happen instead of what happened to me. As I paint them an honest picture of my spiraling descent into drug abuse, their attitudes change from playful ribbing, to disapproval, to curiosity.

Sometimes a circumstance is so extreme it awakens potencies in people that allow them to step out of character. Presented with this family challenge, my parents push their righteousness aside and actively listen. It's not like them to provide verbal comforting. Yet, after hearing my remorseful accounting, they end up validating me and my transparency. They lovingly assure me everything will work out as it is supposed to. It's conceivable they might be infected by the same denial bug that has bitten their son.

My parents offer opinions about how to handle my situation. While I listen with an open mind, my facial muscles flinch unnaturally. Something happens I haven't felt in a while. I feel a warm smile on my face. *Why do they always believe things will work out?* Contemplating further, restructuring my question, I ask myself, Why *don't I* believe? If I'm going to be in Lola's life, I need to start building an arsenal of optimism.

I could start with being open to trying new perspectives.

I *could* talk to people at meetings, let them get to know me. I *could* build a support group, including asking for a sponsor. I *could* talk to men who are knowledgeable about divorce and custody. I *could* become willing to plug in and grow roots.

My parents call Patrick and Carol to let them know they'd like to see their granddaughter when they get into town. The four grandparents have always got along fabulously. Whenever my parents are in town, my in-laws meet them for lunch or dinner. The same applies when the in-laws are in Las Vegas. The call is seen as an olive branch. Both parties agree to stay out of our affairs instead of allowing our drama to become a point of contention between them.

Patrick and Carol promise my parents I'll be allowed to see Lola at their house. How fortunate am I that my in-laws admire and respect my parents enough to promise this? The miracle I'd been praying for managed to come from an unlikely source: good ol' Mom and Dad. Their arrival can't come soon enough.

~

With nine days of sobriety under my belt, my stinking thinking returns. It wastes no time in doing its part to sneak attack the better habits I'm learning by going to meetings. However, I'm sick and tired of being sick and tired. I'm done trying to win battles on my own, so I get up the courage to ask a man in recovery to be my sponsor.

Matt and I were acquaintances. We worked together at the online university. Nearly every time I took a bathroom break, he'd be in there, too. We'd talk and joke, usually about partying too much. Then, during my first stint trying to stay clean, I ran into him at a meeting. Knowing each other's sordid past, our work conversations from then on changed to recovery. He continues to stay clean. Knowing him prior to my life being turned upside down and right side up and then seeing him again after a year away from recovery is too coincidental to ignore. I'm told these serendipitous events are called God shots.

Matt gives me assignments right away. Write out the twenty-five ways my life has become unmanageable, and twenty-five reasons why I'm powerless over using booze and other drugs. He suggests I read about my disease and to get a service position—volunteer duties helping others. I take over his position as the person in charge of making coffee for the hundred-plus regulars at WRGO, the meeting I've decided to call my home group.

~

My parents call from their hotel room to invite me to dinner. I'm always happy to see them, but the fondness doesn't always last. We eat somewhere close to their hotel because they're heavy smokers who don't like to wait to get their cancer-stick fix. Seated at a restaurant booth, we discuss our strategy regarding Lola.

"This is killing me, not seeing her."

"We know, son. Just be patient," Mom says.

"No, you don't know. Neither of you has ever gone through anything close to what I'm going through."

My mom inhales a shortened breath. She's about to say something, but my dad grabs her hand. She exhales without a word.

"You're right, son. We're just trying to help. You'll get to see her tomorrow. Everything will work out like it should," my dad responds. His demeanor and calm are atypical. He's speaking in a voice I've never heard him use.

The table starts vibrating from my foot at its base. *Work out like it should?* I would rather ride a motorcycle full throttle into a barbed wire fence than hear that damn saying again. One thing I don't need right now is the fluid of their passive proselytizing dousing the flames of my testosterone-fueled virtue.

"We don't know for sure we'll see her, though," I retort.

"You'll get to see her, son," is my dad's willful reply. He's as optimistic as any good contrarian. A seasoned provider of the proverbial coin's other side.

"I don't trust them. They're going to pull something."

My fingernails start to leave indentations in my palms. To keep my dry throat from foaming, I gulp down icy water. My glass is covered in condensation. It almost slips from my grip onto the table. Cold droplets of water roll onto my wrist, irritating me further.

My dad restates his point in a more combative tone. "Just let it work out how it's supposed to, and it will, son."

He rubs the back of his neck. I chew the inside of my cheek. My mom spins the lighter atop her cigarette pack on the table.

"I don't know how you can say that," I reply in a snarky tone.

My parents aren't budging. I excuse myself to call my sponsor. My wrist quivers as I punch-tap Matt's digits into my cell. After leaving two messages, it's up to me to know what to do next.

"God, grant me the serenity to accept the things I cannot change, the courage to change the things I can, and the wisdom to know the difference."

To be fair, my parents have no idea what the last two weeks have been like. I don't share details because I still feel the need to have the "look good" part down. Neither parent knows how destitute I've become. I'm a drug and alcohol abuser who, after a soft-fought battle, lost everything that matters. On the outside, it's not easy to see how my downfall comes from the inside, the result of being impervious to my own actions.

Having them arrive during this particular chapter is remarkable. All too often I blamed them, among others, for the bulk of my negative predicaments. Mom worked too much. Dad was too critical. I didn't see them as fallible humans doing their best.

Sitting with them at dinner, being disagreeable, is commonplace. I still feel like a teenager whenever we get together. Like I'm still rebelling and they are still asking me what I'm going to do with my life just so they can tell me what foolish choices I'm making.

To this day, when they ask about me or offer help, I resort to putting on the suit I'm most comfortable in: the victim suit—casualty jacket, helpless tie, and pity-party shoes. I haven't uncovered enough insight to understand why I prefer this well-worn pattern. Being defensive is my way of showing them I'm not a quitter. I just don't know when to give up.

Reaching into my spiritual toolbox, I discover two things. First, I need more tools. Second, I need to look at the positive, no matter how unaccustomed I am to doing so.

I have to be willing to reach for tools instead of what I want to reach for. I was born with a disease that wants to undo, undermine, and undervalue everything about me. A clever enemy of life, it wants me to die, but only after a great deal of suffering.

My propensity to engage by lashing out is innate. I don't do it to protect, preserve, or provide a stance in defense of my deepest values (even though I'm very convincing otherwise). I do it to end up broken and alone. I have a disease that, battle after bloody battle, claims itself victorious over my spirit, eroding it down to a dying nub. This disease fights a war knowing it can't win, outside of death.

After years of degradation, however, my disease still hasn't managed to strip away my core strength—the aspiration to survive, be a better person, think and feel deeply, and persevere. This is something parents instill. Mine taught me unconventional ways to be tenacious. A learned behavior.

In my mom's unpublished memoir, she writes how her dad was convicted of and imprisoned for molesting his own daughters. Her mother died months later from an infection left untreated due to their severe poverty. She was thirteen. The Catholic Church took all six sisters into the East Harlem Children's Center on 104th Street in Manhattan for a year, but then placed them in different orphanages. My mom was sent to St. Agatha's Home for Children in Pearl River, New York. One thousand kids watched over by ninety nuns. She lived under tyranny, abused like Cinderella without the payoff of the Grand Ball. She's never spoken of the cruelties endured at the mercy of the nuns, other than how it turned her away from ever believing in God again.

At sixteen, my dad was abandoned by his mother. Grandma Lily left the rural trappings of Pearl River, New York. She fled to Florida with the milkman, taking my dad and his little sister, my Auntie M, with them. It was a ploy to secure alimony and child support. Once the checks started coming in, the lovers bailed. My dad came home to a twenty-dollar bill and a note that read, "Take care of yourselves." He retells this period of his life with excitement. Being a teenager on his own felt like a dream come true. He and my aunt lived without rules until he was severely beaten for having lunch with his best friend Preston, an African-American kid whom he invited to sit with him at the "white counter" of a diner. My dad soon after returned to New York to be with his father, who got remarried. His wife, Betty, was the only grandma I ever knew.

While sitting in the dean's office waiting to be admitted back into school, my dad claims to have been "hit by a lightning bolt in the heart" the moment he saw my mom. My grandpa, a workaholic with his own printing business in Manhattan, was probably too critical of my dad for them to remain close. A series of events sent my dad into rebellious criminality. He joined the service the day after marrying my mom. They had two kids while my dad was stationed in France.

Upon his completion of enlistment, the family of four piled in a car, and with fifty-eight dollars moved to the Golden State, the promised land of California. Within months, they were living on welfare. My dad eventually found employment. He transferred to Las Vegas, Nevada, so he could indulge in his vice of choice: gambling.

On my first Christmas morning, my dad brought home a tossed-out tree he'd found, just so my brothers and I would have one. On my third Christmas, he drove us to Barstow, California—the nearest town that would take his credit card—so we could have bikes. Yeah, my parents have been through some shit.

~

We walk out into the warm Beaverton, Oregon evening. As my parents inhale repeated drags off their cigarettes, I entertain a thought. *Since they don't understand my disease, I should share what I know.* Because they find it hard to believe I have a problem, I'll explain how my disease works.

They sound receptive, so I run to my car and get out the various books and pamphlets powering my recovery. We meet back in their room. Rushing my words, I read the first chapter from an anonymous textbook.

As both sit listening on either side of the king-sized bed, neither seem as onboard anymore. They're quiet, except for the lighting up of each other's cigarettes between sips of booze. I read nonstop through ten or so pages. Usually, one or both would interrupt or have some remark by this point. After finishing the chapter, I press the issue.

"What do you think of what I read?" I ask. I sound like a zealous boy in church, proud of his limitless inspiration to attain the glory of God by reciting biblical verse.

"Ugh. Hmm. Well. What do you think, honey?" my dad asks. He leans his knees toward my mom, but doesn't look at her. I can't recall a time my dad *couldn't* offer his opinion.

"I'm speechless."

My dad picks up the banner with confidence now. He's been trying to be considerate, what with the fragility of my predicament. It's not who he is. The gentle, piercing tinkle of ice rotating in his vodka glass as he brings it to his lips is like nails down a chalkboard. Its sound always precedes his staunch criticism.

"Yeah. I had no idea. I mean, it explains some of the reasons why we never understood you."

My mom takes a drag as she nods in agreement. I brace myself. Her energy is too built-up to restrain. She exhales pensively, drag freeing her lungs to take over the conversation.

"Do you mind if we're honest?"

"Of course, I don't mind," I reply. I invited them to express their reactions, remember? *If they only knew how many times I've wished I would've said, "Of course I mind. Keep your opinions to yourselves!"* But my predisposition to be berated is automatic.

"Those people you just read about?"

"Yeah, Mom?"

"They sound disgusting!"

"Oh! Yeah, what a bunch of losers!" my dad chimes in. "I'm glad we were never like that."

They clink their vodka glasses together. A toast to supporting one another. My dad pats my mom's free hand. I sit in the repulsion I feel toward their gloating. Like their secondhand cigarette smoke, it's not ingested willingly. I'm reverting into feeling my usual doormat self. Feelings I get whenever we have a serious conversation: ganged up on, and belittled for having ideas, opposing perceptions, or dreams. Less than.

"But Mom, Dad, they . . . are *me*. I can finally define who and what I am without exaggeration or glorifying. The kind of person described in this book *is* me."

The horror on their faces is indescribable, yet somewhat impossible to understand. Not to downplay how traumatic it can be when told a loved one has a disease. Not to understate how alcoholism and addiction cause indelible pain within families. *Don't my parents see how healing and change begin by identifying the problem?*

"For the first time in my life, I recognize what's wrong with me. This is what I am. Mom, Dad, I am an addict. I see on your faces how disturbing this is. I admit it, I'm hurt, so I'm going to go now. Not to make you feel bad. Just know I'm okay with however you feel about me, having shared these truths with you. I love you both. Good night."

I hug and kiss my parents, then leave. I call my sponsor from home. He tells me he's proud of me. I'm confused. I go to bed praying my parents might someday accept me for what I am. I pray for Lola, then fall asleep.

17

The Wait

Just after sunrise, I drive to my drug dealer's house with a premeditated thing I need to get off my chest. Mikey is excited to see me as I pull up. His southeast Portland bungalow front door opens wide, dollar signs in his eyes.

"Nice of you to stop by, bro. Been a while."

As I walk up his driveway, I'm forgetting why I really came here. My disease's dogged determination? To test myself? Yesterday I wondered whether I'd ever be free of the desire to use. How could I know for certain if I have enough willpower to be around dope and not give in? A question which can only be answered truthfully by showing up here, now.

Indicative of our routine, he invites me on to his porch. It is customary for us to go from here straight to his bedroom. There, he'd have a line out, chopped up, ready for me to snort before weighing out whatever amount I came to buy.

"What can I dooya for?" he asks.

Ahh, his usual question. His words, tone, and blank facial expression are a déjà vu. I cross my legs and lean against a pillar on his decayed wooden porch. Within steps of completing the relapse sequence, it dawns on me. Self-will has taken over. Twelve days clean isn't long enough to have all the answers. I've deceived myself, again. I honestly believed the only reason I came here was to talk to Mikey as a friend.

My nose starts to run, as it always does when drugs are about to be snorted. I step forward to follow him in, then stop at his doorway. My head tilts down.

"Nah, I'm good." I say, raising my right hand, palm facing him. He's never heard me use these three words.

Mikey is strictly business. He's never taken an actual interest in my life. He probably thinks he *is* my life.

I can't believe I brought Lola here nearly every time I scored. By having her with me, I reasoned, the police would give me a pass. If I got pulled over leaving, or was here during a raid, the cops would never suspect a guy with a kid to be a dope fiend.

Now I see what I thought to be genius—using my kid as a decoy—was actually one of the stupidest, most farfetched ideas. I'm blessed my theory never got tested.

Mikey again gestures for me to come inside. He's concerned about arousing his neighbors' suspicions. It won't be long before they get wise to his dealings like those at his previous rented home did.

There he had engineless cars and bicycle parts strewn across the yard. Out back, towering makeshift tent structures composed of throw cloths, plastic tarps, pallets, and vinyl banners filled the space. All erected to temporarily house homeless drug fiends who owed Mikey money. Inside, heaps of knick-knacks, mismatched kitsch, tools, artwork, and supplies are piled up, exchanged for dope by insatiable, penniless addicts.

"I'm not here to pick up anything this time, man. Nor will I ever be. I'm here to ask you . . . . umm, as a friend, not to sell to Lola's mom anymore."

"Hmm, let me think about that. Really?"

My lips stretch downward as his reply registers. This being one of just a handful of times he's ever looked me square in the eye. What a set of balls I have coming here to ask him this favor. Any other drug dealer would've threatened or actually taken my life for making such an asinine request. Seeing my regret, he offers a sly smile.

"Well, Paul, this is what I do. I mean, what are you asking me?"

"I suppose, well, I'm asking you not to sell dope to her because, well . . ."

This was a bad idea. Another huge gamble made with a bad hand.

"See, man, we got into a really bad fight. She's taken my kid and won't answer my calls. So, if she's getting high while she has Lola, she's endangering our child."

"I don't want to come off as a dick," Mikey says, "and I sure as hell ain't wantin' to get in the middle of no family shit, but how is her coming here alone any different from when the two of you were coming together?"

Touché! Drug dealer logic.

"It's not, honestly. But—no. You're right, it's not. When it was both of us, I figured it was okay. You know, our attention combined equaled one complete person watching her."

Drug addict logic.

Oh, the shit we addicts come up with. Denial = Don't Even Know I Am Lying.

Mikey nods. "Sure, man." Then goes back to whatever it is he's doing, which is always a thousand things, leaving me standing at his door with not so much as a goodbye.

~

My new assignment is to call my sponsor once a day for thirty days. Not an easy task. I don't mention my futile morning mission. Nor is much said when custody is brought up. Matt's doing most of the talking. With the resources to pull myself up out of a funk right here at my disposal, I fall back into thinking nothing good comes from anything I do, including asking for help. So I don't ask. Tentacles of this disease are fast working their way into every toehold of my development. Matt explains how to apply principles of the program.

"Do you have or believe in a Higher Power yet?" he asks.

I don't grasp the concept. Most of my past beliefs turned out to be falsely-lit dead ends. I've yet to name my Higher Power. I don't want to call it the God religious people call God. Not because I feel better or less than, but because indoctrination isn't for me. He continues, "Where's your Higher Power in all this?"

I shrug my shoulders. "Would a power greater than myself actually be present, involved with *my* life?" I retort.

"Do you believe your Higher Power brought you all this way just to let you down?"

I have to think about that, even though the quick, automatic answer seems obvious. Before I respond, he adds, "No? Well, then trust in your Higher Power. This is all going to work out the way it's supposed to."

Yes, he used *that* phrase.

~

I stop to pick up my parents on the way to getting to see my little girl. They want to eat dinner first. I'm nervous, anticipating the grandparents will pull some kind of crap. I don't want this to end with my tail between my legs.

I'm more wary of being misdirected by my will. I'll try harder to let go and let God, to trust in and accept outcomes that have nothing to do with how much strength or willpower I can muster.

On this comfortable, warm afternoon, I walk my parents over to the nearby diner. As we're being seated, they mention the smell of roasted pig coming from the two Traegers barbequing out front. I haven't even noticed.

My parents' restless mannerisms suggest we're about to get into a heavy conversation. I'm bracing for the letdown. *What if they've changed their minds about seeing Lola? What if Carol talked them out of it?*

"We thought about what you read to us last night, son."

"Yeah?" My forearm muscles tense. My brain readies itself to be defensive, to hear for the millionth time what a loser and fuck-up I am.

"Yeah."

"And?"

The buildup before the kill. *Just spill it, parents. Let me have it. How bad has your son disappointed and embarrassed you?*

"And, well, your mother and I talked. And, I don't know how to say this." My dad turns toward my mom, who finishes his sentence. "Son, we're really glad you read that stuff to us last night."

"Glad?" I swing my open hand to the center of my chest. My jaw drops.

Leaving their hotel last night, I was given confirmation. I—stated as "people like that"—disgust my parents. Then my sponsor pointed out two things. First, only I decide how I choose to feel about myself. Second, my parents have every right to feel however they want.

As my defenses come down, I see where they're right. I *have* been living a life I could call disgusting. Here I am, ready to get upset with *them* over how they felt the term *disgusting* was proper. Yet here they are for me, possibly providing my only chance to see Lola.

"Why do you say that?" I ask.

"Because what you read to us explains so much. We know our reaction bothered you. But at the same time, it helped us see you. It helped us see who you really are, not who we want to see you as. It gave us an explanation. This is a prognosis no parent ever wants to learn about their kid. We didn't want to hear it, but now we know. You have a disease. And we truly are happy you have a program. We really hope this program and the people in it will help you."

"Thank you," I whisper.

We finish dinner, then drive to Patrick's and Carol's. Looking down at their front door stoop, I knock, then back away precipitously like I'm trying to unsee a bad omen. I'm holding back a bit of resentment. Hopefully, it doesn't show.

18

Reunited

"Hi, Paul. Hi, Marge!" Carol says. She greets my parents with hugs.

"Lola, come out, honey. Your dad is here."

There's something mean about how she says, "your dad." Grandma Carol has always called me Daddy around Lola. Perhaps this is no longer the case.

"Where's my little wonder at?" I call aloud, proud parental joy in my voice. I'm anticipating the sound of running feet coupled with an excited cry of "Daddy!" When I don't hear anything, my focus pinholes.

"Where is she, Carol?" I ask. A pit forms in my gut.

"Lola. Come out now. Your dad's here," Carol yells with irritation. She's trying to get caught up with my parents, and here I am, interrupting their time together.

"I don't know, Paul. She's around here somewhere. So anyway, Marge . . ."

"Little lady? Honey Jaybird?" A squeak escapes as I call out.

My blood begins to heat up, reddening my earlobes. *Why would my own child hide from me? What have they said to her?* Before the spinning can clear away reasoning like a tornado, I pause.

Expressing irritation will only prove the point they'd love to make: I'm incompetent to raise my own child. I won't give them the satisfaction. I have to find a way to snuff my wary insecurities and take the high road. Digging in to a place deep down for something to regulate my burgeoning outburst, I scream a prayer within. As I do, everything around me blocks out.

Steam fogs up the inside of my glasses. Wiping them allows for a few seconds of reflection. *Waiting for her to come to me first isn't really showing her how much I've missed her, is it?*

An idea pops in my head. I'll turn whatever Lola's doing into a little game of hide-and-seek. Make it fun. I pretend to go looking for her.

"I sense a Lola Jaybird." Trying to convey gladness through my vocal inflection, I ask, "Am I getting warmer?" As if we're two children playing a game. She's winning.

"I know you're around here somewhere. Are you in here?"

Carol whispers to get my attention. She points inside their converted garage where Lola is hiding behind some boxes stacked on a dusty treadmill. I move my mouth to say, "thank you", without letting on I know where she is.

Our reconnection is predestined. I know it in my heart. I have to stay with the frivolity of the moment. If I make it any heavier by centering on reasons I hate being in this predicament, it will only make Lola feel worse than she already does. She's not even four. It's unforgiveable that her innocent trust is stolen forever. The best I can hope for is that, by keeping my spontaneous idea light, she'll see that what we have was never lost.

"Is she in here?" By poking around, playacting like I'm sure I've found her, I reach out to grab for her aimlessly, exaggerating how I'm getting nothing but air.

"Is she over here?" I say, making an increasingly comical effort. Lola lets out a giddy giggle. She always likes it when I'm playing a buffoon.

"Hmm," I say, pursing my lips, furrowing my brow. I stand up straight, then raise my pinky finger to my lower lip, Austin Powers' style.

"Where could she be? Oh wait! I know. She must be in here." I lunge toward yet another vacant space.

Hearing Lola's carefree toddler's laugh is a symphony to my ears. My every hardship melts away in an instant. My heart is rapt in ways I'm light years from understanding. But I don't need to. By believing in *something* other than myself and my ego, an avenue for us to reunite presented itself. The grace of being here came because I made the effort, not the path.

"Wait a minute. I could swear I just heard somebody. I know you're in here somewhere. Aha! I caught you!" With both arms extended, I reach with wild grabs into another unoccupied hiding place. Lola laughs outright. She sees me seeing her, yet I still pretend not to know where to find her.

Then she comes out from hiding, boasting joyously, "I'm right here, Daddy!"

We run to each other. I drop a knee so we can hug tighter. But she holds back, a little put off, distant, uncertain.

Alarms go off, blaring in my head. Whatever it is, it'll have to be dealt with later. I'm here to make the best of this.

My baby girl and I look each other deeply in the eye. Lola backs away from our face-to-face, closes her eyes tight, then thrusts forward to give me the sternest bear hug ever, as if she'll never see me again. I breathe in her unique scent, savoring the aromas of her baby-shampooed hair and juice-box breath. The ends of her hair tickle my nostrils. We erupt in unbridled laughter. Neither wants to let go.

"Can we go outside to look for la luna, Daddy?"

As Northwesterners, we typically don't get to see the moon because of constant cloud cover. Whenever feasible, I'd take Lola on walks to observe the night sky. From watching *Dora the Explorer*, she learned to say *la luna*, Spanish for moon.

I don't think things through before granting Lola her wish. Halfway out the door, we're waylaid by my dad. He pulls me aside. In private, after taking a sip of vodka, he questions my intentions. His face exudes a "What the fuck do you think you're doing?" aura. He demands I make sure it's okay with Carol. *This is my kid, not hers. Whose side are you on*? Because I want to show gratitude for this opportunity, I do as he suggests. After all, whose actions got me in this predicament in the first place?

"Hey, Carol, is it okay if we go outside to look at the stars?"

"I don't know. Where are you gonna be?"

"We'll just be out in your front yard."

"I guess so, for maybe like ten minutes."

"Okay, cool."

"Ten minutes, son," my dad adds, with a stern stare. His enforcement of what should be my opportunity to build trust feels like a screwdriver jab into my ribs.

Lola and I hold hands, skipping around, laughing, and goofing around childishly. One-hundred percent uncomfortable and awkward. We do our best to make it not so, but it is.

We sit cross-legged, then lie back on the damp grass, gazing up at the twinkling stars in the cloudless sky. We're side by side, holding hands, like so many other nights. Not enough nights.

My soul beams at how fluid she is at retaining this moment. We've always been this close. It feels like I've gone months without her. In the development of a child's brain, who knows how much crucial time has been lost for good?

Stress, confusion, and negativity have been budding lately like mold in an incubator, multiplying each day Lola misses her intact family. She's visibly changed. Her spirit, formerly a beacon of light that held fathomless optimism, has dimmed. Her eyes, once freely shining, amorous content budding within, guarded.

I can tell. I've really fucked this up. It's *good* to recognize my shortcomings, even when my ego defensively points out that it took two. I was supposed to take care of the side of the street I'm responsible for—mine. I let it go to shit in an epic way.

~

Whenever I look at the stars, I think of an astronomy class I took while attending the University of Nevada, Las Vegas, ten years earlier, during an overly busy period of my life. Burning the candles at both ends as a full-time student with part-time employment while playing music in three bands, four nights a week. I managed through "disciplined" drug use. That is until the discipline resigned. Burned out, I withdrew before earning a degree. Gave up just before enjoying the results.

Locating constellations, I point them out to Lola, teaching her their names and what person or animal they're supposed to represent. The moon is in a new phase, so we're not able to see la luna as hoped. We both become quiet. I wonder what she's thinking.

"Paul. It's time for you and Lola to come inside," Carol shouts from her doorway.

"We're just chillin', looking at the sky," I answer, smiling deviously at Lola.

"Son, you need to come inside if that's what Carol wants you to do," my dad reinforces.

Ugh!

I lift Lola up and carry her inside. After setting her down, she strides right through the living room toward the bedroom she's been staying in. *Good to know*. This new information feeds resurging vengeful musings of abducting my kid and disappearing altogether.

Be in the moment, Paul.

Lola has an agenda. My little girl lies on her temporary bed, then pats the top covers, hinting for me to lie next to her. I do so with apprehension. She's re-creating what used to be our pre-bedtime regimen: resting at each other's side, talking without limits about anything we wanted.

One night, to enhance our bedtime convo, I attached a bunch of tiny glow-in-the-dark stars to her bedroom ceiling. At bath time, I'd leave her lamp on to activate them. Then, as part of "lights out", we'd lie on her bed and marvel at them.

We squeeze in together on her narrow single bed in Grandma's spare room. Per our regimen, I trim her fingernails and toenails, which haven't been cared for. Lola speaks with uncertainty, discombobulated. Her usual free-thinking short-circuited. Our routine never should have ended; not then, not now, not ever.

I make up a stupid-sounding word, hoping to spark a conversation.

"Barooga," I grunt aloud, jutting out my lower lip. It's a skill of mine, to act a fool.

"Daddy!" She elbows my side, embarrassed.

The bedroom door is swung open wide. Hallway light floods the room, exposing us like a prison tower spotlight captures an escapee.

"All right, Paul!" Carol says emphatically, slicing away at the braided fabric of our bond.

"Lola, your dad's gotta get going. Come out and say 'bye to Grandma and Grandpa."

"Okay," Lola answers, disappointed. She looks at me with her best sad puppy eyes.

"I'm going to miss you, Daddy. I love you."

"I love you too, honey. I will see you again soon."

"How soon?"

"Soon, honey. I promise. You and I will be together, okay?"

"Okay."

There's my optimist.

"Pinky swear, Daddy?"

"Pinky swear."

We put our pinkies together, put each other's hand to each other's face, then kiss each other's pinkies.

"Daddy, you look me in the eye?"

"Huh?"

"I see you," she says, expecting my reply.

She remembered!

I swear, I can feel an electric tide of endorphin jubilance sizzle in my brain. Lola remembers! Our game from over a year ago. From the last time my mind, body, and spirit were temporarily free of ruinous substances. She remembers the vibe I exuded. How I tried to make up for my emotional neglect; how I tried despairingly to be drug free.

Thoughts that ours is an unbreakable bond are cementing. Nothing can sever our connection, not even me. Never. Not by taking this moment for granted and making a mess of it. Nor by going back to being steeped in my addiction, overdosing, or ending up in jail. Not by succumbing to my fictitious fears of how Leann, her family, or the state will pry Lola away indefinitely. Nor if I were to relinquish any parenting expectation, responsibility, or accountability by running. None of these things could deny the fact that Lola defines my legacy.

In this pivotal moment, my purpose-driven spirit awakens. The connection I'm aiming so desperately for is already made. Any length of time, distance, abandoning, severing, or lack of inclusion from this moment on is one-hundred percent *my* choice.

I could do anything and don't have to do anything. This is my kid. She will always know I am her dad. With this knowing, today, I *get to* do the right thing. All I have to do is want to, figure out how to, set out to, then I'll get to.

And I want to. More than anything else ever, I want to be my kid's dad. But there's more to it than wanting. Now I know that, without a doubt, without any rationalized lie or denial, I either make myself significant or irrelevant. I accept and pledge allegiance to the purposeful carrying out of duties necessary to earn my Parent Card. What I do with this moment, from this moment on, matters. *Please don't let this thought be another grandiose best-intentions speech.*

Before we have to part from each other for an indeterminate amount of time, Lola reminds me of our unspoken bond. She wants me to know, because she's unable to explain it. She relates to me on deeper levels.

To reciprocate our union by showing her I, too, remember, I get down on my hands and knees. I look her in her eyes so she internalizes the sense of security she gets from knowing I am clean. Lola then crawls toward me, plunking her forehead against mine. By widening her tractor-beam gaze to meet mine, she opens a conduit of unexplainable energy. Undoubtedly, this soothes her soul, as a loving parent's nurturing deeds should.

"I see you," I reply.

"I see you, Daddy."

We laugh. Our goodbye is shorter and less painful, for now. I thank Grandma Carol on the way out. Lola gives my parents big, strong-armed, loving hugs. I climb into their rental car, waving to my baby with Disneyland character exaggeration.

One hundred yards down the road, the all-too-familiar berating starts.

"What the fuck was that about?" The demeaning cruelty intended by my father's tone is unmistakable.

"What?" I answer, a sneer visible.

"Son, we're here to help you get Lola back. But you've gotta do things the way Carol wants. She's setting the rules, not you. You've got to play your cards right. What part of that do you refuse to understand?"

"What did I do wrong?"

"You can't be lying on the bed with Lola."

"What? Why not?"

"Because. It's weird. It's inappropriate."

My mom injects her high-octane additive to the fire. "Yeah, son, I was gonna say—"

"Inappropriate? How? She and I used to lie down together every night. That's how I would get her to go to sleep."

"Just don't be stupid."

"How am I being stupid?"

I'm angry beyond caring how defensive I'm coming off. I unbuckle my seat belt. With a grip on each of my parents' headrests, I pull myself up closer to them—nearer to confrontation.

"By lying alone in the room with her, people might get the wrong impression." My dad's voice raises, then backs down.

"Don't you see? You don't want to go and blow whatever slim chance you have of seeing her."

I bite my tongue, and then I don't. But for the most part, I do.

"How is lying next to my daughter something that would give someone the wrong impression? Jesus, she's not even four years old. Only a sick fucker would think something as innocent as that is inappropriate!"

Perhaps it's in the pitch I use to make my point. I'm not willing to back down. My parents know me better than anyone; more than I'd like to admit. They see how worked up this has me.

What my parents don't know yet is how I intend to do everything in my power to make sure Carol feels comfortable. She's the gatekeeper whose trust I must earn.

From my parents' point of view, I shouldn't be in this fix in the first place—a drug addict struggling to recover in order to have the privilege reinstated of seeing his own kid. I'm trying to keep it real, not insincerely ideal. From my point of view, why can't a father show affection to his child without slander? *Is it possible we're both right, each seeing this situation accurately, but from a different point of view?*

In their hotel parking lot, I hug my parents and tell them I love them before heading home. Gratitude dampens the angst flowing through my veins. Had my parents not been here, this brief reunion with Lola would've been left up to whether the courts deemed me safe. There's no telling if that will ever happen. Leann has all the rights. She gets to enjoy suspicion-free custody based on her accusations, and maybe a little bit on gender.

My vow to do whatever it takes to get Lola back keeps getting tested. I admit, I got a little selfish and self-righteous. But in a healthy way compared to how I used to be, I remind myself. After writing my journal entry, which concludes with the statement, "I wanna die", I fall asleep full.

19

Master and Servant

While at work, I receive a phone call from Leann. Answering it would be a clear violation of the restraining order. Not knowing what to do, I let it continue to ring. My eyes leave the road to follow the vibrating phone as it nestles itself into the back cushion of the bench seat. No message. She calls again. *Does she want to be back together? Maybe something's wrong with Lola? Maybe she revoked the restraining order?*

Curiosity proves too much. Regardless of the signal my gut sends, my hand reaches for the phone. Talking while driving is against the law and the terms I agreed to in order to get the temp agency to hire me. Sliding into lawlessness is double-triple foolish, but telling myself it's for Lola's sake makes it feel a little less self-serving.

"Hi Pauly."

Right off the bat, I'm resentful she's so upbeat while I'm fearing for my livelihood, parenthood, and freedom. As mellifluous as her voice is, dark thoughts tug at the knot in my stomach.

"You know we're not supposed to speak to each other, right? I could go to jail, right?"

"Um. Not if I call you."

"Is this a trick? Because that would *not* be cool."

"No. It's not a trick. I wanted to tell you . . . I really need to see you."

"What? Why? Is something wrong with Lola?"

"No. I just really miss you."

What are the odds love will prevail here? I'm smart enough to know better. I've seen where that takes me. Going back for more abuse is stupid. The twist is, I'm telling myself it's a good thing to have a soft spot for her. The heart wants what the heart wants. I'm not worthy anyway.

"You know, I could be arrested if I see you. Don't you care about that?"

"I'm sorry about that."

"Sorry? Well, why don't you have the restraining order dropped?"

"My dad won't let me."

"Your dad?"

"He said something about finding a way to break you."

"Not if you don't let him. This is *so* not okay. Will you get it revoked?"

"I want to, Pauly, believe me."

"Then do it. *You* are the only one who can, you know?"

"Can I see you?"

"Why?"

"Because I miss you."

"And I could be thrown in jail for seeing you!"

"I'm sorry about that," she says with the same lack of sincerity.

"Then change it," I repeat.

"Can I please just see you? I really want to be with you!"

"I don't think that would be good for me."

In turmoil, my heart and head concede. Stalemate. My self-esteem disappears like a mirage in the desert. Now it has sunk beyond recognition. Why don't I foresee remorse for setting myself up for failure one more time?

"Please."

"Why?" I ask, sighing. I'm not stalling to toy with her. This much I know.

"Please?"

My brain feels like it's been dipped in lighter fluid—the slightest impulsive thought could torch it. The hiss of the phone against my ear sounds like the onset of vertigo. I can't explain it, but it feels like my knees give in while I'm sitting behind the wheel.

I reason that if I refuse her it could backfire in ways I'm unable to anticipate. I'm just not sufficiently prepared for the outcome. The potential fury frightens me. *What's the worst that could happen?*

"No. I can't."

She hangs up. Heartache cracks open my chest. My abandonment issues get triggered. Did I just seal my own deal? Is it over? Should I call back? Risk jail? My emotions feel shackled and I'm too stunned to sort out which is more affected, my thoughts or my feelings.

~

For most of my adult years, I boasted of living the commitment-free bachelor lifestyle, waving that banner high and wide until it became old and dilapidated. My dating modus operandi was to be physical first, then live together, then maybe get to know each other, depending on how well we got along (which really meant how much the other person could tolerate me doing whatever I wanted).

Why then, after so many imploded long-term relationships with altar-bound women, did I tie the knot with *her*? Oh wait! I remember. Leann found me worthy. Not only of procreation, but also of conjugality. Leann didn't just wake up one day and decide she wanted a kid; she wanted to have *my* kid.

Seeing the wondrous gift of pregnancy through to birth was among my reasons for getting married. I couldn't bear going through certain motions again. I'd been responsible for other conceptions in the past. Each represents a special affliction I'll carry to my grave via termination guilt. Parenthood promised somewhat of an alleviation.

Empowered by Leann's naïve devotion, I believed I could will myself into a lasting state of commitment. But—like with everyone else I chose with trepidation to get close to—I went and dismantled things. Placing the burden of internal transformation outside myself, I expected her juvenescence to overhaul the parts of me I could no longer stand. The responsibility was on her to be motherly enough while simultaneously equipped with the youthful vitality she'd need to save me.

By the time we met, I'd already made many bad choices. Avoiding making more bad choices became my way of making new choices, which it turns out, were just as bad. The culpability, brick by brick, stacked up to erect the fortress that hid my heart.

~

"Hello? You still there?" I ask.

Moments after convincing myself I don't have deep feelings for her, here I am, bawling my eyes out at work. Without a crutch to shift their weight onto, I'm forced to stand in my feelings; unable to snuff the pain down, dilute it, or chase someone or something to replace it. My semiautomatic way to address pain is to see myself as the victim. But telling myself God never liked me isn't the truth, and I know it. There's no containing this much pent-up agony. My legs and arms fling about, directionless, shaking and swatting at thin air.

The one time I have the self-worth to say no to her, to summon the inner strength to decline her enticing offer, I regret it with every fiber of my being. A maxim so familiar, so reinforced in my brain, it repeats itself: I'm doomed to never get what I want as long as it's something I really want.

The phone rings again. While wiping my eyelids to see who it is, my heart ramps right back up into the red. It's her. Wandering from one thought to the next, I notice how this exhilaration is similar to the kind I get when my dealer confirms he has dope.

I answer.

"Please," she whispers.

"What?" I reply, being blunt, feigning how much stronger I am than this, than her, than my own emotions. A wildly stubborn bull, fraught with conscience, gored by denial. Behind me, a lifelong trail of broken china in shards of disrepair. *This isn't my doing. I was misled* is my testimony. Like any good narcissist denying accountability.

"Let me see you," she pleads, using the soft tone of a seductress coupled with an implied subjugation of a mistress, both effectively targeting my weaknesses.

"Where?"

"Is that a yes?"

"Sure, but where? It's got to be someplace public. This is extremely risky for me. You know that, right?"

"Yes, but . . . please?"

"Okay."

Hearing her vulnerability, sensing broken defeat mixed with eagerness, knowing the person preoccupying my emotions is as helpless over me as I am over her, maybe more, is enamoring. There's an undefined pleasure in knowing I matter this much to her. Still, there's never enough proof.

How did I get this dysfunctional?

~

As I drive to meet Leann, working on recovery with my sponsor last night springs to mind. The timing of his talk about how there can never be enough dope, attention, conquests, or material wealth to fulfill an addict's insatiable emptiness resonates. Matt calls it a God-sized hole.

"Are you willing to admit that you've tried every way you could think of to use drugs and alcohol successfully?" he asks.

"I guess so."

"Well, have you been able to use successfully?"

"No. Look at where I am."

"Are you willing to admit your life has become unmanageable?

"Again, look where I am. Yes. My life has come apart at the wheels."

"So then, Paul, would you say you are powerless over drugs? Are you ready to surrender to that truth?"

"Yes, Matt. Absolutely."

"Great! By admitting this, you are declaring your readiness to receive help. By surrendering, you are, in effect, opening the door to a power greater than yourself and your addictions. Congratulations on taking the first step to freedom."

I'd partially expected a Mormon Tabernacle-sized choir to fill my ears with a resounding "ahhhh." The skies didn't open up. Beams of light didn't come down, transcending me into nirvana. Space aliens didn't show themselves among us. I simply admitted I couldn't win a battle with drugs.

Any time I use any drug, I'm contributing to my life becoming more unmanageable. There's no such thing as controlling my using. I accept that now. I know if I use again, whatever justification I concoct preceding doing so will be a lie. My next hit, if there ever is one, will undeniably come with a shit-ton of baggage.

As I stood to hug and thank Matt, I knew my smile had yet to reach my eyes. Even so, I held up a white flag. By giving up, I allowed my life to be thrust forward . . . and I had no idea what any of that truly meant.

~

Leann and I agree to meet at the Eastbank Esplanade along the Willamette River. Public enough, yet spacious. If she's baiting me to meet with her just to concoct a story later that I initiated this or harmed her, it won't work. Someone, especially in the very liberal Portland metro, would report me on the spot. Even in unmistakable stupidity, I try to think strategically.

Finding a bench that overlooks the river wall and the insipid downtown Portland skyline, I sit and wait. For fifteen minutes, practically getting whiplash from looking over my shoulders, I wait. The longer I'm here, the more it feels like I'm being set up. It's not okay. I'm on the clock, far from my delivery route. Maybe it's a meaningless temp job, but I need it more now than ever.

She walks up the esplanade toward me. I smile. She's wearing a miniskirt, tank top, and open-toed shoes with heels—not her normal attire. Pulling on my lust strings? *Well played.*

We hug, speak a few words, then teasingly kiss. It's both dangerous and delightful to hold her again, to feel her close. But even though my arms wrap around her, it's like they're folded—like I'm gripping an imaginary iron plate across my chest.

I wouldn't exactly call what I'm feeling love. Nor am I picking up on any hints of a deep connection. In the back of my head, back beyond the lonesome thoughts screaming for me to do anything she wants so I can have sex again (it's been close to a month), I'm feeling awkward. This is wrong.

The voice of reason is calling from a distance. It's muffled.

I plead with her to drop the restraining order. If only I had something to barter with to entice her. I don't feel confident or powerful enough to try using sexual charisma, my usual go-to, to persuade her. So, I petition her heart.

"We can be together again and have *this* as much as we want if you have it removed."

"But I don't trust you."

"What do you mean?"

"You'll take Lola and run. I just know it. You're going to take her and disappear."

"You mean like you did to me?"

She places her hand high up my thigh, just below the hemmed opening at the bottom of my shorts. Implying everything she means it to imply. *This* is what she came for. Not me. A rush of warm blood is finding its way into all the right places. My flesh is weak—always has been. Showing weakness seems to be an aphrodisiac for her. Yet, no matter how weak or insecure I am from one moment to the next, my body responds by instinct.

Despite my body's reaction, I see through her ploy. Her intentions are not the same as mine. Opening up and giving in to what I saw as her needing me was a bad idea. I pull the illusory thick, cold, cast-iron lid shut, covering my heart indefinitely.

"All right, I have to go back to work."

"Why?" she asks in an underage Japanese school girl voice.

I try not to allow this to sound sexy to me. She's only using it as ammunition. However, it's alluring to know she wants to break open my carnal fantasies to get her way.

Enchantment, meet entrapment.

"Why?" I ask.

Leann and I spent the last two years snorting, popping, puffing, and sipping away our future. We purged our daughter's savings as well as every last cent of the payout we received from selling the only place Lola ever called home. All because we'd rather sit around and get high than work. Even if I didn't prefer the lifestyle, I chose to go along with it. This is where I ended up.

"Why?" I ask again, with sarcastic inflection. "Because I have to earn a living if I ever want to take care of the family I plan on having back by my side, that's why."

"Oh yeah, *that's* what my dad told me." She pulls away from me to scoot up to the front edge of the bench. *Did she even hear what I just said?* Turning her body toward mine, she adds, "He said he was going to break you financially so you'll never be able to see Lola again."

"Wow! Why would he say that? What did you tell him?"

"I don't know. I was angry. I said a bunch of shit. They talked me into doing the restraining order, Paul. It wasn't my idea. They said they'd disown me if I didn't follow through on it."

"Obviously!"

I hear my angry tone rising. A bicyclist rides by. I wait, then continue.

"But you can change all that." I grab her hands. "Look, I forgive you. Just go back to court and have the order dropped."

She stares away, more interested in watching the dragon boat team practicing on the choppy Willamette River. She seems to be processing an answer. I push, but to no avail. Now I really have to get back to work.

"Your dad paid someone to serve me, didn't he?"

"How did you know?"

"He isn't filming us talking so he can get me thrown in jail, is he?"

"No!" she yells. Her first adamant answer.

I give her a hug to prove, just in case we're being filmed, that we are parting amicably. She falls to the ground, crying. I help her up, uncertain if this is an act.

"What's the matter?" I ask.

"It's just that you look . . . well, you seem happy."

"I'm starting to have clarity."

One last embrace, then I jog back to the work van. Now I'm behind in my deliveries. At my next stop, it sinks in. I just majorly screwed up. Will I ever learn there are consequences to chasing the things I want?

After work, I go straight to a meeting. Trembling, I vent about how I may have ruined my chances for good this time. Afterward, a few men offer advice, having been through similar situations. Addiction, divorce, rewritten relationships, hope, and recovery—my new life and family. I'm advised to seek additional legal counsel and a support group.

An advocacy group called Kids Need Both Parents (KNBP) comes to mind. They help men who want to be in their kids' lives. Men who have hit a wall emotionally and financially. Men up against a system that favors one parent based on genitalia, even though there's no scientific proof either can provide better parenting, loving, nurturing, security, or stability.

I wake up in the middle of the night, paranoid I'm about to be arrested. I'm delusional, believing that meeting Leann was an elaborate setup. Every rustling noise outside is the police forming a perimeter around my apartment. I lie still, awaiting the instant they'll kick the door in, drag me to the ground, cuff me, and haul me away.

Eventually, my spinning head laughs at its own thoughts. Consider the source. Years of addiction left an indelibly distorted seed in my brain. Psychosis, paranoid hallucinations, self-destructive solutions, conspiracies, and an apathetic lack of worthiness, to name a few.

~

A few days later, I sit in with KNBP. Five men attend, including Jim Whinston, the organizer. I met Jim while playing music along the course of the Portland Marathon. He asked my band to play a fundraiser for his nonprofit group. I've also been a guest on his college radio show. We've talked about the shrinking rights of males before I was a dad. My perspective is much different now.

What strikes me about Jim is how effeminate he is. Soft-spoken, gentle, caring. I can't picture him going through a divorce or having custody issues with anyone. He's energetic, persistent, and passionate about making the world a pillar of equality and justice for all.

The experiences of the group members scare the crap out of me. As we go around the table, each man introduces himself and what he is going through. Every one of them describes in detail the sheer hell of his custody battle and divorce situation. Each is a father wanting to be present in his child's life. Each claim to have spent between

$30,000 and $80,000 in legal fees, only to be granted weekends and every other Wednesday to parent his kids. Each is paying alimony in addition to child support.

I want to ask, "What kind of crap did *you* pull?" But as each man reveals more of his personal story, I think it's better to ask, "What kind of demon did you marry and make babies with?"

Not for me to judge, but oh, the fear this puts into me. I won't see $30,000, much less eighty grand, for who knows how long. Maybe my parents are right. I've got no leg to stand on. I should lie down and accept whatever slim chances I have to be part of Lola's life.

I peruse the plush boardroom we're meeting in. On each man's face resides bitterness, frustration, and disbelief. In many cases, divorce is hopeless for men. Most don't know how to fight. Many would rather not. Most bow down, letting their distraught, vindictive ex or her lawyer destroy their present and future relationship with *their* kids.

Lola doesn't deserve that. I don't either. But it doesn't change how terrified of the process I am. One man curiously asks, "Did she get a restraining order on you?"

"Yes. Why?"

Every head nods in disapproval before the eyes dip down to the slick, shellacked boardroom tabletop.

"That's not good," chimes one.

"You're screwed," replies another, in a matter-of-fact James Earl Jones' voice.

"You know, the judges hand those things out like candy, right?"

"They do?" How have I been so . . . *protected* from this reality? I should've experienced being purged like this by a woman long ago. I have not been a good man. I've never been held accountable for the verbal abuse, physical altercations, or mental warfare waged. It seems odd I'm facing the Law of the Harvest this late in life. I've dodged a magazine full of self-inflicting bullets when it comes to relationships.

"Yes. A judge will issue a restraining order on hearsay alone. It will remain on your record for a decade, no matter what the outcome is."

I'm screwed.

I'm in an ominous daze. Jim hands me a bumper sticker. Kids Need Both Parents. A slogan for everyone to see.

My generation of men was told by the previous one that if we didn't run the household, we weren't manly enough. Now we're not feminine enough to raise our kids? Criticism is everywhere. Funny how I never noticed any of this belittling bullshit until after I became committed to being a *good* man and father.

20

Between Something and Nothing

With just over three weeks off of drugs and booze, I get to have my day in court. The thought of being punished with a criminal record for something I didn't do has loomed like a funnel cloud. It will either grow more destructive or calm will prevail.

Who better to represent me than Monika from the law firm I found the morning after Leann disappeared with Lola? Monika's the lawyer who generously offered an hour of free legal advice. She predicted, among other things, that I'd be served. Upon informing her of my upcoming hearing, she cautions me not to risk going to court without representation. At her insistence, I retain her as my lawyer.

On the day of the hearing, we meet at the courthouse cafeteria. Monika is a witty, eloquent, A-type personality, and a woman. Perfect for my case. Leann arrives soon after. She sits a few tables over with her best friend and using buddy, Jessica. The two carry on, laughing and gesturing, disrupting lawyers and clients discussing cases.

Leann is not wearing her wedding ring.

Monika asks if I'd mind if she walks over to the girls to say a few things. If there was such a thing as a gauge to measure trust, mine would read Not Detectable. I've always been the one to rock the boat. All of a sudden, I'm afraid to. I hesitate to answer. Not one to be held back by a client's dither, my hired gun—the alpha bulldog representing me—gets up to approach their table.

"Hi, which one of you is Leann?" Monika asks, holding out her hand, offering a friendly handshake. Sliding down into the wooden booth, I make myself inconspicuous so I can admire from afar. Leann's complexion shifts to a beet color so positively porous that her concealer surrenders.

"I am."

"Hi, Leann. I'm Paul's lawyer."

"Paul got a lawyer?" Jessica exclaims loud enough to hear across the room. The smirks on both their faces disappear.

"Yes, he did. But I don't see one here with you. You *have* retained representation for the hearing, haven't you?"

"Representation?" Both girls' jaws drop.

"I'm going to assume by your answer you have not. I highly advise you do. I take my profession very serious. I'm going to walk into that courtroom and do everything I can to prove my client is innocent. Just so you know, it could get dirty in there. I like to fight. But I fight fair. I can ask the judge for a postponement until you get a lawyer to represent you if you'd like. Because I promise you, you're going to need one."

The bailiff calls our case into the courtroom. There, Leann's testimony, handwritten on the Restraining Order to Prevent Abuse, is read aloud. Full of panic, forecasting a disastrous outcome, I look over at Leann. Our eyes meet just as the judge reads some of the really terrible things written about me. Leann tries staring into my eyes but looks down, then back toward the bench. Her complexion turns scarlet again.

If the judge judged solely on body language, her honor would see through this charade. I'm guilty of not being able to hide how I want payback for the family time I lost. I want validation for the hoops I've had to navigate, the costs, the changes. A voice reminds me I am not here to destroy the mother of my daughter. I'm here to clear my name so I can have my relationship with my baby restored.

The judge presents a question in a voice that feels like an accusation.

"How do you plead to these charges, Mr. Summers?"

My lawyer replies, "Your honor, my client pleads not guilty. I would like to add that my client has been drug free for nearly a month now and is desperate to have his parental rights restored. However, if I may, there is the matter of Mrs. Summers. She has not acquired representation. We spoke earlier, and she would like to seek council before proceeding. At this time, we are asking for a postponement."

My pulse races faster than a proton in a particle accelerator. *What the hell? We're spreading this out farther? I've waited weeks to be with my daughter. Am I supposed to be okay with this?* Postponing my day in court while Leann continues to use and live it up, placing Lola in harm's way, is unacceptable.

The muscles underneath my eyelashes tighten close to my nose to send Monika an angry glare. One that she not only picks up on but expects. "Trust me. Keep quiet. Now watch this . . ." she whispers.

"Do you agree to this, Mrs. Summers?" the judge asks, prepared to hand down a ruling and move on.

"I do."

"Well then, the State of Oregon versus Mr. Paul Summers is postponed for three weeks, until August seventh."

August seventh!

I look straightaway at Leann, conveying the utmost pain through my eyes. She knows exactly why. On the afternoon we met in secret at the Esplanade, she confessed through heavy tears how much Lola misses me. Her Uncle Phil confirmed this multiple times, yet won't facilitate me seeing her. Due to the order, I'm not allowed any unsupervised contact whatsoever. Without knowing a person legally approved to supervise, or being able to afford one, access is denied.

Leann has never been a heartless woman like those depicted in the men's group I attended—women who believe their children are, by some manifest destiny, *their property*. Is she immature and ill-prepared? Yes. Is she a druggie immersed in active addiction? Absolutely. Is she unfeeling? Not yet.

Handling a distressing moment with decisiveness, Leann chooses to do what is right for Lola.

"Your honor. Your honor. May I say something?" she utters.

"Yes, go ahead."

"Well. August seventh is after our daughter's birthday. Is there any way Paul could see her on her birthday?"

"No!"

My heart sinks into my colon. This isn't going as planned. Although I'm making an effort to do everything right, I'm the one living under biased scrutiny. I don't know how long I can keep it up. In protecting my name from defamation, I've been logging my whereabouts, events, and conversations. All this to be told no?

Is this my opportunity to practice letting go by allowing a power greater than myself to restore my life to sanity? There's no time like the present. Time to show my Higher Power I'm willing to trust and have faith.

Yet, with one negative word, I'm ready to throw away all progress—go right back to believing in only me. Faithless, insolent, I tilt my head up toward the ceiling tiles to enquire, *How could You keep Lola from me one more day?*

The judge skims over the allegations written.

"No. Absolutely not."

Leann glances over, making certain I see her whisper, "I'm sorry."

Monika, Leann, Jessica, and I freeze in place.

The judge adjusts her gown, sits upright, then calls out, "May I have both parties approach the bench, please?"

"Here we go," Miss Monika mutters. A boastful, sinister smile fills her face.

I'm clueless and holding back fiery anger. A voice inside says, "Let it go." This is like running a red light. There's as much potential for disaster as there is for success.

"So, let me get this straight, ma'am. You're saying you would like me to alter this order whereas Mr. Summers could see your daughter on her birthday?

Leann answers with an uncertain tone. She's terribly awkward in social settings as it is. Her brain can't process in time.

"Yes . . . ?"

The judge, mechanical in going through the legal motions up until now, reacts with exasperation.

"Ma'am, let me remind you, you have made some serious allegations against this man. To use your own words, you're "certain he'll kill me and take our daughter and I fear for our safety." Now, was that an accurate statement? Were you lying under oath to get this petition filed?"

"No."

"Well, you can't have it both ways. Either he is a threat or he is not."

Leann answers by showing indecision. She believes being button-lipped is the best riposte. She turns away, toward the exit, then back to face the front. The judge has grown impatient.

"Okay. Well, I'm going to grant Mr. Summers the ability to see his daughter on her birthday. However, I'm going to continue to enforce noncontact. Is there someone who can facilitate picking up and dropping off your daughter?"

"Yes. My mom."

"Good. I'm going to allow email contact only, for your daughter's sake. You both can work that out. Any infraction of this standing order and I *will* hold you in contempt," she says, looking at me. "Do you understand, Mr. Summers?"

"Yes, your honor. One of Washington County's finest made sure I understand."

"Mrs. Summers. Do you understand?"

Leann can only nod in agreement. Any verbal response remains in her throat.

"Good. I am going to leave you two with my personal recommendation as follows: I don't see this as a salvageable marriage or family. I think you both have growing up to do. It is most unfortunate for your child. I see an amicable divorce as her best chance for a healthy future."

The judge's gaze is on me the entire time she hands down her opinion. With hunched shoulders, I absorb the news. I get to bring my little girl home for her birthday!

Outside the courtroom, I hug Monika, praising her for her cleverness.

~

As I'm driving home from the courthouse, my cell rings. It's a blocked number. I pick up, thinking it's work. It's Jessica. I'm not allowed to speak to Leann's friends. Another setup?

Wait. She's calling me from an unknown number. How can I do anything about that?

"Hello."

"Dude, what the fuck is your fuckin' problem?"

"What?" I have no idea why she would be this pissed. I'm expecting a punch line.

"Who do you think you are, making Leann look like a liar in there? All that shit in the restraining order is true, and you know it!"

"No, it isn't, and she knows it."

Distorted screaming comes through the earpiece. Vile words. Normally, I'd volunteer to engage. In fact, had this call come at any other time, the desire to scream back, make threats, and obsess with hatred would've taken over until every last drop was wrung dry. Not now.

This time is mine to celebrate victory and not let anyone destroy the joy I bask in. It's my reward for staying clean, working a program to the best of my ability. With a gentle tap, I disconnect, then turn off the phone.

Once home, I review the day's events from a fresh vantage point. When I thought I wasn't going to get what I wanted (to see Lola), I nearly gave up on my Higher Power. Then, against piercing outcries from my will, I waited to see what would happen next. Later, when an opportunity arose to march in and do battle, I chose to turn the other cheek.

This isn't like me.

Why did I see a dad being arrested for drugs while his little girl looked on? Why do I keep having thoughts I've never thought before? Why am I taking actions I've never taken before? Instructions seem to come from somewhere or something outside of me.

I'm doing things differently.

Instead of isolating, I seek fellowship. Instead of sitting in pain or resentment, I call my sponsor or other men in the program. Instead of holding on to being right, I'm learning it's okay to let go. Each time I do, my trust is reinforced and faith builds. There's hope that I'm not too old, nor too far gone, nor in too deep a hole to ever change.

I don't know what my Higher Power wants from me, nor what plan It has in store. When I try to put the data in boxes, I come up with the need for more data. All that is asked is that I'm open to it. Just a few weeks ago, I had nothing to lose. Today, I opened a new door to give what's inside a chance.

21

Tenderness

"This year, your birthday is such a big deal, honey, you get to celebrate it at *two* houses!"

"I do, Daddy? Yay!"

Lola and I sit across from each other in a booth at a McDonalds with a PlayPlace inside. Grandma Carol thought it would be good for Lola to spend time with me *before* her birthday party. She arranged for us all to meet here.

Patrick and Carol sit a few booths away, talking while observing. Keep your friends close, your enemies closer. I get it. But if I think about it the wrong way, I'll get resentful. I'm grateful for every minute.

How I've waited to do my goofy dad thing. I climb through the play structure tubes, chasing after Lola. We slide down together, screaming the whole way. My aging body doesn't like this. Nor do the women who are here with their kids.

I can only guess what they're thinking. Their faces speak volumes. They seem annoyed, probably jealous because my kid has an active daddy in her life. Maybe they're concerned I'm some sort of weirdo. Their judgments won't stop me.

Carol gives us her ten-minute warning. We climb up and slide down the longest tube together, Lola on my lap. She's the happiest kid on earth. I carry her like a sack of potatoes to our table so we can bond just a little longer. When I set her down, she tries to drag me back to the play structure.

"No, honey. Let's sit." I pause, wanting to switch to a more serious heart-to-heart. "You know, Daddy's really going to miss—"

"Let's play."

"Honey, sit down." I force the tension around my face to relax, then try again. "You know Daddy's really—"

"Let's play."

"Honey, I said not right now. Grandma needs to get going, so we only have a few—"

"Let's play!"

"Lola. Honey. I want to tell you something before you gotta—"

"Let's play!!"

"Honeeey, Daddy—"

"Let's play!!!"

"No, Honey, Daddy needs you to—"

"Play!" she demands, yanking on my sleeve.

"LOLA!"

My raised voice projects with such sternness that it ricochets off the glass windows surrounding the play structure and booths, carrying above and beyond the noise of a dozen shrieking kids. Lola's body is frozen, except for a trembling chin.

Out of the corner of my eye, I see Patrick jump. The lines on his forehead snap up to his receding hairline, lifting his eyebrows. His knees bang against the table bottom. I realize right away I didn't use an acceptable parental tone. Next, regret washes over me, concerned I may have triggered Patrick's PTSD. He's a Vietnam veteran, a decorated Marine with a Purple Heart. The unpredictable, short-fused burst known as my temper found a way to do harm.

Lola starts to cry. Instead of remorse, I'm filled with excuses for raising my voice so I can come out of this smelling like a rose. I pick Lola up, gently cradling her with my forearm. I explain how she wasn't listening. Between pants, she lets me know I scared her. A monster doesn't make excuses. My apology is sincere.

"All right, Paul. We gotta get going now. Say goodbye."

Lola's cheeks are moist with tears, her nose runny. How the hell did I fuck this up? If my drug-free brain can't cover for me, what do I do? *Deal with it.* Okay.

"Give Daddy a big hug, honey. I'll see you in just a few days for your birthday."

Her facial muscles strain hard not to give in to letting me see her smile. I lift her so we're at eye level. She closes her eyes, then dips her little head into the safe harbor of the nook beneath my neck.

"I don't want to, though."

"I know, sweetie. I won't be gone long this time, honeybee."

Her little body shakes as she pouts. Patrick and Carol look on. I assume they're rethinking this arrangement. As in never again.

"Wait! What's this?" I ask.

I set Lola on her feet on the floor. In dramatic fashion, I pull my T-shirt out away from my chest, then look down at it. There's a wet spot on it where her nose was nestled against me.

"Lola. What is this?" I point to the rounded wet area. A genuine, tiny smile loosens itself on her face.

"Naw. You didn't. Did you?"

Her smiling eyes are unable to hide what's coming.

"You did. Lola . . . you sauced me!"

She laughs at least twice as loud as my bellowed outburst moments ago.

"Awww mannn. Really?"

Her exaggerated nod up and down confirms she did it on purpose.

Through this skit, I've convinced Lola I'm not mad. The grandparents, however, are dumbfounded. What they're witnessing is too telling. Denying the bond their granddaughter and I share would be unreasonable.

Lola runs to hug my leg, squeezing with all her might. I walk toward the exit with her hanging on like a koala bear. She's heavier than I remember. Inside, I'm breaking apart like Tillamook squeaky cheese, but I have to be strong for her sake. I kneel to hug her back while looking at Patrick and Carol. *That's right! That's exactly what I want you to glean from this. Look at what you'd be destroying by separating us.*

"I don't want to go, Daddy."

"Honey. So many people love you so much, including me. You be strong and I will, too. See you on your birthday. I love you. Mwah!"

"Mwah!"

~

Lola's fourth birthday is as joyous, carefree, and memorable as I can make it . . . just in case we won't get to spend another one together. The bar had been set pretty high. Her previous three birthdays were huge events, considering my family traveled from Las Vegas to shower her with gifts and affection. Concerns whether she'll notice we're not *all* together as usual wane once the party starts.

There are moments when I lose focus or become restless, waiting to have Lola all to myself. This is the first birthday of hers experienced without drugs. Still, putting on the festive face for five hours isn't easy. The parenting stamina I used to have has diminished. I push through to show myself it can be done. Living "as if." I've been clean thirty-eight days, each morning not knowing if I actually can—each based on doing what I did the prior day to get through.

My friend Mykeal, his wife Deb, and their son, Oden, are among those attending. Mykeal's been my drummer for years. He struggles with alcoholism. Some say the opposite of addiction is connection. Sober events like this are good for us and our families.

Lola and her friends start off in her room playing dress-up, then go outside for hide-and-seek. The cake and ice cream and gift opening cause a buildup of sugar energy, which she releases by splattering a princess piñata all over the courtyard. I hold on for dear life. Me, in charge of eleven wild children.

As the party nears its end, I allow myself a sense of accomplishment. I handled invitations, decorations, and organized festivities with just a few days' notice. Not bad for a single dad.

Then there's the letdown. Lola and I only get a few moments alone before I have to take her back to Patrick and Carol's. Being back home around her stuff again brings up some difficult feelings. Separation and divorce tears kids' hearts up in ways we adults can't begin to fathom.

"When do I get to sleep in my bed again, Daddy?"

"You will, honey. Right now, I'm just not sure when."

Her eyes look for a point behind her forehead. The gears are turning, trying to get an equation to compute. You can put sugar on logic, but it's still going to taste like crap.

"But I miss you singing me to sleep."

"Oh, honey, I do too. Sooo much."

Having to drive her to Grandma's is hard. By letting go of control, I'm showing trust in my Higher Power. Things that don't appear to be working out actually are. I got to spend Lola's fourth birthday with her when all signs pointed against it. Accepting how my life, left up to me, will always be unmanageable is a big step. Life happens even when we don't want it to. So does recovery.

~~~

At the retrial, Leann enters the courtroom with the support of her parents. Rather than remain beside her, however, they take a seat in the gallery. She still does not have a lawyer. Today's hearing is more formal.
~~~

Through emails and conversations, I've been building a case. Leann hasn't been parenting much. In fact, her family complains *to me* about how little she's ever around. I had hoped the grandparents had come to testify today, under oath, providing their own eyewitness accounts. Perhaps they don't have enough confidence in me as the obvious alternative parent for Lola. Sometimes blood is thicker than reality.

The judge reviews her notes before asking how things have gone with the email contact-only parenting plan. Monika responds on my behalf, then asks that the restraining order be dismissed. She adds, "Paul's parental rights should be reinstated to the tune of four days a week."

"Do you have any objections, ma'am?"

Just as in the first hearing, Leann answers with a questioning tone.

"Yes?"

Leann's maternal uncertainty doesn't sit well with the judge, who seems to evaluate her intentions based on her mannerisms. Leann isn't exhibiting traits of a mother vested in the well-being of her off-spring. She may be falsely telling herself she is and doesn't even know it.

Back when we were getting loaded every day, we believed we were present "enough" to parent adequately. This wasn't nearly enough by any measure. While the two of us were high, we'd argue that Lola's safety, well-being, and whereabouts were *always* at the forefront of our thoughts. But thoughts are just concepts. A child can't be raised on concepts apart from action. The judge knows this.

"I am going to dismiss the temporary restraining order. Also, it is my judgment Lola Summers spends three days a week with her father."

I sigh an extended expression of relief. Not the four days I asked for, but I'll take it. My little girl will finally spend the night in her own bed in her own room. Leann is stone-faced and motionless at the stand. I'm at a loss. Why didn't she get legal representation? I'm sure her dad would've paid for it.

On an oak bench in the courthouse lobby, Carol and I work out the new parenting plan details per the judge's ruling. Leann is absent, which makes me suspicious. I'm worried about Carol going behind my back to make a ploy for custody.

Later, the negative voices continue their pummeling. Why? Soon I'll have fifty days clean. False thoughts—*Lola would be much better off with the grandparents*. Despicable thoughts—*You're not doing this for Lola, you're doing it for your own selfish pride*. Drug thoughts—*Once you get full custody, you know you'll slide back to using, just like before. Why wait?* Down the rabbit hole race my thoughts. Up and out to a meeting I go for reprieve.

~

Per our arrangement, I arrive early at McDonalds PlayPlace, expecting to pick up Lola from her grandparents. I walk in to find Leann and Jessica—a plan change that feels menacing. Even with the restraining order dropped, I still feel powerless, less than human, blindsided.

"Give your mom a hug," I say. I'm robotic. It makes my skin crawl to play nice. I walk Lola to my minivan, buckle her in, and go. After exhaling tension from the moment, I turn to give Lola a smile. Driving away, removed from imagined danger, I'm free to be with my kid.

But less than a block away, I sense someone tailgating me. In the rearview mirror, I spot Leann and Jessica. They're hysterical, pointing at my Kids Need Both Parents sticker. I can't help feeling attacked, considering all I've been through to earn this opportunity. Brief freedom dissolves into sustained bitterness.

I'm indebted to Lola by choice, not by right. I make a mental pact to prove to my daughter, my ex, her family, my family, our community, the world, universe, and God how a man can raise a child every bit as well as a woman. From this day on, I dedicate my life to it.

Such are the extremes siphoned out of resentments.

22

Taking Care of Business

I must've skipped the "think things through" part when it comes to figuring out how to take care of Lola with my already full schedule. On top of working fifty hours a week and attending meetings, I'm placing additional pressure on myself to get my act together . . . for Lola's sake, my sake, the sake of single dads, and the sake of recovering parents.

Drug excess has a substitute: overextension. Although I'm learning to trust outcomes and to believe things will work out as they should, I need to be careful not to get to the point I'm overcome. Being overwhelmed gives my disease a foothold. If I take on an implausible amount of responsibility, I set myself up for failure. For this addict, overextension can be a place where using is inevitable.

The daily application of "deal with it as it comes up" is beginning to appear more credulous than pragmatic. I've never been consistent with following to-do lists, tasks, and goals. Now I'm foreseeing a need to do so. "Playing it by ear" is a musician term. It means we'll make it up as we go when we get to a certain section. I've literally survived by this desultory rule.

I'm told to ask sober single moms how to do this.

Simple. Yet not.

It's not exactly safe for me to interact with women. You see, I'm an addict. Sex is gratification. My disease doesn't want me to figure out one is too many and a thousand is never enough. It wants me to think if one is good, more is better.

My sponsor suggests postponing major life-changing decisions for a year, including relationships. Any time I crave something that even hints at being pleasurable, my disease perks up, scheming ways to indulge to excess. My libido is alive and well since the removal of drug use; strengthened, emboldened, and providing an ever-increasing indignant hankering. *Thanks dick.*

How I view women differs from most men. I don't see females as notches, trophies, or sex objects, nor as placed here to serve a need I *have* to meet. It's off-putting to hear men who brag about or detail their sexcapades.

Playing the courting game has never been enticing. It comes fraught with too many possibilities of rejection. Looking back to when I first became sexually active, women (like drugs did later) provided a temporary satisfying of the emptiness within.

Being a charming, witty, hip, and handsome musician didn't hurt. Pile on the popularity that comes with being onstage and you have a perfect storm of overcompensation. Suddenly, the insecure, attention-needy boy on the inside becomes this intimidating, attractive man on the outside. That created opportunities to get what I wanted as often as I wanted. Now that I'm clean—without my brain being altered—those opportunities have all but dwindled.

It's frustrating at times to sit in a meeting with women who I know are addicts. There's an unspoken presumption that those present are unfulfilled fiends like me—as if we're all insatiable beings who are hypersexualized once the popping release of endorphins which came from dope were removed.

The nervousness I feel about asking a woman to help me is too intense. I have to wait until a day comes when obsessing over thoughts of a sexual nature are minimal.

Nearly a week goes by before I get up the courage.

~

The topic for this evening's meeting is powerlessness. I share my situation with more transparency than usual, which feels great. Afterward, I'm more confident than usual. I walk up to a woman I admire. She's standing outside, flanked by three other single moms. I ask how she does this parenting/full-time employment/recovery thing. All four women chime in with different perspectives. Two offer to babysit. One tells me about a government program, then remembers it's not available to men.

The passion and intensity of our riveting conversation is momentarily derailed when the fourth woman goes off into man-hate village. The salty criticism some women have of men, the vendetta they carry for the men they make babies with, their exes or what some crudely call baby daddies, can be brutal. When I hear men talk about moms with such malice, it's usually in the context of parental alienation or being deprived of time with their child.

That said, unless a child's dad is making an honest effort to take part in every facet of parenting, he should be called out about his absence—especially by *other* men. If that's not the case, criticizing dads publicly and privately is inadvertently a form of child abuse. Especially when it comes to moms raising boys—demeaning the male role model is sexist. It ultimately hurts the kid.

"Paul, when you shared about how you've been praying for God to remove craziness from your life, it really resonated with me," the first mom says, adding, "How troubling it must be, seeing your wife now. For you to draw the conclusion that every time she comes around God is showing you an example of the insanity of your past behavior was well said. Especially admitting how you're grateful for it."

"You wanna know what's funny, but not ha-ha funny?" I ask. "She doesn't want me to bring Lola to meetings because she doesn't want her to be anywhere near 'those fucking drug addicts.'"

"I was in her shoes at one time," offers the woman with the most clean time.

"Really?"

"Yep. There was nothing anybody could say or do to get me to believe I was a bad mom. *Nothing*. The way I saw it, nobody better ever dare try to take my kids from me. *One* thing kept me enabled, in denial, and stuck in active addiction. That one thing was being able to say to myself, 'I am a good mom. I don't have a drug problem. Look, I still got my kids.'"

As we part, I express appreciation. Overall, my fact-finding session was well received. The support that women are willing to offer a man who's trying to be present in his kid's life is astounding.

~

I'm back to playing Whack-A-Mole with my recurring self-deprecating thoughts. Just as one self-undermining fire drill is handled, another pops up. My disease keeps conjuring up alternating pathways to counter effective safeguards.

So, I go out on a limb. I acknowledge my habitual fear by addressing it through quiet meditation. I'm new at this. First, I get my head clear. Next, I pray for openness to solutions. I start with a few words aloud, take some deep breaths, then position myself comfortably on my knees until the tension in my body softens. I close my eyes, hold open my palms. Seconds pass.

The silence is overwhelming. Reclaiming their territory in my head is a splattering of babble chatter, intertwined with task-oriented thoughts. I'm soothed by the reacquired noise and chaos. I open my eyes, then concede to consciously allow for whatever to happen rather than force something to. Without a frame of reference, I'm unable to interpret what any of this means. I get up off my knees and go about my day like nothing happened.

Before long, I manage to move on from judging or expecting results. Then the temp agency calls.

"A full-time job just became available. You'd be starting at six a.m. Interested?"

"Yes! I'll be here tomorrow."

"Great. You will need to take a drug test."

"Great!"

On my forty-ninth day clean, I put my application in for a temp-to-hire job. If I do well, they'll hire me permanently. Days later, they call back, offering me my first job interview in two years.

~

Leann's been unpredictable. I've been doing my best to trade niceties. Every time we talk, she degrades into innuendoes alluding to us hooking up. Recently, she complained about not being able to look for work because of getting stuck watching Lola during the day. To help, I paid for a five-day summer camp. Lola was never taken. I'm always asked for gas money, but as far as I know, Leann never goes anywhere. She calls in the middle of the night, demanding money for groceries, then doesn't show up to receive it. Yesterday, she offered to watch Lola later than the arranged time so I could get to my interview.

As I'm driving there, she calls. I debate answering, but cave.

"Good luck, Daddy!" Lola joyfully screams into the phone before it goes silent. Nice touch. Got me weeping. I have to compose myself before walking through the doors.

The man interviewing is a real hard-ass. He tests my reactions and responses to uncomfortable scenarios. Drew reminds me of my dad. I like that he's direct. It's unlike me, but any joking and people-pleasing is kept to a minimum. This job is that important to me.

My resumé raises flags. It speaks of inconsistent and meandering employment. It's not who I am today. I'll prove it, if given the chance. Lying won't benefit me like honesty will. In response to gaps in employment, I describe my life as a musician. Drew lifts his head from the notes he's taking, smiles, then tells me about his years playing saxophone with Ray Charles, Tommy Dorsey, and Heart. He ends the interview, saying, "I wish all interviewees were as good as you."

I thank him for his time on the way out. Before starting my van, I sit with the moment.

~~~
~~~

Afterward, I take Lola with me to a meeting. The topic is about surrendering self-will. The person sharing, Eric, relays a revelation, an insight given by a power he, too, struggled to understand.

Humbly, he admits, "Through working the program, I'm given tools that help me become aware of my efforts to control the world around me. You guys taught me that having control is never sufficient enough to achieve serenity. I always end up either afraid my schemes will fail, worried or angry when they don't work out, or guilty when I actually pull them off."

I feel he's speaking directly to me.

Through Eric's disclosure, I'm able to better understand my addict brain. A complex, confining structure; an enigma prison. I won't ever be free of my disease. Today, however, I can start inhibiting it instead of the other way around. The key is not to get out, but to let others in.

By sharing the mindset I'm learning from those doing the work, I'm giving myself the best shot at being drug-free. I'm reading recovery literature. I have a Higher Power. The program I work is one where, as a group, we collectively come to find solutions to our problems. It is one where, as an individual, solutions are sought by working one on one with a sponsor, which I'm doing. My home group—a meeting I attend on a regular basis—is where I feel comfortable letting people get to know me, people who contact me when I'm absent and guide me when I'm wavering. I'm giving back by taking on a service position. And I've become willing to take suggestions.

Still, the passing of time hasn't made the desire to use vanish entirely. Not yet, at least. Right around the week I take my sixty-days key tag, the cravings return. Like Autolycus, my disease is a cunning, formidable adversary. I can't get complacent, yet I've never practiced vigilance. This is all so new.

An unforeseen ordnance in my arsenal against negative self-talk is the turnaround I've made as an advocate for my daughter. That's measurable proof. Gratitude is emerging. However, I still get tinges of fear, the worst of which comes from an ongoing illusion that forces may exist that will target Lola as a way to break me. In these moments, I'm afraid my right to parent her rests precariously on thin ice. If I lose Lola, I may just say, "fuck it" and lose everything.

Just as unconditional surrender is the only chance for survival against a more powerful adversary, the only way to combat the illness residing in my thoughts is to accept them. Their symptoms were caused by my actions. They can only be reversed by the actions of future choices now unfolding . . . staying clean among them.

23

Down With the Sickness

Leann exhibits palpable signs that indicate the progressive disease of addiction. She calls or emails every few days to ask if I'd mind watching Lola for her. She's either "too tired" or "not feeling well." Sometimes it's to hang out with her friends or "run errands." I'm not sympathetic because she's home all day, unemployed. Every time we start to discuss parenting, something happens to her phone, or she has to go.

One afternoon, Leann arrives late to pick up Lola. She's flustered and impatient. I try to hurry, but as I buckle Lola in, Lola starts to cry. This happens each time we make the exchange.

"Why does this kid gotta fucking do this shit to me?" Leann caterwauls. It's ear-piercing. From the driver's seat, she lunges back and forth. The full force of her body slamming into the seat shakes the car.

Lola's cheeks turn pallid. She raises her arms higher at me to bring her to safety. She doesn't want me to leave without her. I remove her from her child seat, cradling her at my side like a mother.

"What's up? Are you okay?" I ask once Leann calms down.

"I've just got a lot going on."

I try to change the subject.

"What did you have an appointment for yesterday that you couldn't pick up Lola on time?"

"I had to meet . . . I was supposed to meet a lawyer."

"For what? Are you divorcing me? I mean, are we getting divorced?"

"No," she whispers. "No."

"If you want a divorce, I support you."

"No! I just, um . . . since the restraining order got dropped, any chance I have of getting money from DHS is ruined. I'm hiring a lawyer to help get assistance. I have no money. Jessica keeps acting like my husband. The more she pays for stuff, the more she expects."

"When were you getting money from DHS? Never mind. None of my business."

My upper lip rolls over the bottom one.

"Well, listen . . . we're bound for life by the child we brought into this world. We should always think long-term for her sake. Remember when you told me you really needed to be independent? I don't want to get back together until you've proven to yourself you can be. Not that you're asking."

Her eyes glaze over. My attempt to offer encouragement feels ignored. I pull her attention the only way I know how.

"It's fucking lame when you call me, crying about how you're in dire straits and need money for gas and food, but completely avoid talking about parenting. It hurts." I pause for effect. "I won't do it again."

"Do what?"

"Give you money when you're crying."

"You don't know how hard this is. Everyone keeps telling me 'Get a job,'" she says in a sarcastic, annoying voice. "Get a job? They're not my fucking bosses. I do what I want. Nobody's supporting *me*. I've done so fucking much for you. I deserve sooo much."

"I'm not saying you haven't done a lot for me. In the past, yes. You have. I am saying it feels like you're using me now."

I sense her walls going up, defenses emboldened.

In comparison with the hold drugs have over her, anything I say or do is irrelevant. I'm as powerless over her disease as I am my own. A normal person must realize this when dealing with an addict. Families are destroyed by this disease. Especially the children held at ground zero. As usual, I'm in tears when she drives off with Lola.

When it comes to getting away with as much as possible, Leann never tires. Her excuses for not holding up her end of the parenting plan are a waste of her time, for they fall on deaf ears. An active addict can't bullshit a recovering one unless they want to be bullshitted . . . another reason the recovery community is so valuable. We don't cosign each other's fake-ass, manipulative crap. We use it for training purposes. It helps us learn to identify how *not* to be!

One situation when Leann let her parenting card expire stands out. Lola had come down with a bad cough, which turned into pneumonia. I took her to a doctor. She prescribed antibiotics via a liquid medicine that had to be kept refrigerated. While staying with her mom, Lola's symptoms worsened.

Jessica calls. With a bossy tone, she tells me I need to come pick up Lola right away. I assume it's to cover for Leann being dope sick or staying somewhere with some young stud again. I don't react with a sense of urgency.

Upon arrival, Jessica brings Lola out. My baby looks anemic. She can barely say hi. She's too weak to perform her usual run to hug me. I squat to hold her. She's unable to fully open her arms. My hug is reciprocated, but it's feeble . . . lighter than an air hug.

Leann pulls up. I can tell she's been up all night. Only after I pry and prod does Leann confess that she left Lola's medication in the car, out in the heat. It's no good anymore. Because of this, she hasn't administered any medicine for two days.

Doesn't everyone know when you start a regimen of antibiotics you have to follow through until it's all gone or you run the risk of contracting a much stronger, more resistant bacterial infection? At least she told the truth. Had she told me two days prior, however, she could've kept Lola from getting sicker. It's difficult to stay objective while Leann steers clear of her responsibilities as well as the fallout from her oversights.

I buckle Lola's limp body into her seat. She's fast asleep. Her hands are too weak to grip the tippy cup of juice. Her cup falls to the floor of the van.

Within minutes, I arrive at the nearest Quick Care facility. I unbuckle her, then lift her out. My cradling barely wakes her. The electric doors part as we enter. Before I'm halfway inside the lobby, the receptionist jumps up from her seat. Hearing the commotion, a nurse also responds by bolting from the back of the office.

"Turn right back around and go to the hospital emergency room!" the nurse shouts, pointing toward the exit behind me.

I must have the deer-in-the-headlights look. *My baby is that sick*? Dutifully, I twist my body around, then head back through the double glass doors, still electronically held open. Lola's tiny cough is getting worse by the minute. I speed to the Providence St. Vincent hospital on the hill. I tell the receptionist I've already been instructed at urgent care to come straight here. They take Lola to a room right away.

I text Leann that we're at the hospital. She texts back an hour later. She'll try to come after she cleans Jessica's mom's house.

A trainee checks Lola's vital signs before we're placed in our own room. There, the RN takes over.

"Sir, how did your baby get to be this sick?"

"I'm not really sure. How bad, or rather, how sick is she?"

I'm guarded about what is said and discussed openly. Lola might panic if the nurse has bad news. Carrying myself as if there's no need to stress or worry or be afraid might help. If I appear worried, Lola might go into a tailspin, which could compound her illness. On the other hand, I can't appear too nonchalant to the nurse. I know the answer to her question. My baby got to be this sick because her mom skipped the administration of two days' worth of antibiotics. However, I choose not to make Leann look bad, nor myself look good for that matter, by coming to my daughter's rescue. While I'm forming sentences to address the issue, the nurse continues her tirade.

"You know, sir, you can't just ignore symptoms in babies? Kids get worse and can even die if you don't get them the care they need."

Left alone in a carafe, oil and vinegar separate—one being her personal issues, the other her professionalism. My presence, like her disdain, shakes up the carafe.

"I do know that, I—"

"This child is terribly, terribly sick, mister," she interrupts, her voice raised. "Why is it men wait until the last minute to act? How often were you checking her temperature?"

"You'd have to ask her mom that question, ma'am. Our daughter has been in her *mother's* care the last three days. I would never let it get to this point."

The nurse nods her head with a slow, shaming, left to right tisk-tisk. I have every right to lay into her verbally or complain to management about how inappropriate and sexist her comments are. But I'm here to save my baby's life. To cool my stirred-up blood, I ask God for help not to engage. No single action or quick-witted response could change this woman's convictions anyway.

I'm feeling all alone, but am I? The way the nurse is acting towards me is no different from how any other solo parent gets singled out for child-related circumstances beyond their control. As the responsible parent taking the brunt of blame, I'm a part of something bigger. It helps to imagine myself locking arms with single male parents who have been in this position, and the single women before us who dealt with the same singling out by the old-world, male-dominated medical culture. Count me as one with those who, based on gender, endure similar prejudices and prejudging as single moms have for years.

I hold Lola's hand while the nurse and doctor do their job. Her temperature is 106. They put an IV in her to replenish her fluids.

Once she begins to come back to life somewhat, I carry her down to the radiology department so a doctor can X-ray her lungs. Finally, they write some prescriptions to get her started on a whole new, longer-lasting, stronger antibiotic regimen. We're not released until 3:00 am. There's still no call or text from Leann. I have to work in the morning. Knowing in advance what a tiring day awaits, I'm frustrated.

The following morning, I keep going on just two hours of sleep. Through selfless giving, I feel renewed. By being there for my child, I'm fed from a fathomless wellspring of spiritual nourishment. In becoming the human God planned for me to be, I'm invigorated with hope and confidence that I'll be a trustworthy caregiver for Lola. In the meantime, I will continue working to provide her the life she deserves.

24

In Between Days

I'm losing interest in living on the edge. I've regained shared custody of my daughter. Lola and I have a roof over our head, food in our fridge, clothes on our backs. I've been hired full time for a family-owned corporation which offers benefits and random drug testing. I'm responsible, productive, and accountable. Things have aligned pretty well.

Yet I feel I have to protect myself.

I'm fearful my every undertaking is being judged. I worry about Leann's family filing a new restraining order in an attempt to pull Lola away. Because of this fear, I won't even allow Lola's friends to come over to play in her room unless another parent is present. This is one difference in single parenting as a man.

Living in the "worst-case scenario" mode is debilitating and draining. At least twice a week, I make journal entries detailing and accounting for my whereabouts. I've gone as far as to itemize the meals I cook for Lola in case her dietary health is ever called into question. Doing so, I'm afraid, is necessary in case more lies are concocted.

The journal proves useful as an overview for deciphering patterns. In the midst of the day-to-day chaos, it's difficult to notice how often Leann's behaviors repeat. Through closer observation, I see I've been part of her ongoing drama, no matter how far I try to distance myself from it.

I'm not keeping track to take her inventory. It's to protect myself.

In the last ninety days, she's emailed or texted nineteen times, claiming to be too exhausted or too sick to watch Lola. On twelve occasions, she showed up later than the agreed-upon time, half of which resulted in me being late to work. Six times she's asked for money, each solicitation enhanced by flirting and sexual offers. Three times she's complained she didn't have a place to stay. Three times, because of her no-shows, I needed her grandparents to care for Lola. Finally, I've tracked twenty-one instances of Lola losing control of her bowels—a physical symptom of the hell she's going through with her parents' marriage dissolving. Each time I'm rinsing feces off undies, it reinforces the idea that I am failing as a parent. The nights everything goes well feel like pure bliss.

One particular drama-free evening, I call Phil. I'd like to repair my relationship with him. He'd like this to work out for everyone, especially Lola. He voices concerns about how uncomfortable having Leann stay with him is.

Vindictiveness bubbles up within. I want to react with, "I told you so," or "payback's a bitch, ain't it?" It's unnatural for me to be tolerant. I give it a shot anyway.

"Hey man, hold tight. I'm coming over."

I surprise Aunt Darcy and Phil by bringing Lola with me to their Murray Hill home—an olive branch extended to express forgiveness (and maybe a tinge of showing off how much better Lola is doing under my care). Aunt Darcy pulls me aside to explain something face-to-face. The reason she didn't show up in court to testify on Lola's behalf was because she couldn't get on the stand and lie. I'm hesitant to believe her. Then my eye-to-eye contact with her softens. I'm doing my best to show, by example, that actions speak volumes, that I'm not the monster I've been made out to be.

Uncle Phil and I talk while playing a game of pool in their garage. The fan I took out of the window is still lying on the workbench. I try to hold back a devious smile.

"Hey, man. You know Leann's seeing someone, right?" Phil asks.

"I kinda figured. Why?"

"Oh, okay. I didn't want to get shot down as the messenger. Did you know he's married?"

"So is Leann."

Before emotions get overwhelming, we exchange hugs and call it a night.

While driving home, Leann calls. She needs to talk—right now. I pull over.

"I'm ready to come home," she says between sobs.

We meet at a park. Lola grabs my wrist and pulls me toward her mom, who is slow to get out of her boyfriend's SUV. Lola grabs her mom's wrist, then puts our hands together with her own and yells, "Family!"

I put on a grin for Lola, but inside, I'm overcome by profound melancholy.

Then Leann takes over.

"I need groceries," she demands, her tone cold.

"Okay, make me a list. I'll buy them and bring them over."

"And my car is almost out of gas."

"Okay. Whose car is that?"

"A friend's."

"I'll follow you to the gas station and fill it. Now, what's this about wanting to come home?"

Fidgeting in place for a minute, she then power walks to the slide where Lola's playing. Left standing, I think, *Filing a restraining order against me is the biggest mistake she ever made. If she hadn't drawn such a divisive legal line in the sand, I would've been fooled into giving her anything.*

The woman I married, the mother of my daughter—I never took this shit lightly. It's painful to watch. The firepit of addiction consumes her life. She's lashing out, unaware of how it's herself she's actually hurting. I feel like Neo in *The Matrix,* discovering the power within was there all along. Being clean and focused on my parenting responsibilities has given me the ability to preemptively figure out what Leann is trying to get away with. I just need to get Lola out of the way before she's collateral damage.

The three of us play until I need to leave. As Leann buckles Lola in, she asks, "What's that spiral notebook there? Are you keeping track of me?"

"No. Actually, yes." *Busted!* "It's for my step work."

She looks curious.

"Can I read you something? It'll only take a minute."

This is the first time I have had her undivided attention since she left me. While she stands on the gravel lot outside my minivan, I read my first recovery assignment to her. I read two lists; twenty-five reasons my life is unmanageable and twenty-five reasons why I'm powerless over drugs. Most of my answers express the regret I carry for forcing this situation. Others express owning my part in how much I make life intolerable for anyone living with me.

Reading what I've written is not meant to be an indirect amends to her. It's so she doesn't think I sit around every night reciting some "fuck that bitch" refrain. I'm reading to her so she knows I'm not plotting vengeance after all she's put me through. This might just show her the ways I'm taking responsibility for my part in allowing anger and drugs to destroy the well-being of our family.

I read both lists, hoping she'll see that she, too, can benefit from recovery. My tears make the ink in my spiral notebook run. I look at her to affirm my feelings. Sweet and soft, I say, "I'm not your rival or adversary."

"Okay. Well, I gotta go."

Vulnerability never felt so wrong.

She adds, "Unless . . ."

"Yes?" I ask.

"You *knowww*, we are still married. We should hook up."

I respond by starting the van and rolling up my window.

Being indirect is the safest way to treat a self-centered person bereft with the need for instant gratification. Head-on refusal or denial of their needs is often met with tantrums, hurtful words, sometimes violence. Her proposition feels fake, anyway. She's catering to my ego only to secure her future wants. No further mention of groceries or gas or moving back in is made.

I'm dead inside. I take the long way home to sort my thoughts. Lola perks up from napping in her car seat directly behind me.

"We need to go to the store, Daddy!"

"What do we need to get at the store, honey?"

"We need to get some answers."

~

Weeks later, Leann and I meet to take Lola trick-or-treating. Halloween is Lola's favorite holiday. After walking Carol's neighborhood, we head up to Aunt T's where there's more wealth and better candy. We wrap up the night at her house.

Leann's in an extraordinarily chipper mood. I assume she's high on pills, judging by her mannerisms. Lola and I are by ourselves, playing in the living room. Before long, I notice we've been left alone. Feeling ignored, I go looking to let everyone know we're leaving. A cloud billows out as I open the garage door. Phil and his underage son are trading bong rips with Leann. Two adults pretending they're seventeen. I leave, taking Lola and her pillowcase full of candy home.

Minutes later, I get a text from Leann:

I would like to have non-committal marital sex with you.
I'm not ready for that, I respond.

~

Just before Thanksgiving, my health benefits through work kick in. My first order of business is to get my teeth looked at. Meth addicts are notorious for their missing teeth. I resemble that remark. In fact, when I was up for days on end, I avoided brushing, showering, using deodorant, checking the fluids in my van, and paying bills. Life maintenance took a backseat to drug maintenance.

X-rays yield a whopping six cavities, two extractions, and five crowns to save what can be saved. Thousands of dollars in repairs. I start with a few fillings and a root canal. My sponsor suggests letting the dentist know I'm a recovering drug addict because special concern should be made when prescribing narcotics. I notify her, but it doesn't matter. She prescribes them anyway.

We're not supposed to be martyrs in recovery. We are allowed to follow doctor's orders. Taking any drug—even a prescribed dosage of one, it turns out—is dreadfully trying. The body doesn't know the difference between a drug taken recreationally and one taken therapeutically. But even though taking opioids helps to manage pain, mentally it feels like my relationship with God is severed. It awakens my addiction like a bear poked near the end of hibernation. The more I pray, the more my addict brain unloads a whirlwind of mad posturing. One can become delusional to the point of believing the temptation to take more than prescribed is *impossible* to resist. My best thought is to ask my sponsor to help.

"Are you sure you wouldn't be okay with aspirin?"

"Probably. I didn't take any painkillers at work today."

"Well then, why don't I come over and we'll dump them?"

"Sounds good."

~

In meetings, we're told we can only keep what we have by giving it away. God finds me a good place to start. My friend Mykael has been binge drinking again. Fatherhood, meth abuse, a dissolving marriage—we have common ground. He's quit everything but the booze, because it's legal. His wife has asked for my help. Deb thinks I'm a good influence. That's a first!

After church, we get to talking about the control our vices have over us. In a loving, nonjudgmental way, I remind him alcohol is a drug. He runs his hand through his hair and scratches his jaw. He tells me he doesn't have a problem. I know not to push. I'm of no use to him, save by example.

One night I pop by unannounced. I need some of my belongings I'd stashed at his house back when my apartment was still susceptible to Leann's looting. I've come with an ulterior motive—to invite Mykael to a meeting. This is at Deb's request. Since Lola and their son, Odin, have fun playing together, I figure it'll be a win-win. Standing on the porch, I tell Lola to ring the doorbell.

"You're such a jerk, Daddy."

"I'm not a jerk, Lola. Who said that?"

"I did."

Interpreting her innocent comment, I angle my head back to the left. I smile while kneeling down at her level to get her to focus on our conversation. I heed Parenting 101 advice: Don't make a big deal out of bad words lest your child latches on to them and infinitely repeats them.

"Where did you hear that, honey?"

"Momma."

"Momma's been pretty mad at Daddy lately, huh?"

"Yeah. And you're mad at her!" Her inflection of excitement is hard to interpret. She's at an age when learning to communicate is crucial.

"No, sweetie. Daddy loves momma—he's not mad at her."

"Okay."

"And . . . Daddy's not a jerk, sweetheart. If Momma says Daddy's a jerk, say to her, 'No he's not, Momma, he loves you.' Then make this face."

We're laughing at my silliness when Mykael answers his door. Turns out tonight was bad for him. I'll have to save what I have to give away some another time.

~

The enabling and tolerating of Leann's actions by loved ones around her are about to reach critical mass. She's pulling her shenanigans more often. I fear they'll soon become tolerable and acceptable. Once this "new normal" is established, it's doubtful anyone will make the effort to curb her behavior. They'll say it's too late and give up.

Were my loved ones forced to jump through the same flame-laden hoops? Can someone who is too inebriated, co-piloted by denial, and downplaying matters even tell? I've lived the lie on the one side and now I'm living the pain and confusion on the other.

Addicts are inconstant. We take advantage of distance and time to create confusion. Often we don't know we're doing it. For example, since Halloween, Leann seemed to be doing better. Weeks went by without drama or absence.

Just when responsible behavior was becoming consistent, Leann pulls another one of her disappearing acts. Three days later, she calls. Hearing her complain about how overwhelming watching our daughter would be for her right now, I offer to keep Lola another night, provided she picks her up early.

It's 5:30 am. Leann still hasn't arrived, breaking her promise. My boss threatens to write me up if I'm late again. I'm cast into crisis mode. Carol is my only option. Our phone conversation sounds more like code.

"No show."

"Bring her."

Click.

After work, I return to pick up Lola. She's been with Leann most of the day. While we're driving home, Lola blurts, "Me and Mommy and Jerry fall asleep in his bed watching movies together."

This desert camel has but one spine, a broken one. I call Leann to address the ongoing bullshit once and for all. No answer. Five months straining to quell, contain, and direct my anger in a healthy manner gets the best of me. I leave a message. Trying to sound like I'm in control, I spout off seven key points.

1. You're only a mom for three days a week. Quit yer bitchin' and get a job.

2. You need to respect my time.

3. You're hanging out with boys, doing drugs around *my* daughter.

4. I've given you a lot of leeway; not anymore.

5. If your boyfriend wants to spend time with Lola, he needs to meet me first.

6. Maybe I should let him see the text you sent about wanting sex.

7. One day you'll know how much this hurts.

I should be proud of myself for getting my true feelings out. But then I don't hear from her for days. The fear that my text will be used against me takes hold. I've become afraid that whenever I defend myself, it's perceived as a threat, which then justifies the use of a restraining order. I call the county courthouse four days in a row to ask if a new order of restraint has been filed. The Serenity Prayer has been recited so many times it seems to have lost its effect. So, I come up with my own:

"God, please watch over my child so the wreckage I created in my active addiction is minimized by the progress I make each day in my active recovery."

I don't hear anything from Lola's mom's side of the family for a week. *What did I do wrong?* After the restraining order fiasco, I can't be idle. I won't just sit around waiting to see what trouble is in store.

I call the grandparents to check in. I tell Patrick everything. He doesn't seem the least bit surprised, but he's hard to read. Maybe I've hit a dead end here, trying to get the family to see I have Lola's best interests in mind. As I'm about to hang up, Patrick stops me.

"Carol and I are completely disgusted with this whole situation. We think you should go for full custody. We still want to babysit our granddaughter, though. Leann don't wanna look for a job or get out and do anything. She just wants to lie around and have someone support her. She doesn't even watch Lola when she's here."

"Well, I don't want to talk bad about your daughter, Patrick. I'm looking out for Lola. It would be ideal if she could have her mom in her life, but her mom hasn't stepped up. I'm thankful Lola has you guys. And just so you know, no matter what, I'll make sure she sees you both."

"Yeah, Leann's been talking about moving in with this guy. We won't let her take Lola. We'll call you first."

~

Progress in recovery comes in baby steps. I'm impatient to get on with healing the pain I've caused. Although making amends is a ways down the road, I can't help looking ahead. It's my nature. At times, it's all I think about. My sponsor assures me it's best to trust the order of the process.

"But this is how my brain works," I joke. "Ready. Fire. Aim."

We both laugh.

"You're going to need to forgive yourself first. If you can't, you won't have a concise understanding of what it is you'll be asking of others." Matt's logical, useful information seems so simple. I'm surprised I haven't thought of it on my own. I've prided myself on being a gifted overthinker. Strategic, empathic, influential, logical.

Suddenly, it clicks. Only through interaction can we bear witness to how the program works. Only through one person being transparent with another can the veil lift, or at the very least, be pierced. If I want to be of service and heal others, I must first work on healing the person I hurt the most: me.

I'm asked to decide for myself whether or not I'm ready to turn my will and my life over to my Higher Power's care.

I'm ready to decide, but . . .

My understanding of who or what this Power is isn't fully formulated. I'm *ready* to believe, but my perception of truth changes daily, sometimes by the minute. It depends on where I'm seeing things from. I'm either acting "as if" I'm ready, procrastinating being ready, or feeling too cocky to think I should be ready.

Matt asks me to note all the new things I've been willing to trust in that *are* working. There, I find proof. It's through people and in how my attitude and actions are evolving. Besides, wherever this program is taking me has got to be better than where I've been.

Before finalizing my decision, I search outside the program for community, fellowship, and additional spirituality. It's nice to have Lola at my side on this spiritual quest. Our little family. Through volunteering and sitting in on a wide variety of religious denominations, I find a church that aligns with the newfound values I want for us. In practically every sermon along the quest, I hear the language of the program; I hear God asking me to trust Him.

By committing to make a consistent effort of asking for help and pursuing faith, I decide. I'm trusting my Higher Power, whom I'll call God, allowing Him to place the loving guideposts I believe will lead me toward spiritual principles. By doing so, I'm claiming some level of dedication to do the next right thing, not to sit back and expect everything to be taken care of. No. It's up to me to be willing to ask of and listen for His will, make a continuous effort to stay on course, get out of my comfort zone when suggested, and do the work. Simple, but not easy.

Decision made, my will is turned over to God. Matt congratulates me. Coming from a lifetime of instant gratification, I'm in awe of how fulfilled I am by the gradual, subtle, "high" of daily progress. My next assignment is to dig deeper into discovering who I am by writing out a thorough inventory of the liabilities and assets of my thoughts, feelings, and past actions. Through writing these out, I should have the freedom to see the pieces of my personality that drugs prohibited me from seeing.

25

Uncontrollable Urge

Over the course of the many years I played music in Portland, I never achieved the "big fish in a small market" status I'd earned in Las Vegas. Nevertheless, I built lasting relationships with local musicians. I never wanted to be the center of attention just for the attention. I wanted to somehow "keep it real." In the music business, this meant I'd remain unknown.

When my addiction took over, it replaced the devotion to my life's first passion, music, with getting loaded. This passion, along with every other feeling, got blocked out. Now, as I've strung together some clean time, my soul yearns to express itself. In equal measure with the written word, music is my natural pathway toward meditation, healing, and mindfulness.

Fortunately, my musician friends come a knockin.' Two brothers, Dale and Bones, are persistent with their invitation to jam. Seasoned players like me don't jam; we're paid to show up. When you've toured the nation selling your own music or backed up someone selling their music; when you've opened for headliners like Devo, Sublime, Julian

Lennon, Al Green, Black Flag, the Smithereens, .45 Grave, and others at venues holding over 3,000 people, it's beneath you to jam.

Without rehearsing, we book a gig at a little restaurant on the Multnomah Channel in Scappoose, Oregon. Money is money, but my soul aches to bleed some blues out through the strings. Mykael is busy, so I call Matt. He, too, played drums through some of my worst highs, lows, and drug-fueled drama. I have to convince him I am clean before he'll do the gig.

It's a lot to ask of recovery folks to come to a bar. Fortunately, the brothers bring heaps of friends. A few Wednesdays into this thing, we are a steady local draw.

Sometimes, just the thought of being in touch with those raw things called *feelings* is scary. That which I yearn for is also what I'm terrified to seek. Playing music not only invigorates my soul, it reinvigorates my libido, long since defiled in dereliction by drugs. I look forward to playing; to feeling again.

Arranging to have Lola at Grandma's, being up late playing music, then working the next morning, is no easy feat. In the past, it was rare to play all night without taking something "to spread out the energy." I've never been able to come home from a gig and easily fall asleep. Now I only have natural inner strength to rely on.

There's a contagious liveliness around people filled with spirits. Additionally, profound sexual energy emanates from uninhibited dancing and flirting. This hasn't changed with sobriety.

Tonight, either my loneliness or onstage magnetism bring an attractive woman's attention my way. Her friend approaches first, offering to introduce us.

"I don't want to just come out and say she's interested. She likes to play hard to get, but I can tell."

"This may sound precocious, but I already knew," I answer.

"Ooh. She'll like your confidence."

Call it a radar thingy or musician-in-tune-ness. Even if she makes it blatantly obvious she is mine for the taking, it hasn't been since before I met Leann over five years that I've sought out a new . . . anything. I'm not ready. It's too soon.

Her friend then pulls me by the wrist to their table to introduce us. Georgia and I make small talk. I can't tell if there's actual chemistry, supercharged particles of lust in the air, or if I'm just reacting to the long-overdue absence of connection with flesh. Whatever the case, I go from "be patient" to "gotta have" mode the minute she laughs at one of my silly anxiety-alleviating jokes.

Georgia gulps down her drink. She bangs her glass down in front of me. It's a hint.

I have a rule. I don't buy women drinks. Two decades of observing gullible guys used for free drinks in bars will do this to you. I tell her I'm sober.

"Oh! That's sweet. I don't drink that often. I could stop anytime I want."

Why do people in bars feel the need to get defensive when another patron claims sobriety? A sober person in a bar is like a deaf person at a rock concert—they still feel their feelings, minus the booze. But to a drunk, a sober person on their turf somehow triggers the Inquisition. Newsflash: A person owning their sobriety has nothing to do with you, or how you'd like to quit, or how you don't really have a problem.

Georgia plays aloof quite well. My mission becomes one of bringing this to a point of no turning back. She mentions getting over a recent relationship.

"The best way to get over a man is to get under a man." I flash a fake smile as my brain screams, *ewww*! I'm out of practice.

She smiles anyway.

I leave her table to play our last set.

On my way toward the stage, a drunken regular pulls me aside.

"Hey. I see you're hooking up with Georgia tonight."

"What? No, I'm just talking to her."

"Yeah, right. Well, you can thank me later, bro, but be warned . . . that bitch is crazy."

"Define crazy."

"Shit, bro. You know what I mean!" He gives a wink wink, nudge nudge. I don't follow his drunken gibberish.

"No, I don't."

"Hey. I'm just trying to help you out. That psycho bitch stayed the night with a friend of mine. Three weeks later, he's gotta call the cops to get her out. Some of his shit was missing, too. She had dope dealers coming over all the time. Bitch is bad news."

"Yeah, okay. Whatever."

"Don't say I didn't warn you."

Fuck.

A few songs into our set, Georgia comes and dances with her friend in front of the stage. Watching her hips sway, her long tan legs turning about in her short dress, is too much. My brain tells me, *go for it.*

I'll deal with the consequences later . . . if there are any. I make sure she sees she's got my full attention. Her friend keeps elbowing her. Georgia plays it super cool, nonchalant. She ignores my stalker-like focus. Good game.

My head fights the medium fight. I follow her around the club until I realize doing so *isn't* in my best interest. So I do a little nonchalant ignoring of my own.

I grab my gear, then trek up the dock ramp to my van. Her friend helps by carrying a guitar. We discuss what the guy in the bar said. She puts my mind at ease, claiming it was all a misunderstanding. I'm apprehensive as hell.

"Georgia really wants to be with you. I think the fact you're not a drunk impresses her. She's just super heartbroken and wants you to make the first move."

"I'm recently heartbroken, too."

"Well, if you want, I'll tell her I can't give her a ride home. She's been staying with me, but my husband's getting tired of her."

"Whoa! She can't stay with me. Nope. Ain't gonna happen."

"What time do you go to work? I could come get her first thing."

This woman just became my best friend. Or she's duping me so she can pawn Georgia off. The angel on one shoulder, devil on the other battle begins.

It's a clear, moonless night. We walk down to the boat launch area. Some drunken straggler is there, sitting next to Georgia. He's trying to make a move.

I walk toward them. He dismisses himself. She almost collides with me, then wriggles her way beneath my arm. I reciprocate, holding her close. We stare at the stars for a minute, then embrace. I'm uncomfortable, guarded. I turn to say something to her friend. Nobody's around but us. Well played.

We take the steps adults take to hook up. In the back of my head is a feeling of wariness as to just how fucked up this could turn out. If there are obvious cues to cut and run, I ignore them.

It's nearly two in the morning when we get into my bed. Not to sound like a man, but moments after we're done, I'm honest with myself about what a bad idea this was. Knowing I have to work at six, I go cold. I can't sleep.

I wake Georgia at 5:00 am. She's full of questions.

"I have a daughter. You can't be here when she gets home."

"Why can't I stay and get some sleep until then?"

What I was hoping would be a reprieve from life's seriousness just got serious. I sink into fight-or-flight mode. I seldom set out to be a dick, but I usually end up here. I've had women become belligerent when casual sex didn't turn into more. I've been accused of using them, which is offensive, really. If two people consent to hook up, how does one feel "used" afterward?

I would never demean or disrespect a woman for being intimate with me. That's why making the first move is extremely rare for me. But last night I did. Now I'm reneging on the proclaimed attraction.

I want to be kind, but I can't be soft. I don't know who this person is—at all. What happens if I give an inch? I can't take that chance. How do I kindly tell her I can't leave her here in the sanctuary I've taken enormous steps to build for my daughter?

"It doesn't matter what time. You agreed to leave in the morning. Your friend promised she'd get you," I say. I sound mean.

God, I feel like shit.

"Okay, okay! Just give me a minute." Her voice reflects disappointment, like it's commonplace for men to treat her the way I am.

Georgia gets her things together while texting her friend. When she's in the bathroom, I open her purse to check her phone, just to be certain. She's being honest.

Her friend texts back:

How was he?

I laugh, then tell myself I don't deserve to know her response. I don't need to. I know I was lame. This was lame. Being subjugated by the aching in my loins and allowing it to predicate my actions is lame.

Chasing pleasure, regardless of consequences, is old behavior. She's being mature about this, and I'm in a panic. A firehose couldn't wash all the shame, guilt, and self-icky away.

I can't keep from reading Georgia's texted reply:

Very average.

After her friend comes to pick her up, I pretend to leave, then circle back to my apartment. I do a walk-through, ensuring nothing's stolen. *I trusted her enough to sleep with her, but not enough to let her stay?*

My eyes well up. My stupidity is heartbreaking. Have I changed at all? What about Lola's heart? I'm a wreck who can't deal with feeling this shit. Every feeling is felt deeper now that I'm clean.

I call Matt.

"What did you learn?"

Of course, he's going to ask the question I don't want to answer.

"What's the right answer?" I ask.

"You tell me."

"I don't know. That I'm a fuckup? That I get lonely and horny? That being single sucks? That I put everything I worked so hard for, for Lola and me, at risk? That I'll never do it again? That my disease is always looking for an opportunity to get me to feel this way about myself?"

"Yes."

"Okay?"

"Yes, but you left out a few things. You're human, so you *will* fuck up. Part of being human is feeling lonely, horny, hurt. Another part is making mistakes . . . then learning from them.

"Before you got clean, did you think about Lola's needs? No. Would the thought of anything other than getting what you want have crossed your mind? No."

I hold my breath, wanting to absorb every word.

"Progress, not perfection. You're growing, my brother. Growing pains are a natural part of what?"

"Growing?" I answer, shoulders drooping toward the carpet.

"That's right. Give yourself a break. We still make blunders in recovery. We learn the hard way what not to do, hopefully for good."

"You got that right. Thank you Matt."

"Oh, we're not done. I'm going to add to the assignment you're working. I want you to make a list of all the women you had sexual relations with. Write down their names first. Next to their names, write out what harm was caused by the interaction. Next to that, write about how it made them feel, and last, write the end result. We'll go over it when you're done. Be as thorough as possible."

26

Bitter Sweet Symphony

The daunting process of deciding amongst numerous daycare facilities brings about a rude awakening. Most are either grossly mismanaged, micromanaged, or priced beyond what I can manage. Picking one out after work is both exhausting and hopeless. Another lesson in how to prioritize while juggling an already full plate.

Through perseverance, I find an affordable, clean daycare. Colleen, the owner, seems friendly and good with kids. I contract with her for three days a week. Even with a loose game plan, things are falling into place.

From the onset, it appears Colleen and I could become good friends. She's gracious enough to let me drop Lola off before she opens at 6:00 am. Most kids are napping when I arrive to pick up Lola. This gives us time for chit-chat.

One afternoon, Colleen isn't her usual reserved self. Using discretion, she shares details of how her daughter died of alcohol poisoning. Then the tears come. Wanting her to feel comfortable about what she is revealing, I inform her I'm in recovery.

I explain to Colleen how her daughter's demise is not her fault. I share what I'm learning. Her daughter died of a disease that has no known cure. Once Colleen better understands this truth, she'll know there's nothing she could've done—even if she knew about alcoholism, even if she did everything completely different.

"I really appreciate talking with you," she says. "This isn't something I normally ever get to do. All my customers are moms. You don't know how refreshing this is. You're not only helpful, you actually listen. Unlike most men."

Colleen's train of thought undergoes a conversion. Her head tilts off to the upper left, followed by a deliberate raising of her eyebrow. I know the face. She's off to man-hate village. The topic changes into a rant about her ex. She's still upset over his cheating and absence from their daughter's life after they divorced. I interrupt her fierce, hateful words.

"Why choose to carry a torch that still burns you up inside?" I ask.

Before she can respond, one of the youngsters she cares for appears, asking if nap time is over.

Mental note: Don't drag deep-seated hatred around in *my* situation. It serves no purpose to seethe relentlessly about Leann's personal choices. She's the one missing out on time with Lola. Milestone moments pass, never to return.

I admit, however, every time I overhear Lola crying in private, it's easy to hate Leann.

~

The adult conversations Colleen and I succumb to each time I pick up are borderline platonic—words laced with enough sexual innuendo to go either way. Months later, Colleen invites me and Lola to dinner. Two other kids she watches join us, making it appear, on the surface at least, innocuous.

I get a bad feeling in my gut.

When we arrive, we're blitzed by the bouquet of garlic, olive oil, mozzarella, and basil. Aromas replaced by alcohol when we're brought to our booth. Colleen's there, already buzzed on white wine. I give her a cautious look. She's forthright, patting the seat beside her for me to sit.

"So we can keep an eye on the kids, silly," she proclaims, to excuse her overt advances. She doesn't know that I'm no stranger to presumptuous women, especially those uninhibited via liquid courage. She's immediately forward enough to eliminate any doubt that her intention is to have me go for it. Two lonely adults. What harm could come of it?

This question is best answered with the head on my shoulders. I have everything to lose if I lose sight of Lola's heart. A meaningless one-nighter with a trusted female could destroy every bit of progress I've made toward restoring Lola's fractured psyche. But saying no is new to me.

Resisting Colleen's drunken advances does not fare well. She rises from the table. In doing so, she puts an abrupt end to dinner and interrupts any subsequent conversation between the kids. Under her breath, she whispers a few snide remarks. She insists on paying. I offer to leave a tip, but she refuses to look me in the eye or hear me. I do anyway. Exiting the tall wooden front doors, we're a silent group. We continue on our separate ways without formal goodbyes.

I had hoped Colleen would put this behind us and professionalism would prevail. I had hoped she'd do the right thing—err on the side of her business reputation. On the morning of the first return to Colleen's care, she doesn't give so much as a nod to me.

That afternoon, a mandatory work event comes up. My only available option for childcare is Grandma Carol. The event ends late. From my van, I call to thank her for picking Lola up from daycare and tell her I'm on my way.

"Leann picked her up," Carol says.

"What? Why?"

"Isn't that okay?"

"Leann is not on my list of safe adults approved for pickup. No, it's not okay. Why would Colleen let her go without asking me?"

"Because I was there with her, silly."

I shut off the engine.

"You should've seen Colleen's face when she met Leann."

"What do you mean?"

"Colleen was in tears. I guess Leann is the spitting image of Colleen's daughter. You know, the one who died."

"Huh."

"And don't worry about picking Lola up tonight, Paul. She can stay here and I'll bring her to daycare for you tomorrow."

When I arrive at daycare, Lola runs at me. She gives a bigger than usual great big hug, then runs off to gather her belongings. Halfway down the entryway to Colleen's office, I hear a familiar laugh. It's Leann.

She and Colleen are inside, enjoying each other's company like two long lost best friends.

"Paul. I brought Lola this morning. This is a great place for Lola. I've been here all day helping out. That's okay, right?" Leann asks.

The look on my face is her answer. I glance at Colleen. My warnings about Leann's substance abuse and neglect, given in confidence, must've gone out the window. I'm afraid to reveal my thoughts or take action. If I do, I'll tempt them into proving my worst assumption—that they'll gang up on me.

Here I am, standing alone in my despondency. Alone before two women avowed to sisterhood. Smiling wide, boisterous, their intertwined female energy dances amok. Their celebration ominous.

Instead of being seen as the knight come to save his princess, I'm cast into a lesser role as interloper. The cold shoulder Colleen's been giving is problematic, but this just made it worse. I don't want it to alter the current arrangements. My feet are locked in place. Life is too busy to devote my attention to strategy right now. I work hard to provide a stable routine for Lola, not to feel impotent. Maybe it's an act for Leann, but Colleen lets on like she's repulsed by my arrival.

The fox guards the henhouse.

Lola is quiet on the drive home, which is odd. She then breaks down in tears. Because of all the spinning going on inside my head, it takes a minute to register. Her outburst is out of the ordinary. Our drives together are always chockful of silliness, pranks, and laughter.

I determine her moodiness is a result of seeing her mom. Perhaps it reopened the wounds left by her intact family's separation. It's hard to handle her crying. I ask what's the matter three different times in three different ways. It's typical for Lola to take her time responding, for her brain to process, especially when it's something serious. I've learned to be patient, however, she resists telling me for a longer time than ever before.

"Why do Mommy and Colleen say mean things about you?"

Hearing this, voiced through breathy hiccups and sobs, I can't believe my ears. Lola's mother—who kidnapped my daughter in a power-struggle chess move, who uses Lola as a means to ensure her partying lifestyle continues uninterrupted, who emptied every last penny of our savings and Lola's college money, who falsified legal documents to restrain me from seeing my kid, who is not present in our daughter's life—sinks to a new low: badmouthing *me* in front of Lola at the daycare facility I pay for because I can't rely on her to be a mom?

How much more can one take?

To punch the dashboard with my rage-propelled fist is the burgeoning reaction. Instead, I take a surreptitious lungful of air, exhaling slowly and controlled. This way Lola can't tell I'm using breathing to calm down.

In the rearview mirror, I verify my ears and cheeks are flushed. It feels like I'm burning from the inside. Even if I want to play this off for the sake of Lola's nerves, she's a perceptive child. My lips purse to manufacture a docile tone.

"Why, honey? Did you overhear something?"

Lola sobs uncontrollably, profuse tears flowing. I pull over to unbuckle her and cradle her in my arms until she catches her breath. Minutes pass before she's calm enough to speak. Meanwhile, I'm melting inside, trying to hold back the bitter flame smoldering beneath the surface. I feel it in my earlobes.

Because I'm certain she will internalize my animosity as her fault, I self-declare I must not show my little girl the combustion consuming me. Studies show how it will result in her feeling bad about speaking her pain in the future. Going against all the demons I've fed my entire life, I tell her in the sweetest daddy's voice I can muster that it's okay.

"We don't have to talk about it right here, right now, honey."

"They were making fun of you and saying mean things about you, Daddy."

I won't allow the daycare duo's deplorable insensitivity to become my daughter's problem. Not if I can help it. She gets a big, tight squeeze of a hug.

"You know Daddy loves you, right?"

"Yeah."

"Yeah, well, you know Mommy and Daddy are not together because of problems between *us*. You know you had nothing to do with that, right?"

"Yes, Daddy?"

"Yes, honey. Both of us love you very much. It's not because of you that Mommy says mean things. She and I don't get along. That's why we're not together anymore. Now, as far as Colleen, hmmm, what should Daddy do about Colleen?"

"She's a meany!" Lola's little lip juts out.

Pouting is a notch above crying, so I take it as progress. I wipe the tears from her cheeks with my index finger, then kiss them. She'd like me to believe she's all better. I get a deeper sense she's not.

"Tell you what, honey. Daddy will let her know it's not okay to say mean things. But don't you worry. She won't know you told me. Okay, honey?"

"Okay, Daddy."

"I love you, Jaybird."

"I love you too, Daddy."

We stop for ice cream on the way home. I can't afford two cones, so I go without.

What Lola revealed eats at me, but I keep my composure long enough to complete the evening's parenting responsibilities: reading to Lola, tucking her in, kissing her good night.

The minute I flick off her bedroom's ladybug light switch, my sympathetic nervous system tightens up. Fight mode. I start to obsess about resolving matters.

Calling Colleen to verbally smash her would be a great release. Anger, risen to this point, feels impossible to contain. Elaborate fantasies arise in which I'm able to get away with doing nuclear actions without fallout or repercussions. I imagine myself as a mighty bull. It's muscle-laden chest pummeled by sword after sword. A capable bullfighter and her accomplice stand proud, as if victorious—that is until I'm granted an *indultado,* or pardon, by the bullring crowd. Fantasies of atonement bar a good night's sleep.

In the morning, I have a word with Colleen. We address the issue head on. She shrugs her shoulders, holding her palms upright, feigning as if nothing was said about me at all, neither in front of nor in the vicinity of Lola. She then goes for the jugular.

"Wow, Paul! Do you really think you're so important that we sit around here and talk about you all day? Someone's got a huge ego." She snorts. "Nothing could be further from the truth."

"I didn't say that. All I'm saying is I would appreciate it if you could resist saying negative things in front of Lola."

"That would be unprofessional. I'm insulted you would accuse me of such a thing. I've run a successful daycare company longer than you've been a parent. Give me a little credit. I know what is best for kids. I'm not so sure about you, though. Maybe you'd like to take your business elsewhere?"

"I'm only asking you to be considerate of Lola's feelings and to avoid saying things with her mom that would upset her."

"Yeah, and I'm telling you I would never do that. What did Lola tell you?"

"Nothing! I just . . . I got the impression from how you guys were acting yesterday."

"That kid has a pretty good imagination. Have you considered she might be making it up? Kids do that, you know? No. You probably don't know. Maybe you shouldn't be so paranoid. Maybe you should think before you accuse people of saying things they didn't say."

"All right. Well, I didn't come here to argue."

"Well, if you're done, you know where the door is. See you Tuesday."

When your gut tells you one thing, your head another, conflict looms. I'd rather not continue to bring Lola to a care facility owned by a woman who holds such hostility toward men and indifference toward their kids' hearts. Even if I can't prove it.

Yet, I can't continue to deny my gut feeling that Colleen's growing relationship with Leann, whom she has taken in as a living substitute for her deceased daughter, could so thickly cloud her judgment about the harm done by talking about me in front of Lola. The question that plagues me, contributing to my hesitation, is how am I going to find an affordable childcare open during the hours I need?

With the economy suffering a downturn, I'm expected to work more overtime. I have little left in the tank by the time I pick Lola up each day. We still have months to go before public school starts. I want to find a new daycare, but I'm reluctant to keep bouncing Lola from one place to the next. She's been through more change than any kid should have to go through. In less than four years she's endured four moves, a failed marriage, and two addicted parents—one who's clean, changing from the inside out.

~

Too fearful to engage in conversation, I keep a safe distance from Colleen when picking up and dropping off. When we do interact, it's icy, especially now that Leann's working there part time. What's being said behind my back, I can only imagine.

Lola is my only barometer for measuring changes in daycare dynamics. I notice things. She's not as excited to see me. The same pep to her step she had before doesn't come until we're alone at home.

I'm struggling with this. How clearly can I examine my motives and actions when I'm beset with such bitterness? I'm not the parent who is still using. I'm not the parent whose choices result in seeing Lola less and less. Isn't Leann grateful that I'm providing Lola with stability? Or is she resentful because my values have changed?

For a minute or five, I feel good about myself. Asking myself these questions, practicing an honest internal dialogue, sculpted by tools of recovery, shows growth. But the bane of resentment has already hit my bloodstream, coursing through to my pores. I chase it with the antidote, a serum of Step work—memorized clichés and being of service. Regardless, the poultice of recovery needs to be applied over and over to run its course, for the toxins take time to be drawn out.

Meanwhile, questions thump at my head, fostering the enmity between us. Why am I paying a quarter of my income for daycare when Colleen just takes the money and pays Leann under the table with it? Whose fault is it Leann doesn't have her own place to provide for our daughter? Why, through some sick twist of fate, has Colleen become *her* ally? The nerve of her joining in on the dad-bashing, then indiscriminately funding Leann's using with money meant for Lola.

~

I call Matt to update him. He's unable to hold back laughter. Hearing him do so is strangely comforting.

"What's so funny?" I ask.

"Geeze dude, your life just keeps on getting worse. I've never had to deal with anything close to this."

Not that his comment in itself helps, but to have another person acknowledge my going through this much difficulty does. It gives assurance everything is going to be okay. Things will work out just as they should.

Once my thoughts are out in the open, exposed, transparent, I can move toward replacing them with healthier ones. Matt praises me for choosing not to act in all the unhealthy ways I have in the past. These days, I'm on the tolerating end of the madness. I'm not sure which I prefer.

~

In the long run, drugs closed more doors of perception than they opened. No one starts off making long-term plans to use drugs. I didn't. Having no guarantee the dope I thought I needed to get through the day would be available, I was only able to focus on narrow, short-range plans. I'm super curious to discover what effect staying clean is having. Each day I'm still alive feels like a miracle. Each day I wake up clean, I am astounded by the possibilities of the day ahead. One at a time, I've strung together six months—the longest I've gone without some form of mind-altering substance since my late twenties, when my relationship with drugs began. I was a late bloomer. What is the opposite of a bloomer?

27

Creep

A decade or so ago, I listened to a radio show hosted by Dr. Laura Schlessinger. A marriage and family therapist, she took to the radio with a stern perspective on ethics and values, some of which were controversial. In an incessant culture of weak parenting, she reinforced the values of families seeking to do the right thing while offering reassurances to those who weren't supported when doing so.

When I first heard Dr. Laura's program, I was living with my girlfriend, Candy, and her teenage daughter. As was typical with most of my relationships, I'd never planned on tying the knot. I believed it was practical to live with the person I dated—shared rent, physical benefits, commitment free. Neither of us considered the possibility our relationship was setting an unhealthy example for her daughter. It was my first time living with a mother, but I wasn't the first live-in boyfriend Candy's daughter had to involuntarily adapt to.

The Dr. Laura Program offered a perspective I hadn't heard. She talked about having scruples, aspiring to find a moral compass, and always doing the right thing for your kids. For me, her advice was the proverbial teacher's sudden appearance for the student who is ready. I reacted like a lost entrepreneur showing up at an inspirational conference, slapping their forehead and lamenting, "Why didn't I see this?"

~

My addiction reignited when Candy was prescribed bottomless refills of the drug Ultram (tramadol) for a back injury. I started taking two, three, even four times the recommended dosage. I got hooked on the unusual high I got from abusing it. Using every other weekend turned into every weekend, turned into Thursday through Sunday, which turned into "What does it matter?"

Drug abuse took a toll on our relationship. Sleepless on meth for days, I would be impossible to deal with. Somehow I got away with not facing reality. I went to great lengths to convince myself our troubles were her fault. I couldn't accept any other truth.

As I saw it, Candy was the one with an issue because my "relaxing" bothered her. My mood swings and explosive, angry outbursts were always a result of things *she* did. If I was alone, I reasoned, I wouldn't have these problems. I incited arguments sometimes just so I could get high. Any excuse for sneaking away to the basement for days to escape feeling.

Twisted by drug combinations, I'd dress up in women's clothing, pretending to be the woman I thought all women should be—disobedient like Eve. I played with sex toys, watching porn insatiably for days on end. Under the concocted pretense that I was songwriting in the basement, Candy and her daughter would respectfully tiptoe around upstairs. No matter how hurtful and unfair it was to them, I didn't want to give up my selfish solo sexual routines. The lies perpetuated in the name of my gift were taken advantage of more often than not.

It was around that time when we both started listening to Dr. Laura. Candy took the talk show host's advice to heart. If I wasn't going to marry her, she would no longer live with me. I laughed. *The absurdity,* I thought. *People don't just change their moral compasses overnight.*

"Who do you think you are giving an ultimatum like this?" I scoffed.

My disease is adept at severing feelings before they affect the heart. Then, when it's too late, drugs are sought to keep them from surfacing, from feeling pain.

~

Dr. Laura began each hour saying, "I am my kids' mom." As the number of homes with single parents and both parents working grew, as societal prioritizing of the quest for more money and things increased, the need for a staunch advocate for children became necessary. I didn't have my own kid at the time, but her logic made sense. In listening to her program, I came to find I was among those promoting the problem, not exemplifying the solution.

Dr. Laura came off hard-nosed, unbending, demeaning at times. Not one to tolerate the complaints of women who criticized their husbands, she'd argue with women in ways men don't ever take the time and energy to learn. She pointed out how women don't fight fair, how females tend to use tears, vindictiveness, and withdrawing of sex as weapons to win arguments.

Concerning the feminist movement, she often offered her opinion about how the original, essential message was lost. She pointed out the symptoms: catty women who made babies as a status symbol, then evaded motherhood to pursue selfish goals, emasculating men by shutting them out of their babies' lives because the courts gave them the power to do so; devaluing men in academia because their sheer numbers enabled policymaking to go unchallenged. She called these women *feministas*.

When I first heard this, it appalled me. I believed in and fought for the forward progress of women, for equality and empowerment. So did she. She's among the few media personalities who suggest the equal rights movement slid into bigotry; how women replaced the men they passionately despised, only to adopt the same attitudes.

Men were a target of Dr. Laura's opinions, too. While she stood up for the ones who were present, active, child-nurturing men, she spoke out against the ones she labeled *stud honeys*—males who stuck around, but only to live off their responsible, loving women. Basically, adult boys. The males who just made babies and fled the scene were labeled *sperm donors*.

She became more empathetic toward men because of all the nagging calls she got from dissatisfied women who spoke so poorly of their husbands or children's fathers. She felt the need to defend the men who were becoming more and more disconnected and debased by this upwardly mobile class of women, women who did not seek to be equal to men, but above them.

Denied an engagement ring, Candy broke the lease on our rented house, discontinuing our living arrangement. It made sense. Without being able to admit it, I knew I shouldn't be living with a woman and her child unless we were married. I wasn't ready to make a sacrifice for the betterment of her kid. She took action, reacting to the choice I made—a choice made just so I could be alone to get high without anyone questioning or intervening.

Months later, at the company Candy got me a job with, I met my daughter's mom.

28

Come Undone

"My thoughts are not to be trusted," I say out loud. My shaking left hand holds a pointing finger to my brain. I'm trying to make myself laugh. I'm so caught up in my spinning that I forget I'm in public. But it's fine. No one so much as winces at my crazy self-talk. Either they don't hear me, or they're in their own world. *Am I not the center of their universe, too?*

I'm standing in line at the Washington County Courthouse in Hillsboro, Oregon, awaiting my turn to go through the metal detector. I'm here this morning at Monika's suggestion. She's had enough of my complaints about Leann and how unpredictable her parenting is. I've been begging her for a solution. I don't know what else to do. According to Lola, Leann has been taking her around our old drug-dealing crowd. I don't ask, she just tells.

Monika proposes that I file for an Emergency Order of Custody. This way, something is put in place as a safeguard. It's my last legal hope to protect my kid from a situation where she could get hurt.

I've waited forty minutes. As I near the entrance, my thoughts fire a barrage of internal contradictions without warning. And just like that, I'm second guessing my decision to file for emergency custody.

I flash back to my glory days. Ridin' dirty, intoxicated, singing like a bard to my captive audience of one. Lola loosely buckled in. Her carrier MacGyvered onto the minivan bench seat. My bemused hostage, sitting innocently unaware, sipping high fructose corn syrup with ten percent real fruit juice from her Dora the Explorer juice box holder. Exchanging sips with bites of fish crackers, fallen crumbs littering the stained floor mats ruined beforehand by monthly build-ups of fast food and trash. Messes ignored when I was too focused on getting high to keep clean.

Have I forgotten where I came from? How am I any different than Leann? Am I pretending my behavior wasn't neglectful? Do I really think I'm qualified to carry the torch of righteousness? Is this what I'm taught in the rooms? No.

If recovering is about being better than those who haven't discovered it yet as part of their journey, then what I'm getting from the program is no different from the dogma and judgment of religion. Would my Higher Power want me to cause suffering for another addict? Of course not. Am I enticed by the possibility of having the power to control what happens to others? Well . . .

The only person who has the power to control *my* actions is me. But what are *my* values? Do I know? Have I grown, or am I using this program and sobriety as a means to become a hypocritical judge and jury?

My inexperience at making confident choices shows. Being unable to gauge for certain if this is my will taking over again, I'm unable to answer my own questions. Refusing to take action on a whim, I leave, losing my place near the front of the line.

Back at work, I pray for clarity during my lunch break. Prayer will have to do for now. After a long day, I return to the solitude of my room, then call my sponsor.

"If I turn her in, it could ruin her. I don't feel right about doing that."

"How would it ruin her?"

"Because. Lola is Leann's last reason to at least want to try to get clean. If the state takes that away from her, she's probably not going to make it."

"Sounds more like it's her last excuse. You've stayed clean to protect your daughter, not her mom's poor choices. We don't *know* she's not going to make it. Whether or not she does is not on you. Look. We can carry the message, but we can't carry the addict."

"True. But who am I to come off holier than thou? I don't feel right about turning her in. It feels like I'm punishing her."

"How? By holding her accountable for her actions? This is Lola's safety we're talking about, not some Inquisition judgment-day witch hunt. She has just as many choices and chances to step up and be a parent as you have." He pauses to breathe. "There's a difference. You are taking all the opportunities and risks; she's not. You are being responsible and accountable; she's not. Sorry if this sounds morbid, but how would you feel if she was high on pills and got in a car crash that killed Lola?"

"I'd want to die."

"Right. You'd blame yourself for not doing everything you could. What's different about who you were seven months ago and who you are now?"

"I'm clean."

"And?"

Ugh! I hate it when someone asks me questions they already know the answer to. It feels like the answer isn't mine, like I have to guess what they're thinking to get it right.

With my sweaty palms together, I place my head down on top of them. I really give it some thought before lifting my chin. "The difference is I know what life looks like from her shoes. Now if I point out what she's doing wrong, I'm speaking from experience, not criticism. My perspective comes from being clean. Now I have a different perspective—one which comes from being clean. Now I see that I have to give my testimony because what she's doing is irresponsible. Mine is firsthand knowledge. It's not that of some vengeful spouse out to win a domestic dispute, it's lived. I'm a loving father prepared to do anything to protect my kid. That's the difference. Lola. Caring more about Lola than myself is the difference."

~~~

Back at the courtroom, my case is last on the docket. For two hours, I've listened in on four different women's testimonies before the judge. Each looking to get a restraining order placed on their boyfriend or children's daddy.

Their stories sound like they come from the same coached script. Each describes how her man "seems" threatening. Each embellishes data like a cable news network reporter—highly opinionated. Each testifies
~~~

under oath about how the male "acted" violent, thereby creating a viable threat to her and her children. None were asked questions as to the validity of their claim.

One woman requests that a special consideration be made for her kid's dad to visit his child every once in a while, but be ordered to stay away from her. Nice positioning tool, these restraining orders. Just as the forlorn father from KNBP said: "Handed out like candy."

With what I've been through, even after hearing these women give iffy statements, I still believe a restraining order is a valuable tool for protecting citizens from the potential of violent, criminal aggressions. Best sought as a necessity, not out of whimsical manipulation. The serving of these has sunk to the likeness of crying wolf, which is a huge disservice to women faced with a legitimate threat.

However, how does one excuse the poking, incessant arguing with, making babies with, provoking, and then demeaning a bear, only to call animal control to take care of *the problem*? There's disparity between the way men and women set boundaries, defend themselves, and disagree. True equality is one of my highest hopes, especially since I'm raising a female.

The bailiff calls me to the stand. I state my case for why a legal order is needed. I cite drug use and endangerment, concluding how being in her mom's care is an unsafe environment for our daughter.

"Sir. Can you prove she is still getting high?"

"Well, your honor, my daughter has told me about the friends her mom has been hanging out with. I know these people. I used to run with them. I've been clean and sober for over six months. These people are dealers and substance abusers. She's getting high and who knows what else with them."

"Sir, I asked if you have proof. I'll ask again. What proof do you have that she is endangering your daughter's well-being?"

"Well, my daughter said she has seen her . . ." I hold my palm upright to my face, motioning like a person smoking pot out of a pipe.

"I AM NOT DRAGGING A FOUR-YEAR-OLD INTO MY COURTROOM TO TESTIFY AGAINST HER OWN MOTHER, SIR!"

Point taken. Loud and clear. Would she say the same to a woman about her child's dad?

Her statement burns through my body. I feel like the idiot who came up with the saying "No good deed goes unpunished." If I can't influence the state to protect Lola by entrusting her to her own father's care, I have failed as a parent. That's how convinced I am something bad will happen. The mother of my baby has a knack for making unhealthy choices—me having been one of them. I want to do what's right. But I won't know what that is if I can't sway the judge to help me. I cannot kidnap my own kid, even if it's the right thing to do by her.

In the middle of everything happening, I remember to ask myself the question I was taught to ask myself: Where is God in all of this? Truth is, I don't know how to know. I silently pray anyway, then open my eyes.

The judge blinks rapidly in disgust.

I wilt at the podium. Others in the courtroom are laughing and shaking their heads at my sophomoric effort. The epitome of an idiot man. The dumb male gender who actually thought he would use the system to benefit his kid. He thought he could strip the baby from her mommy's privileged grip. *Ha! That is not the way it works around here.*

At least that's the vibe I'm getting.

Bamboozled for believing in an upper echelon of truth in equality and fairness. This is my reward for thinking the rungs on the ladder of justice have neither top nor bottom. *No, fool. This is the real letter of the law. Live with it.*

The judge's demeanor changes after I finish my testimony. She observes the chastening courtroom reaction, turns a few papers, then clears her throat to get everyone's attention. She pulls her cat-eye framed glasses from her face, then lets them dangle from neck straps. Exhaling through her nostrils, she looks me dead in the eye.

"I will not grant you an Emergency Protective Custody Order; not at this time, sir." Her tone sounds exquisitely sarcastic, as if she knows she'll never grant me one. "However, due to the fact I am a mandatory reporter, and you are alleging that your child's safety is in danger, I have no choice but to report this allegation to Child Protective Services."

Turning to the right, then left, I gauge the temperature of the courtroom. The expressions on each woman's face freeze. Everybody is motionless. The laughing at my expense, silenced.

You'd think I'd be satisfied with the judge's call to action, but I'm not. On one hand, I'd rather stomach being flat out told *no* so I can move on. On the other, I'd prefer some certainty nothing's *ever* going to happen. I'm willing, maybe too willing, to walk away from this courtroom a loser; a slightly satisfied loser.

Then a third side emerges. A side of myself that's confident in taking action for the values I hold; values just months ago I struggled to live by "as if." Preserving the standards I live by today.

I may not be winning my fight for what I believe, but at least I'm not being silent.

I grab my tiny notepad off the podium, then turn to vacate my spot while stuffing it in my work shirt pocket.

"Sir. Stop. Sir, I am not done."

"Yes, your honor." I spin back around like a dizzy Weeble.

"If what you're saying is true, and you really are seeking to protect your child, I would highly suggest you find two other people who would contact CPS on your daughter's behalf. This is the process. You'll need to build a case before the agency will take action. This doesn't just happen because you want it to or because you suspect your daughter *might* be in danger. And you had better not be trying to use the system to get back at your wife."

"I know she's still getting high, your honor. I don't know how I can prove it, but—"

"You shouldn't have come here without proof. You made yourself look really bad. If you're going to fight to protect your daughter, you'll need to do much better."

"Okay," I mumble, then lower my head to her. Like some omnipotent robed goddess, the judge hands down hopelessness and hope simultaneously.

"Once CPS receives three reports of neglect and or abuse, they will, by law, have to do a wellness check to substantiate your claims. I don't envy you, mister. I sincerely hope you are attempting to do the right thing here."

"I am, your honor."

After the bang of her gavel echoes around the fine millwork of the courtroom, she whispers a few instructions into the ear of her aide, who looks in my direction and nods. Then the judge rises up fast from her seat. Her robe flings about like a four-square dancer's poodle skirt.

I remain at the podium, eyes sentenced to tears. Once I regain composure, I turn to find an empty courtroom. I arrived with no prior experience in this arena, no knowledge of these types of proceedings. I'm finding being clean, however, makes me a quick study.

29

How Many More Times

Single parenting is grueling. I get home from work, then go to work. Like most nights, tonight I've made dinner, washed dishes, had Lola help wipe both counters and our tiny two-person table. While she watches a DVD, I do bills, read emails, then check social media.

I post some random rants about how I might move back to Las Vegas. Exchanging seeds of change with old friends back home passes the time before I call for Lola to get ready for bed. We brush our teeth together.

"Tops. Bottoms. Sides. Other sides. Rinse."

Lola runs from the bathroom, leaps onto her bed, patting it on the spot where I'm to come sit next to her.

"I'll miss you tomorrow, Daddy. You read to me?"

"I know, sweetheart, Daddy will. I mean, I will miss you, too."

I feel unbearable guilt that Lola's heart is torn between two homes. Since she's already thinking about the next two nights at Grandma's, I segue, using it as a springboard to talk about her mom.

We say a prayer for her. No action on our part can affect Leann's choices or outcomes. It's risky, but how else can I get Lola to believe in the possibility that her mom may one day be okay? It's better to have hope than sit in hopelessness with a frightening fear of the worst.

Lola climbs under the covers and waits for me to tuck her in. We read *Don't Let The Pigeon Drive The Bus*. I get into character. She laughs so hard she has to hold her belly. My scratchy pigeon voice is entertaining, yet too comical to doze off to. Sneaking peeks at her between pages, my heart is filled with pure joy. The way she listens with wonder in her eyes. Touchstone moments I chose drugs over for three years.

Next I read *Wemberly Worried*, a somber story. It lulls her to sleep. As she drifts off, I kiss her little head. Since she doesn't like the dark, I leave her pink-petaled sunflower lamp above her bed illuminated. I get up gently, quietly pick items up off her floor, and hang up her clothes.

In the kitchen, I return the dried dishes to the cabinets. My day is not done just yet. I look over my income versus bills ledger to prioritize how I'll pay for things this coming month. It's all handwritten, including the grocery list to take shopping right after work tomorrow.

I fill the coffeemaker and then drag my tired body to bed. I lie there, wondering if I'll have enough energy to do this full time—a more challenging routine pending. Downtime is another thing I took for granted while using. I wish I could have that time back.

~~~

I'm up before dawn. I help Lola get her stuff ready for Grandma's tonight after daycare. She sleeps in the car seat on the way. This time
~~~

of year, north of the earth's forty-fifth parallel, the sun rises at around seven. It's still dark when I drop her off.

After work, I go food shopping, make a small dinner, and attend a meeting. I grab a soda and a bag of chips before plopping onto my bed. I'm dog tired, relishing the quiet calm I get in these last few ticks of wakefulness.

The moment I close my eyes, my phone rings. An unknown number. It's after 9:00 pm. I debate answering. One day I'll learn not to. Damned curiosity.

It's Lola's mom.

"Paul! You've got to talk to my mom and dad," Leann huffs. "This is such fucking bullshit!" she screams out away from the phone. Carol yells something back, but Leann's hand over the receiver muffles her words.

"Paul. They're accusing me of getting high around Lola. Can you believe this shit? They're saying they don't think I'm a fit mom."

She makes what sounds like a fake crying sound.

"You think I'm a good mom, right?"

I'm not walking into this trap.

"Who the fuck are they to say these things to me?"

Her angry tone is then replaced by the same uncompromising one she used the night she left. "This is *my* daughter!"

I'm unable to get a word in, not that my response would be heard or welcomed. She's so amped up on whatever she's on that she's irrational. It sounds like she's been called out for doing the things she's been getting away with for a long time. Over the next five minutes, all I can make out are bits of argumentative screaming.

I'm relieved Grandma Carol's fire and fervor aren't directed at me for once. Leann pleads with me to help, as if she's being tortured. My chin presses into my palm, all four fingers resting on my lower lip. I'm not distressed so much because the peace of my evening is interrupted, but because I can only imagine what Lola is going through. I try asking Leann questions, but they go unheard.

The madness and insanity, destroyer of families and lives.

Eight months ago, I was right where Leann is now. I'm seeing the inherent blindness of this disease, the degrading denial drugs have on those of us in our addiction and those who love us. I'm witnessing firsthand the misery I'm missing out on. Misery that could be refunded by choosing to get high again.

The phone goes silent. Dead air. Fear lifts off like a rocket, shattering the stratosphere of my peaceful personal space for the night. I flip my pillow over, the cool side against the back of my head and neck.

Fifteen minutes later, Grandma Carol calls. She's broken up, shaken to her core. She makes it clear how sorry she is for what just happened. Speaking as calmly as I can, I make it equally clear I don't hold her responsible.

"Leann is way too intoxicated to drive. We wouldn't let her take Lola. She got pissed and drove off, leaving Lola alone for the night, again."

The grandparents have had enough. Protecting Lola is more important to them than covering for their daughter. Carol goes on attesting, like she's confessing secrets she's struggled to harbor to herself. On more than one occasion, they've caught Leann being deceitful. I'm guessing Carol's ashamed, disgraced by how her daughter's actions might be seen as a reflection of her parenting.

"And, oh! Paul. This pisses me off so much. Sometimes she doesn't even show up to watch Lola until ten-thirty at night."

Awkward silence. I sense a nudge from my Higher Power.

"There is something you guys can do."

"What?"

How I present this means everything. I have to be careful and methodical, but mostly compassionate. If it comes off looking like what I want them to do is for selfish intent, it'll raise concerns, possibly defeat the purpose. I check my motives before I open my mouth. Lola's welfare depends on my being principled at this yet-to-be-tried approach. I have to be tactical, tactful, and tacit all at once.

"Well, okay, but this is hard for me to say."

"Just say it, Paul."

"Um, well, I just want you guys to know I went to a judge. I tried to get a protective order put in place so I could be granted emergency custody of Lola."

I pause to hear what they will say because I don't want to spew out all of what I've done at once. I want it to sink in a bit. Then I'll relay the result. But I add, "You know, just until Leann gets clean enough to be a good mom again."

"You went to a judge?" Carol asks before I finish my sentence. The alarm in her voice is followed by a long release of her breath. Patrick's monotone muttering is heard in the background. She ignores whatever it is he's saying.

"Okay. So, how did *that* go?"

"The judge wouldn't believe me. She would not take my word that Leann is putting Lola in danger. I don't know what it'll take to get the courts to do something. I keep having this premonition—that nothing's gonna change until after something terrible happens to Lola. This really sucks."

"I don't want something bad to happen to Lola either, Paul. Are you saying there's something we can do?"

"There is, but—"

"Well, what is it? We'll do anything."

"I don't know; this is pretty major. I mean, it would be great if you guys did this, but it's a lot to ask. You don't have to do it, you know, just because I'm asking you to. Never mind. It's a lot to think about."

"Just tell us and we'll do it," Carol announces assuredly. Patrick, overhearing our conversation, verbally confirms.

"Are you sure?"

"We're sure. Tell us what it is. For Lola, we're sure."

"All right? You would have to call Child Protective Services on her."

I turn my head away from the mouthpiece, concealing, for some reason, my own deep inhalation.

A long pause drags on.

"Yeah, I don't know. Really?"

"That's what the judge instructed. Judges can't force CPS to do a wellness visit based on one person's account. I didn't have proof. My testimony, without proof, is considered hearsay, especially coming from me."

"Why especially from you?"

"I guess men do it all the time to make their wives look bad or exact some sort of revenge. They'll make up lies to punish their spouse for their having to pay child support or alimony or whatever. That's not why I went to the judge."

Through the phone, I hear their television over mixed movement and shuffling. Their silence makes me uncomfortable. My paranoia tells me Carol is looking for a way to record our conversation.

"Why *did* you go to the judge?" she asks.

"Because I keep hearing how Leann is still getting loaded around Lola. Lola tells me things they do together. Without my asking, by the way. She tells me who they're around. She names people I know are drug dealers. I went to the judge because I'm scared for her safety. The judge now has to report Leann to CPS, but CPS will need to hear from at least one other person before they assign the case to a fieldworker to substantiate the claims."

"Are you asking us to turn our daughter in? To go to jail?"

"Jail? What? No! Who said anything about jail?"

Although muffled, Patrick's voice comes through. He's clearly having a negative response to what's being said.

"Then what are you asking, Paul?"

"All I'm saying is, if you file a report, they'll send a caseworker out to do a wellness check. If they find that she's being a good mom and providing a safe atmosphere for Lola, then all is well. But if they find negligence on Leann's part, they'll grant me a temporary protective custody order. It's a legal document that will temporarily, not permanently, give me custody until Leann can prove she's clean and safe for Lola to be around."

"Is that all you're after? Custody? How do we know you're not going to get custody and run back to Vegas?"

"You don't."

My remark is intentional. Let her sit in fear and lack of trust. The extra-long silence cooks the blood-is-thicker-than-semen stew I want her to taste—this time with my ingredients. I allow a few extra seconds to pass before I clarify.

"I'm just being honest, Carol. You don't know. But maybe you can take my word. I know I haven't built enough trust with you and Patrick. As far as Vegas, there's no way in hell I'd want to raise Lola in that shithole of a town. Yes, it's true I don't have family here. And things aren't exactly going great, but I can't afford to go anywhere for quite some time, even if I wanted to."

Yes, I said the most stupid thing I could say.

"That doesn't sound good to us. We love our granddaughter. We don't want you to take her away and never see her. That would really hurt us."

There's profound sadness in Carol's voice. Under that tortoise shell is a soft, gargantuan-hearted woman. Only a fool would intentionally attack it.

"This may not mean much to you, but you have my word. I would never do that."

"Fair enough. I trust you, Paul. Patrick and I see how hard you're trying. I'm not saying we'll call. We'll have to think about it."

"That's all I'm asking. Thank you. And thank you for providing a stable place for Lola through all this. I'm sorry you've had so much to deal with."

I give Carol the number to CPS before she hands the phone to Lola for us to say our routine good night.

"Hi, Missy."

"Hi, Daddy."

"How's my little monkey doing? Ooh ooh ahh ahh?"

"Ooh ooh ahh ahh."

"Are you worried about Momma, princess?"

"Yeah."

"Aww. You know what I think?"

"What?"

"I think Momma's gonna be just fine. You know how Daddy has rules for you, like to put your toys away when you're done playing with them? Well, Grandma has rules, too. When Momma doesn't follow them, Grandma has to be Momma's momma. Except Momma growls and roars and snorts back."

I make a gross snorting sound.

"Daddy! Momma don't sound like that."

"Speaking of animals, sugarplum, how would you like to go get ice cream on Wednesday afternoon when I pick you up?"

"Ice cream? Yay!"

"Oh, wait! What's that got to do with animals?"

"I don't know, Daddy, what?"

"Cause' you're my little monkey."

"Ooh ooh ahh ahh."

The evening's drama leads to another in a string of sleepless nights filled with gut-wrenching worry about my little girl. I remember a suggestion made at a meeting. A woman shared how she was taught to pray for those who do us harm. I chuckled along with some of the other addicts listening. To pray for someone who keeps hurting you seems counterintuitive. But what else can I do? Just because I'm familiar with powerlessness doesn't mean I prefer it. Tired of insomnia, I give it a shot.

Whether it works or not isn't the reason to try. Prayer, as I'm beginning to understand it, isn't done to get ensured results. It's an action taken to communicate what we think we want or need, kind of like asking for help, then letting go of the outcome. The outcome is irrelevant—it doesn't change the fact that we put forth the effort. By showing faith in something different from our own controlling will, our spirit finds itself at ease, knowing we're neither too afraid nor too proud to ask. This sense of ease is the gateway to serenity.

While praying for Lola's mom, I realize something. Carol and I switched from being on opposing sides to being on the same side, caring for and protecting this dependent little four-year-old. Without purposefully asserting my way or deliberately manipulating, I made an ally. Patrick and Carol's support has come. Unexpected, and so very needed.

Also, as much as I've wanted to lay it on, as bad as I've wanted to pull some power move so I'd appear to be a force Carol and Patrick don't want to mess with, I haven't. I've become empathetic. I can relate to Carol more now. She, too, is trying to look strong while facing the reality that her daughter's life is falling apart before her very eyes.

In the past, I would've seen Carol's desperation as something to use to my advantage. And I would've used it. I'm no longer obsessing over one-upmanship. By taking personal inventory, I'm able to identify these behaviors.

One thing common with addicts is that we tend to attract people by disarming them with our upbeat, appealing personality. We'll seek to know them by catering to their ego. We gather intimate details so we have something, some stain of dirt on them, stuffed away. Saved for the day we believe is sure to come when they'll turn their backs on us.

We seek to know likes, dislikes, dreams, fears, intimate details about where their life is heading and who or what barrier is keeping them from getting what they want. Extra attention is paid to complaints about specific traits they dislike. Then, by coming off as a tailor-made opposite of that, we appear gallant.

Unless they figure out how to guard themselves, platonic friends or lovers interpret our inquisitiveness and "interest" in them as flattery. We're often commended for being "attentive" and a "great listener." But as the relationship wears on, we're rarely called those kind names. Because we don't even think twice about going for the jugular when we don't get our way, most of those people become the casualties that line the road behind us.

The program teaches us that this kind of deceptive practice is premeditated, deliberate. However, thanks to the denial part of our disease, we're lucky to catch it in time. Once we become skilled at rationalizing, no consequence can deter us.

Healing and compassion are written into the steps. As long as I'm open-minded enough to be aware of those influences, I have a chance I won't repeat those old behaviors. I'm growing up. Different things matter now. It matters that Carol is faced with one of the hardest decisions no parent should ever have to make: Should I protect my daughter or my granddaughter?

It's her decision to make, no matter what I see as right or best. Grandma Carol is a woman of strong ethics and values. That's what hurt the most back when she saw me as the bad guy. Deep down, I knew she was right. She was never *my* sworn enemy. She was the enemy of my behavior—my disease in action. Now that my behavior's changing, we're often on the same side.

Patrick and Carol are allowing me to earn their trust. They're showing a willingness to forgive, which, in turn, inspires me to be more forgiving of myself. I'm beginning to grasp the essence of their bond to my child, how important and necessary they are to her development. The best way I can honor this is by exemplifying how love and family can put egos aside and work hard to stand together, whether the ties are through blood, semen, or adoption.

Every hour I'm not moving toward securing custody, I'm living in fear that bad things beyond my control are happening behind the scenes. It's the ominous potential for things to get worse that I'm not okay with. Which points out just how much I lack trust.

If I don't trust my Higher Power to restore sanity to my life, then I don't have faith. If I don't have faith, then I must not have been shown in a manner clear enough for me to see that God is working. If I don't believe God is working in my life, then I must not have hit my bottom. If I haven't hit my bottom yet . . . wait right there.

I *did* hit my bottom. There's only one place lower than where I was eight months ago. I never want Lola or anyone else to find me there, including me. I don't have another drug run left in me—not one I'd survive.

30

Saved By Zero

Just after work, on a day Lola gets picked up at daycare by Carol, I get a call from a private number.

"Hi. Is this Paul?"

"Who's this?"

"Is this Paul?"

"Tell me who this is first. You're the one calling me."

"I'm with Child Protective Services."

"Oh! Okay. Yes, this is Paul. Who are you?"

"My name is Neil. I've been assigned to be your caseworker."

"I . . . I have a caseworker? Great! Does that mean there *is* a case pending?"

"We can go over that later. Is there any chance I could meet you at your residence anytime soon?"

"Well. I'm just getting home right now. I haven't eaten dinner yet, so, maybe in a half hour or so?"

"I'm here now. Would that be all right? It would just take a few minutes."

"You're at my place? Uh. Yeah, that's fine. My daughter isn't with me right now, though."

"That's okay. I'm here at the bottom of your stairs. If you can come around to meet me, we can get started."

"On my way."

This seems abrupt. Serious. The element of surprise. I shudder at the thought of what I would've done if I were still using. My apartment is a bit messy, but safe. No drugs, no paraphernalia, no porn. Nothing but a single dad doing his best to provide for his kid.

Neil waits at the bottom step, a large black briefcase in one hand, his phone in the other. He's wearing a long black trench coat over a wrinkled suit jacket, unbuttoned dress shirt, and loosened necktie. Is it typical for a social worker to be so unkempt? It's close to 6:00 pm. Maybe he's had a long day. I approach him and introduce myself with confidence.

Keeping his introduction short, his mannerisms imply he's ready to get to the business at hand. He turns to climb the stairs, putting on an air of pushiness. I feel his breath on my neck as I unlock my door. His breath is foul; the odor of a person overworked while postponing eating.

"Whichever way you need to conduct your check, I'm more than compliant," I say, letting him in. This seems to throw him off. There's friction building that I can't identify. I have no idea what it is he's looking for.

I offer him water or juice. He politely refuses. He appears somewhat intrigued by how I've placed Lola's artwork all over our living room walls. His head tilts sideways, his lips purse together. Maybe he's confused. I feel the need to explain.

"The idea came out of nowhere."

The way he continues to stare without commenting is making me uncomfortable. Maybe he thinks I'm weird.

"I can't afford any framed paintings. Maybe you're expecting posters of Lamborghinis or girls in bikinis, like some young bachelor might have up? Not here. I want Lola to know how proud I am of her creativity and imagination."

Neil scribbles a few notes on the faux leather pad folio balancing precociously atop his forearm. *Good notes or bad ones?* I wipe the sweat from the pores of my palms onto the sides of my shorts. He continues throughout the apartment. He inspects Lola's room, her closet, the bathroom, then the living room, our DVD collection, and her books. Briefly, he checks my bedroom. Last is the kitchen before he sits down on my futon.

"First of all, it is unsafe to have a glass mirror in the shower area," he begins. "Kids drop things. The mirror could break into pieces. Besides that, your home passes as far as being in a livable condition for your daughter. Unfortunately, I can't discuss details about the case. Our investigation is currently ongoing."

"Oh. Okay," I say, while going into the bathroom to move the mirror to a stable spot underneath the sink.

"Handled. Well then, Neil, are you saying I can't ask you questions?"

"No. Actually, you can ask me any questions you'd like. You just can't ask me about the investigation."

"Why did you become a caseworker?"

"Hmm. Well, my dad was an abusive alcoholic. He'd get drunk, severely beat my mom, then come after my sisters and me. My mom was too afraid to leave or turn him in, so I did. I guess you could say this is my calling. I was predestined to be an advocate for children."

"That's horrible you had to live through that, man, yet great you choose to help others. I'm not trying to blow smoke up your ass, but I'm grateful for what you do."

Neil rolls his eyes.

"I'm sure you get that all the time."

"All the time . . ."

"I hope you come to find I'm not like that. I'll be completely transparent. Whatever it takes for you to see how I'm trying to protect my little girl. I just hope the state will do something about her mom before something bad happens."

"Like I said, I can't discuss a course of action until we have all the information. If there isn't anything else you need from me, we'll be in touch." Neil stands to leave. "Oh, personally, I like how you put your daughter's artwork on the living room walls. I've never seen anyone do that before."

"Thanks!"

I am so pleased action is finally being taken. I feel like I've made a good first impression on Neil by being myself instead of playing it up as if I'm worthy of some father-of-the-year crown. If I came off weird, it's just because I'm fearful of Lola being taken away. But being weird isn't enough reason to withhold custody of a kid from a loving parent.

It would be nice to resolve this custody equation once and for all. It won't happen on my timetable and terms, so I try to play it cool. Keeping my expectations low makes it easier to pretend to be patient.

At meetings, we learn that how we appear on the outside seldom matches how cunning and baffling our disease is on the inside. There's a saying, "Never underestimate the resourcefulness of an addict." We know—our thoughts and deeds are never beyond suspicion.

I *have* to examine my motives because I'm not in a space where I trust myself. Not yet. Until I get there, I have to deal with a destructive inner dialogue that searches with obsessive acuity for any angle it can find to prove my unworthiness. Every time I dig deep for a fix, I'm confronted by yet another spectacular reminder of how often I opt to hate myself. I don't trust my motives because of how many times I've lied to myself—how I've habitually deceived and deviated with and from my best intentions. One of the many great paradoxes I've discovered through recovery is how I didn't even realize my life was as unmanageable as it was until I hit bottom. Therefore, how can I possibly know if my motives are pure unless I run them by others?

31

On The Radio

I listen to the *Dr. Laura* show while delivering plumbing supplies for work. Each day I anticipate hearing a call from someone in a similar circumstance as mine. When one comes, I labor over each word of advice she gives for any tidbit of info that will help me be my kid's dad again. The advice I really need to hear will just have to come firsthand by calling her show.

I pull over to dial, listening while trying to get through. A woman on the air complains about her baby's father who is out using drugs and not being present or being a provider in their son's life. In a bitchy tone, Dr. Laura makes it clear: "Don't complain about the person you made babies with. He was your choice." Her goal, I believe, based on other calls, is to help this woman see she's focusing on the wrong thing: herself and the defunct union. She's not focusing on her children. The children are suffering much more than the adults. My situation is close to hers, but with the genders reversed.

My second try yields a busy signal. This means she's taping live. I try one last time. As the phone rings, my heart zings; my mouth and lips dry up in an instant. The screener asks for my question, then helps me rephrase it into the form Dr. Laura prefers. There's a long pause. I turn the radio off. I'm up.

"Thank you for calling."

"Thank you for taking my call. It's an honor. I am a divorced parent of a sparkling four-year-old daughter. I am a recovering addict. Her mom is still out in . . . you know, choosing to continue with her active addiction. My question for you, Dr. Laura is, today at school, my daughter's teacher pulled me aside to inform me that my daughter told her that she doesn't think her mom loves her anymore. Every time I set boundaries for her mom, she retaliates by disappearing. This time it's been for six weeks. She finally called yesterday to talk to our daughter and—"

"Does your daughter understand that her mother is a druggie?"

"I think she kind of gets it. That's part of my question—."

"That's not what I asked you. Does she understand? I asked you if your daughter has clarity that her mom is a drug addict?"

"You know, I don't believe so even though I—."

"She needs to, and I'll tell you why. Because when kids don't have reality checks, what they're left with is their imagination. And in her imagination, if she were a better child, her mother would be there."

"Okay."

"They blame themselves. That's why the truth is important." She continues in an affected voice. "We like to protect our little sweet ones from . . . but we can't here. Because then, she really is rejected. As opposed to, she's a drug addict and you need to explain what that means."

"Okay. What I've been telling her is that her mother is making bad choices."

"That is so . . . I don't even understand what that means!"

"She does say 'It's not my fault that mommy hasn't called.' I mean, I take her to meetings so she—."

"Sir, when she tells the teacher that her mommy doesn't love her, that is her fault in her mind. She doesn't think her mother's ability to love is broken, she thinks her lovability is broken. So, you're wrong. She thinks it's her. At her level of psychological development, that is how they think."

"Okay, so the best way to tell her is to . . ."

"I'll leave that up to you. Because you have a lot of experience. I think you need to sit down and talk about your history. Tell her the two of you were way off track and did bad things like take illegal drugs. And that you decided that being married and being a daddy was more important than the drugs. But you made that choice alone."

"Okay."

"And when people are on drugs, this is the kind of thing they do. Drugs become the center of their lives. That's why it's a very bad thing. This becomes a lesson for her about drugs when she gets to the age when people are going to start trying to hand her drugs. She'll know what happened to her family on drugs and she'll be a lot less likely. Especially when she understands that it's not about her. Because when she thinks it's about her, then the likelihood of her doing drugs is higher . . . to get rid of the pain."

"Yeah. I can already see that with people in the program and what they go through with their older kids."

"Right. Exactly."

"I will be very direct with her."

"Yeah. Let her know that you used to be there and why you're not. And the reason you're not is her. Then she'll know, 'I am important! I am important!' And that's very . . . that is so necessary."

"I need her to get there, that's for sure. Thank you, Dr. Laura."

"Right. You're welcome. And congratulations to you, sir."

I'm running late for my next delivery. I start the truck. It idles until my eyes are clear enough to drive.

32

Boys Don't Cry

Not long after getting used to things always being just Lola and I together, a call comes from out of the blue. Leann is nearby and wants to see Lola. I'm not sure how long it's been since she's come around. Weeks? I don't count the days anymore, or resentment will build.

It's 10 p.m. on a work night. But if getting to see her mom means Lola won't be hurting for a short spell, I'll consider it a plus. I wish I could protect my kid from her own negative thoughts; the pain inflicted within—pain she feels each day her mother is absent.

Lola's in bed, waiting for me to read to her. I hand the phone over to let Leann say hi then scramble around like a military person ready for action. I have to think of every possible angle—ways I might need to protect myself and Lola from any further damaging plans devised to strip away the parental rights I've fought so hard to attain.

Somewhere in my hallway closet is something to record with. I dig deep and manage to piece together an archaic setup of music gear. Relics which are starting to feel like the belongings of another person.

A strategically placed microphone plugged into my fifteen-year-old zip disc multi-track recorder should do the trick.

Leann arrives about twenty minutes late. She's with Jessica. The alcohol cloud on their breath confronts me as I open the door. My putting on a welcoming face can't be hiding my disappointment. I don't like Lola seeing her this way. I want Leann to be present in her life, but not like this.

Showing no regard, nor offering an apology for arriving this late past Lola's bedtime, Leann walks right past me. She's here to get what she wants, as if it's owed her. This tunnel vision way of thinking is a hallmark of people who are loaded. In this state, the inebriated person won't even think to ease back their intentions nor bother with social graces.

Jessica, left at my door, is next. She gives me an exaggerated fake smile. She can't stand still. Before I acknowledge her, she puts her head down and stumbles inside. She teeters past me, bum rushing straightaway into my living room.

"Whoa, I didn't say you could come in," I say, albeit quietly.

I'm trying not to be a dick right off the bat. Irritation isn't what I want to feel. But I'm not going to be a doormat either. Between Leann's lack of geniality and Jessica's obstinate demeanor, I think I'd best be up in arms.

"I didn't ask you," she answers. Foolish, drunken bravery. Line in the sand.

"Okay, then. I'm telling you. You can't come in."

Jessica scowls. She looks puzzled. She knows me to be passive. I'm not going with the flow.

Her eyes dart around my living room. I know why. Her hands fidget. I'm extra familiar with the buzzed-brain thoughts. She's looking for ammunition. She's oblivious about how obvious her mannerisms are. Frustration registers, replacing the sheer determination on her face. Still nothing, retort-wise. Then her cheeks draw in—a spark. She's found the comeback her pickled brain believes will be pay dirt.

"What is this shit?" she asks.

"What are you talking about?"

"This. This is fucking *weird.*"

She raises both of her arms to point out Lola's artwork adorning my living room walls. Jessica emphasizes the waving of her index finger to draw attention to each artistic piece. Then, one at a time at each drawing, she waves her bottom three fingers like she wants it whisked away, as if to say, "Off with their heads!"

Okay, enough. Now this is getting to me. Why is my reaction such easy bait? I'm thinking, "Who the fuck are you to call my daughter's artwork weird? And how dare you come in here as if your opinion of anything matters?"

Jessica doesn't get it. Why do I give a shit?

This is my homage to my child, placed in our sanctuary with specific intention. By calling them tiny masterpieces, I showcase Lola's artwork to boost her self-esteem. By displaying something tangible, it proves how proud her parent is of her. Even though I tell her all the time, I want more meaning attached than mere words. I want her to feel, hear, and see how deeply loved she is. This is our insulated universe. One where the outside world that wants to beat us down and tear us apart is not welcome to enter. One I am ruthless to defend and am called to do so more often than a parent should have to.

"This is Lola's artwork. I'm proud of her, so I hang it up. What's weird about that?"

"It's just weird." The disgust in her voice feels like the penetration of a thousand darts into my brain. It takes me back to being called ignorant in grade school; the name caller pursing their lips to the side while twirling their index finger in circles.

"Why would you hang so much of it up?" She looks around, then back at me, then shakes her head and shrugs her shoulders. It's like the emoji of a shrug given when someone does something idiotic.

I've been working on increasing my tolerance and acceptance, harmony, and serenity. Underneath it all, however, I've yet to touch on other necessary work. Namely, addressing the extra sensitive, ultra-defensive, insecure, immature man inside. I'm not trying to demean my deepest self, I'm admitting my truth. Only through admission will I possibly have some humility, which I'll need in order to see where a solution hides. Situations like these provide opportunities to commit new actions to muscle memory.

If Jessica set out to push my buttons, she's found success. Does this mean what it always means? Is it time for unfriendly fire to prove hatred trumps tolerance? Can it mean something else this time, please?

"Well, look, you are not welcome here," I tell Jessica. "You were not invited inside. Now you can go on ahead and take your ass outside and wait."

"I'm here with—"

"Go!"

Using only seventy-five percent of my total possible volume, my voice projects well. I'm fuming inside. The amount of control I'm showing surprises me. In exaggerated slow motion, my finger points toward the door for her to leave.

"Yeah, right," she responds.

I can't tell if she's being defiant or if she believes my command is a joke.

"How about, no!"

In a deliberate physical surge, Jessica stomps like a bull toward Lola's room. I have enough presence to be careful. Laying hands on her by acting on the rage growing within could mean the end of my fathering. I hold out my arm clothesline-style, to keep her from passing through.

All Jessica needs to draw out of me is one stupid choice. It's unbearable, at times, how much pressure I'm under. It's constant. I'm always one wrong decision away from losing my kid. I'm fighting demons even when I don't want to. I have to. The disease in my head has a leech-like appetite. It fastens on to make the worst of this. It begs me to physically threaten her, to show her insolent ass who she should not be so bold as to fuck with.

Paralyzed by indecisiveness and divided thoughts, I'm left vulnerable. Jessica dips under my arm and swaggers her way into Lola's bedroom. If doing the right thing makes me look weak and defeated, so be it. The right thing to do isn't to be passive, it's to reason with myself enough to trust in taking a path I've never taken. Instead of choosing to react to the button pushing and flat-out defiance, I choose to respond.

Looking up at the ceiling, I ask out loud, "How would my sponsor handle this?" The answer comes: He would stay calm and get help. "Thank you," I lip whisper. Is calling the police warranted?

I call Neil. If anything, documenting this is a response. No answer. I leave a message. Time to scale my defensive maneuvering up a notch. Immediate help is warranted. Meanwhile, Jessica helps herself into my sanctuary, slamming Lola's bedroom door behind her so the three of them can be alone. I make the call.

"Nine one one. What is your emergency?"

"Hello. My wife and I are separated. We're working out custody arrangements. Our daughter lives here at my residence. Her mom stopped by, which is perfectly fine, but she brought her best friend along, who is drunk and acting belligerent. I've asked her to leave, but she refuses to do so. I don't want to physically remove her from my property, but I believe she is challenging me to force her. I won't do anything to threaten my position as my daughter's parent, but I need the friend to leave. She's intoxicated. I'm afraid this situation could get out of control. But I need her to leave. She is not welcome here."

"Sir, I'm going to need you to stay calm. Can you try asking her to leave while we are on the line together?"

"Sure, I'll try."

Although I can't help but wonder whether the operator would ask the same task if genders were reversed, a tinge of empowerment comes with knowing I'm doing the right thing the right way. Months ago, I would've happily made sure this escalated. Right now, I just want a good night's sleep so I can go to work in the morning feeling rested.

I knock on Lola's door and then open it a few inches. Someone slams it shut. I open it again, cramming my foot in from allowing it to close. Someone pushes on it as I yell in, "Leann, Jessica needs to leave. You can be here with Lola, but she needs to go."

"Go fuck yourself, asshole."

Here in my apartment, in front of my daughter, my wife's best friend dares to verbally assault me. If the law won't do something, I certainly will. If a brain could grab a person by the throat, mine would do so. It would command my muscles to kick the door in, throw her up against the wall, and scream the word NO so loud into her ear she'd have permanent hearing loss.

Self-restraint won't hold much longer. Jessica and I have bypassed fail-safe. We're beyond the tipping point in which cool heads can prevail.

"Did you hear that response?" I ask the operator.

"Yes, I did. Beaverton Police are being dispatched to your address."

"Would it be okay with you if I keep you on the line with me?"

"Yes. It might also be a good idea for you to leave the house until the officer gets there. We don't want things to escalate. Do you think your daughter will be safe with her mom until officers arrive?"

"I think so."

In just under nine minutes, three squad cars pull in. I lead them upstairs, motioning approval for them to enter with my hands. One officer stays behind to question me while the other two run inside to protect my daughter from a drunken menace. I try to eavesdrop while providing personal information.

The police ask Jessica to come out. She refuses their first two requests, causing them to make commands. Standing on the landing at the edge of the doorway, I'm unmoved, numb to her screaming at them to let her go. The two peace officers walk her past me. Looking more obliterated than I first thought, her face resembles someone who doesn't even recognize where she is. She's too busy fighting with one of the officers. She shouts that his attempts to detain her are inappropriate, his touching her unwarranted. He's doing his best to pull her a safe distance away from Lola.

A female officer comes running up the sidewalk to assist. The two upstairs are left with no choice but to match Jessica's aggression. They lift and carry her down, step by step, before handing her off to the female officer at the bottom. Jessica accuses *her* of inappropriateness and brutality.

As soon as she's shuffled away, I'm told to go back and wait downstairs. For twenty minutes I'm left there. Shrieks and ultimatums coming from the parking lot are overheard. One by one, my neighbors' bedroom curtains are illuminated. They're awakened either from the yelling, the flashing blue and red lights, or both.

The officer I spoke to comes out of my apartment. He stands silent and firm on the steps like he's blocking entry to my apartment. I'm anxious about Lola's well-being. I ask if I can go back in.

"Wait. This is your apartment?"

"Yeah. I live here."

"There's a mom and a kid in there. This isn't her residence?"

"No. This is my place. As I already mentioned to the dispatcher, my wife and I are separated. She's visiting our daughter. She brought the friend with her. I'm the one who called you guys."

"Oh! We got the report a little skewed then. Yes. Of course, you can go in. Wait. Actually, wait here. Let me make sure."

Make sure of what? I wait, pacing back and forth. I doubt Lola is still awake. But if she is, she's probably wondering why I'm not there with her. Fuck this! I don't need permission to enter my own residence.

Just then, the officer returns. He informs me it's taking a while to deal with the situation because Jessica's not sober enough to drive. They're concerned she'll come back to cause more trouble once they leave.

"I don't mean to be insensitive about what's going on with her, sir, but I really need to check on my daughter to make sure she's okay. Do you mind?"

"Oh, yeah. Yeah, yeah. Go ahead. Sorry about that."

Jessica's incessant raging is louder than the clunking sound of my feet jogging up the stairs. My guess is she's biding her time. She's too smart to get in her car and drive away drunk. The cops won't let her stay here, nor walk home either.

There's a clear view of what's going on from the top of my stairs. The cops are performing a sobriety test. Jessica wobbles back and forth. Her noncompliant language continues. A dread comes over me. *What are the repercussions of this going to be?*

The cops handcuff her. She chastises them even louder while they corral her into one of the now four squad cars. It looks like she's earned a trip to the county jail where she can sleep it off overnight in the drunk tank.

After closing my front door behind me, I check to make sure Lola's okay. Leann's relaxed on the bed, talking on her phone. I hear her tell whoever is on the other line how upset with her friend she is. She convinces that person to come pick her up. Through all of this, Lola is asleep. She wasn't exposed firsthand to the madness, thank God.

"Coming over here so late was not okay," I tell Leann. I don't think she hears. Not that she isn't listening. She's not used to me setting boundaries. Neither am I.

In the past, I didn't set boundaries, I set traps. When I tried to set boundaries, they weren't evident until *after* you snagged the trip line. I kept people on edge. Life with me meant walking on eggshells. That is what she's used to.

"I don't want you to ever come here buzzed or high again."

"I'm not high."

Stalemate. Did I forget how impossible it is to engage in a meaningful conversation with someone who's wasted? You have to wait until they're not on something before you can get through to them. I don't know when that'll be. I tell her she has to go.

The next morning, I tell my sponsor the details. He asks what I've learned. I think about it with ferocious honesty. The events that transpired are examples of trying out new living skills. How I handled my part shows how I'm able to set a precedent: standing up for myself without having to get violent, vindictive, controlling, or conniving.

This event adds another anecdote to my story of renewal, one I can refer to over and over. I do not have to manipulate or manhandle. I went through the proper channels to deal with the situation in a healthier way than ever before.

And protected my little girl by doing so.

33

My Own Worst Enemy

Coming up on ten months of being substance-free, I wonder if I'll ever be free of internal doubt. *Am I good enough to be a parent on my own? Do I have to stay clean? Can I ever use drugs again? Not even recreationally?*

The last question sends my thoughts into crazy-land. I know the answer. So why is it I still have the gumption to ask?

While I'm busy juggling butterflies, my disease is conspiring. I step up my meeting attendance as an antidote. However, having never learned balance, strains arise in other life areas. I react like a bull to the muleta.

I'm fine with going to work every day. I'm fine with clothing, readying, feeding, cooking for, cleaning up after, explaining to, nurturing, doing laundry for, reading to, disciplining, and being fully attentive to Lola. But having her more and more often has presented unforeseen challenges.

How do I bring a four-year-old into a meeting where adults are talking like adults about adult shit? Where there's obnoxious cussing, crying, and laughter? Where I'm excruciatingly self-conscious about having this ball of energy at my side?

Most meetings happen after dinner, which is when Lola wants me to herself. Most are an hour long, which is an eternity for a child. Bringing a bag of things for her to color, play with, or snack on only goes so far. She can get restless. I find myself apologizing, certain her moving about is disturbing others, distracting them from hearing the message or speaking freely. As adorable as she is, more often than not, having a child in tow feels disruptive.

At one meeting, I must've looked embarrassed after someone commented, "No one loves your kid as much as you do." It was meant for a mom with an unruly, unsupervised child. Granted, she was ignoring her attention-starved kid. Then a woman with close to thirteen years clean spoke up.

"One thing I love to see in a meeting is a parent here with their kids. Sure, it can be distracting if they're noisy, but think about it: a mom or dad who's in here is not out there using. How many of us come from homes where a loaded parent was neglectful or abusive, or let someone else be abusive because the parent was too high or passed out or doing tricks in the bathroom? A kid here is safe. Parents are welcome. You are in the right place."

Amen, sister.

Her soliloquy is something I'll share every time I see kids brought to a meeting. It's that important. Not only are recovering parents' childcare options limited, but finding a forum of support and connection is as well. The online community is useful, but social media is laced with antagonists who believe in sophisticated theories for recovery. Meetings are where fellowshipping and accountability are learned. A parent who can't get to meetings might not stay clean.

~

The quest to attain a healthy balance exposes a need to have more in my toolbox. Without tools, our disease is apt to force our will to run lopsided. We've got to be careful not to obsess on any one particular behavior, even a beneficial one. If we obsess to the point where our overall well-being starts to get run down, drugs or booze will appear as a viable panacea.

Negativity, self-destructiveness, giving up my clean date . . . these are the thoughts creeping in. People with long-term recovery describe being on a "pink cloud" when referring to the exuberance of early sobriety. The floating sensation dissipates. Reality sets in. Then what?

I can't say I was ever on a pink cloud. But life for me has fallen back to being bland and mundane. This is a time of concern for addicts. If we start to label the unpredictable stunts we pulled as harmless, or we view the freedom we were once willing to hand over for a bag of dope as *missing out* on excitement, we're in big trouble. It helps to remember the deceptive nature of our disease. While we're busy figuring out what's happening to our brain in the present, it's working on glorifying our past—as if chasing a bag in desperation every day *wasn't* repetitious and routine.

Writing out an inventory is supposed to help iron out this kind of thinking. My disease keeps me from seeing how well-worn the patterns of immoral motives that lead to wrongdoing are. It hides from me how often I think the same way I've always thought, how often I've behaved just like the same people I've blamed for how I behave. How I've held resentments near and dear. How an unwillingness to forgive myself causes resentments to mushroom into stubborn self-hatred. And how self-hatred leads to outward disdain.

I'm willing to change.

I'm willing to try to do things a different way because I'm grateful I hit my bottom. If all I'm ever going to do the rest of my life is revert to things perennial and familiar, I'm afraid that one day—based on my past—I'll just say, "Fuck it!" and give in to using.

~

Fears of reliving the pain of active addiction are fresh in my memory. Time for preventative care. Precautionary actions. I ask Matt over.

"Imagine yourself in a situation where you'd normally lie. Now imagine how it would feel to tell the truth," he says.

"So, we're back to living *as if*?" I reply. It's a little smartass sounding.

His stone face answers.

Why have *I lied so often?* Easy. To avoid conflict. I want what I want via the path of least resistance. Because I'm avoiding any chance of rejection, I never state my desires or needs up front. I lie to bypass all tension, presumed or perceived. Then I go deeper.

I want to be liked. I'm afraid of being alone. I'm scared of not getting my needs met. I have constant fantasies of dying, coupled with nightmares of having led an unnoticed, meaningless life. Then it goes deeper still.

Some of my modes of pretext are obscure. I really don't believe in myself enough to feel certain I deserve to get my way in the first place. Yet, I use subversive tactics to get it. As much as I want to pretend I don't think I'm special, I walk, talk, and move like a person who does. This could be why it was easy for me to act "as if" at the beginning of my recovery journey. I've been acting as if I'm someone else my entire life.

One trait we addicts have in common is self-centeredness. Coming to rely on it like any other survival skill, we use it as a form of protection from having to accept reality. Mine often manifested itself through defiance. It kept me from feeling the guilt of my blithe substance abuse, further enabling the insulation of my insanity. I lied to myself each time I said, "I don't give a fuck." My actions proved otherwise. One had to be paying attention, though, to notice. Which is both all I ever wanted and the thing I despise the most.

Matt and I pray, then go over the inventory I've spent weeks writing out. Each character imperfection I've listed is meant to help identify patterns of harmful behavior, even the ones I no longer wish to act out on but can't seem to stop. We discuss the detriments and benefits of each one so I can see how some are assets. For example, my list includes hubris. It's typical for me to counter my inflating ego by beating myself up. This time, however, identifying flaws is done with a healthy goal: balance.

Matt has me read through each item aloud. This way, I'm acknowledging my behaviors to God and another person. Hearing my voice speak these further allows me to see patterns I couldn't detect before.

"Are you powerful enough to remove the behaviors you listed here?" Matt asks.

"Hell no."

"Can you think of anyone who can?"

The answer is obvious—God. I only know this through all the other paths I've tried: therapy, an entire bookshelf of self-help publications, religion, one guru infatuation, another guru speaker, agnosticism, psychedelic retreats, prescribed numbing, harm reducing substitution, burying of self in work, and many more. None has worked. Personal experience is the most reliable answer. I've got to go with what's been working—trusting my Higher Power.

"God. Only God can."

~

From a college-ruled spiral notebook, I tear out the pages of a letter Matt had me write to God and fold them into an envelope. It's coming with me on a spiritual quest. Tonight, there's a full moon blanketing the sky in pure light. Driving toward remote farmland in nearby Yamhill County, I find somewhere secluded to pull over. Outside, a brisk pace is kept to stave off the chill in the air as I wander around. The smell of cow manure enhances the raw, earthy nature of what I'm about to do.

To create a spontaneous, sacred space, I'll begin by getting on my knees and praying aloud. Using my most humble voice, my prayers are to God to remove the defects I've written out. In the full lunar light, I dig a hole, bury them, thank my Higher Power, brush the mud from my pants, and drive home.

I'm skeptical.

Days pass. I feel the same. I'm thinking and acting the same. *Where's my miracle overhaul?*

My sponsor suggests some new literature. I need every bit of reinforcement I can get. Before cracking open the new book, I say a prayer, then write a note in the back.

I want to be free because

I want to love you (God) with everything I am and have.

Because I loved me with everything, and all it did was hurt.

But it didn't just hurt me.

~

In the weeks leading up to my one-year clean milestone, my thoughts are getting squirrelly about continuing with the program. Why, I wonder, can't there be some magical wand which, after a certain amount of time and effort, gets waved, then, *poof!*, I am free of my disease? I know the answer deep down, like an organic, universal truth. Addiction is the hand some of us are dealt. Which explains why, after coming so far, my brain dares to entertain thoughts that dance so close to the edge of starting over again.

Never mind who is doing this thing to the best of his ability. Who prays after reading recovery affirmations daily. Who has *two* service positions—coffee person and operator for the anonymous helpline. Who has a place to live and a car with his name on the paperwork. Who is still employed and whose hard-earned money pays bills via a legit bank account. Never mind who has been granted shared custody of his four-year-old daughter.

Yet my head tells me I'm not good enough. It recycles fantasies of how good it would be to have just one pill, or one line, or one hit, or one shot, or one sip. I've been cautioned about this. It's been suggested I might be holding onto a reservation.

A reservation is a place in our recovery reserved for relapse. It's a forecasted "what if" event where we've preapproved reexamining the validity of our reasons for staying clean and the necessity of recovery. Instead of living "as if" to manifest living clean, a reservation allows us to set up a "what if" event or construct. It's an aside permission predestined to open the door for using. A reservation could be a situation we believe might be too difficult to get through sober. Or it could come during a time of complacency when we've been coasting on our laurels and we tell ourselves we don't have a problem anymore. Losing a loved one or winning the lottery are extreme examples of situations in which we tell ourselves we "might" use.

Our head never stops lying to us. If you hear a lie enough times, it starts to sound true. Whenever I try to ignore or refute the lies, I get outnumbered. The disease murmurs in stereo with deafening whispers.

I'm pretty sure I'll reach my one year, but then what? Can I use again? Haven't I proven I can beat drugs? There's no way I'd lose everything again. I'm not that stupid, right?

We have the only disease known to humankind which deceives from within by devising specific thoughts designed to coax the afflicted and our hosts into believing we are not sick. Why else would I get these naïve impulses to partake? Why else would dope management seem possible, contrary to what years of evidence proved otherwise time after time?

I can't forget to remember.

I once heard a guy named Eric say at a meeting that recovery is like walking the wrong way up an escalator. The minute you stop climbing, you start lapsing. He called our disease *The Underminer*. I pictured a surly WWF wrestler in a leather mask when I heard that. The image (and name) stuck with me. I later asked Eric for his number. Whenever he shares at meetings, he says what I need to hear. He speaks eloquently about dealing with negative thoughts positively.

I'm not ashamed to admit I need more tools, so I call him. Eric listens carefully as I recite my resurfacing doubts. He has questions.

"Where is God in all of this?"

I'm stumped. Faking like I know the answer would be a disservice to myself. It's hard to admit I don't know, but I do anyway.

"What are you currently working on?"

People working the program ask each other these types of things. They're a way to evaluate if a member is doing the program or doing their own thing. It's not to judge or criticize, but to assess the principle or step that could be used for guidance.

"I'm making a list of the people whose lives my behavior created wreckage in."

"Very good. How's it coming?"

"I haven't started it yet."

"Well, do you think writing out a list of the people you've harmed will help you see why going back to using is a bad idea?"

"I don't follow you. Yes?"

"Out of all the people you harmed, everyone you burned, or stole from, or chose drugs over, whom did you harm the most?"

"My daughter? My parents?"

"What about you? Didn't you harm yourself?"

"Oh God, yes."

While answering him, something clicks. I see myself as the last person to ever give a fuck about me. Which sounds all good and dramatic and emo, but it's a lie. Well, it's not a total lie, there's just more to it. I'm good at shoveling shit atop aspirations which start off as self-care—of piling an ever-increasing burden of diversions upon them—until the load is no longer bearable. Do it 'til it hurts. Pleasure, taken to extremes, has always been my way to care for myself, no matter the consequences, no matter who gets hurt or what's left damaged—including me. Because of ending up in it so often, living in pain became my preference.

But now I'm seeing other reasons why I end up in painful predicaments. They're a means to an end. By undermining my goals, relationships, or best intentions, I *created* a place to run from. I set my sights on my own demise because, from there, I'll be in pain and I'll need to escape. I'll make it bad so I can make it good. But the good is actually bad. My addiction doesn't give a fuck about me. It wants me to believe getting loaded appears to be the only option. Drug and alcohol abuse are not the solution, I am. If I'm not aware of the part I play in undermining my potential for success, I won't have the mindfulness to temper my thirst for failure.

Over the last eleven months, I've practiced habits that would help me move beyond this affliction. But my disease doesn't forget. It hasn't forgotten how it has brought me to the teetering point over and over. Up to the edge I've often danced upon, until saying, "Fuck it."

"Well, brother, it will serve you well to write it out. Remember, you don't have to worry about how you're going to make the amends, you simply need to be willing to. The *how* will come. Just make your list based on what you've already identified as times you acted out in unhealthy ways, causing you to harm others."

"So, by remembering the pain I've brought, or caused, I'm less likely to repeat it each day I stay clean?"

"Yes."

Hitting my bottom was actually a gift. It ripped my custom-made, drug-stained goggles away from my head long enough for me to see what I was really doing to myself. Without hitting bottom, I wouldn't have been able to look at, first of all, my obsession with putting the goggles right back on. Second, how—contrary to internal opinions—it *wasn't* too late to admit I needed help. Only months later, after having the tainted eyewear removed, am I able to discern once and for all that I am powerless over *and* under the influence of drugs. God saw something in me worthy of saving, perhaps to write these pages. I only wish hitting my bottom would've shattered those goggles forever.

If God sees me fit to save, why can't I see myself fit to save?

~

I know where to drive to for a fresh perspective, a respite from the intermittent frequency of mistruths in my brain when it gets distorted. There's a meeting across town I've never been to. It's held in an old basement crammed with fusty old sofas and loveseats. It reeks of coffee, waterlogged wood paneling, unwashed resale clothing, and nicotine-stained wallpaper left by ghosts of smokers.

A series of six 16x20 photocopied posters hang on the ceiling. Mugshots taken of the same woman over the course of five years. They're a photo diary of the progression of meth abuse. The first one is of a normal-looking, attractive young lady. By the sixth image, her face is deathly withdrawn. She is covered in pockmarks and scabs. The skin is stretched taught over her cheekbones. There's no expression. Her hair is choppy and burned by bad bleach jobs. Stillborn is the life her eyes once carried. The dark, dilated pupils are like those of a shark sleeping in the deep, cold throes of an ocean of addiction. A grim reminder of what's waiting for me out there.

A guy with dreadlocks and tattoos timidly raises his hand at the beginning of the meeting when asked who has less than thirty days.

Andre has recently gone back to using after accumulating some time. Admitting relapse should never keep a person from coming back to seek a solution. Addiction is dehumanizing and debilitating enough—we don't need to add shame to it. I, among others, commend him for being courageous. He clears his throat to share, and by doing so, speaks my truth.

"After I took my one-year coin," he says in a voice filled with regret, "I was convinced I was no longer an addict. I was cured. I figured I could have 'a' drink of wine with dinner. So I did. My wife and I ended up getting super drunk that night. The next day I called in sick. I lay in bed all day feeling, you don't even know . . . so shitty about myself."

Most heads nod in agreement. We do know.

"I went to work the following day, but I couldn't get out of my head. I had lost not only my clean and sober date, but my self-respect. So, then I was like, fuck it! My wife and I got one of those boxes of cheap wine and got drunk again. This time I didn't want to be sick, so I drove over to my old dealer's house to score a bag. What did I have to lose anymore, right? That's exactly what I told myself. By the time the sun rose, I was still awake, ready to score more rock. Guess who ended up missing work again and didn't give a shit 'cause he thought he had nothing to lose? That's right. Me. It is just like we hear in these meetings, man. Our disease picks up right where it left off. That shit is true! Once I took that drink, I swear I couldn't remember a damn thing any of you had to say anymore. My head was so loud with my own shit." By now, he is sobbing through his words. "I'm here, though. I made it back! I'm gonna lose my job 'cause now I've missed too much work. I can't lose my job or we'll lose our house. My kids don't deserve my . . . This disease ain't no bullshit. I really fucked up."

Andre is crying so hard that he can't continue to share. Those of us who have been there offer a heartfelt silence. What a mess he's made in just a few short days. I bring him a tissue, then hug him while thanking him so he knows how grateful I am to hear his message.

I thank my Higher Power. Hearing this young man's story at this particular meeting on this particular day as I near this particular milestone is meant to be.

Like him, I've been taking my recovery for granted.

My disease is planning my dishonorable discharge. Like a bear building a den to hibernate in, it's putting the final touches on its nest. A cozy place appearing so hospitable that, on either a good or bad or mediocre day, I'll feel welcomed into an early slumber. All I have to do is say, "I don't give a fuck!"

Andre will never realize how influential he is to my recovery by sharing his story of relapse. A lot of people don't make it back to tell theirs. His misfortune, while unfortunate, isn't lived without meaning. His slip-up solidifies my commitment to persevere. In ways no one understands entirely, a life lived provides learning. My favorite inspirational speakers cite failure as the single greatest motivational factor for growth. Recovery isn't just built upon the shoulders of giants. Proportionately, it's built upon the shoulders of people overcoming broken spirits and lost paths.

We open our mouths not only to be fed, but to give back what was freely given to us: the tangible, living story of how we *earn* hope. Hearing how someone else felt or feels, hearing what they did with those feelings—then having the freedom to incorporate or ignore suggestions for learning from their experience—is priceless.

It helps to be in a state of open-mindedness to hear encouragement in the message Andre shared about his testing of the waters. It also helps to be willing to look for the "neon arrows" guiding us to do things differently than we did before, and to trust that, by doing so, we'll achieve different results. In this light, even the discouragement of failure can be the trial and error another person doesn't have to suffer through. Human interaction is key to getting the benefits. Without each other, recovery is a feat close to impossible.

34

When Doves Cry

When the pain becomes too great, we will surely change.

These words, meant to motivate, prophesize an undeniable truth. By avoiding or putting things off, we're inviting more difficulty. Life always brings challenges, and acceptance isn't always the fancied path for addicts. Not as long as resistance and retreat are options.

With five more months of Colleen's hostile daycare to endure before school starts, I lean on my will to help me keep on keepin' on. By biding my time and suppressing my intuition, I'm allowing choices to be made for me. Out of laziness, I'm hoping things will work themselves out. This accomplishes nothing. The discomfort of indecision doesn't just go away on its own. Something must be done sooner than later.

Picking up Lola from daycare is trying. Maintaining a distance is hard for this social butterfly. Unless Colleen engages conversation, I don't deviate from my usual hurried entrance and exit.

This afternoon, using her smarmy voice, she asks me to stay. Her bright, glossy eyes lend sexual overtones to the openness purposed on her face—a look she hasn't shown since our "playdate" dinner.

I'm kept at bay in her office doorway after I send Lola to grab her belongings. In privacy, Colleen discusses how Leann acted the last time she came by.

"She was odd?"

"I don't mean to alarm you. She was just a bit off."

"It must've been enough for you to pull me aside. What do you mean by 'off?'"

"Like maybe she was on something."

"What makes you think so?"

Many addicts and alcoholics, myself included, can detect with notable accuracy someone who gets loaded. We're proficient at identifying other users. But people the program calls *normies* are not as adept. A normie is a person who can have one drink and not need to have five more. They can try cocaine or crystal meth and say, "Wow! That was fun!", then go on about their life, maybe trying the drug again just for kicks. I don't suggest anyone casually try drugs to find out. Some are so addictive that just one use can release enough endorphins to cause a destructive spiral, even in a normie.

Colleen is a normie hell-bent on showing the world she's neither weak nor less than anybody, especially males. Self-made, she loves having little kids' minds to shape and mold. They're too young to challenge her. Adult males are another story. She uses flirting and exposing ample cleavage to soften the men she interacts with. In my book, Colleen's a bona fide man-hater normie.

"Leann wouldn't look me in the eye. She kept looking down. Then, when I did get a good look at her face, her eyes were bloodshot. Her pupils were dilated," Colleen replies.

"Really?" I say, acting surprised. "What did you do about it?"

There haven't been many chances for me to practice setting boundaries. Insecure and uncertain, I stay stuck in a constant state of reactionary self-preservation mode. It would mean a lot to me to change this mindset. In this instance, however, the best I can do is put her in the position she always puts me in: feeling the need to be defensive.

"What did I do about it?" she asks. Her right hand clamps onto her watchband and rolls it around and up and down her wrist. "I didn't do anything."

"No?"

"No. I'm telling you about it. That's what I'm doing."

"Yeah, but aren't you a mandatory reporter?"

Colleen's face, neck, ears, and chest turn a watercolor palette of red shades. Her chin dips downward. Her soft eyes get hard.

Trap set, vindication exacted.

I can't not bear a grudge. Colleen's trustworthiness flew out the window the moment she found herself a buddy to go dad-shaming with. She chose to partner up, regardless. It's not like I'm void of empathy. I'm taking into account the daughter Colleen lost to the same disease I'm arresting a day at a time. But my compassion was assassinated the afternoon Lola wept uncontrollably after overhearing Colleen's unkind words spoken about her rock: me.

Game on.

"Yes, but, no! Not in this . . . are you serious? I don't have any *real* proof. What? Do you expect me to call the state every time someone shows up here with tired eyes? Oh my God, that is pretty stupid, now isn't it?"

"You're the one who brought it to my attention. For what reason?"

Lola happens to walk up at the perfect time, thus denying an elaborate rebuttal from Colleen. I grab her little hand and leave. After buckling my kid in, out of the corner of my eye I see Colleen standing at the entrance. From twenty feet away, I can feel the veins in her neck pulsing, her eyes uttering death threats.

It's gratifying to watch her squirm. I don't know if I'll ever understand my propensity to lock horns or rub someone's nose in shit. It never feels better afterward. My aggravation is with myself for not choosing a better caregiver; one who is intelligent enough to side with me, the responsible parent. Or maybe I just want her to like me?

~

My primary focus is caring for Lola, recovery, work, then myself. My sponsor points out I have it backward. "If you don't take care of yourself, how can you take care of anyone else?"

This concept is hard to grasp. I've always thought self-care meant indulging in anything and everything that feels good. This isn't my way of thinking anymore. But now this is wrong, too? *Haven't I been my main focus all these years? Wasn't selfishness behind opening the door for this disease to take over?*

It's tough to measure what self-care means. The definition changes as I grow. The strides made just months ago are nothing like those I'm making today. Because of this, I can't help but wonder what I'm unable to see about myself right now that I'll discover tomorrow. There is no graduation from recovery. It's an ongoing progression. There is no quick fix. I'd like to stop looking for one, but the temptation to return to what's known is perpetual. Being in a healthy state is unfamiliar.

One way unhealthiness has manifested itself is by procrastination—how, for one thing, I'm dragging my feet over finding a new daycare for Lola. My putting stuff off leads to feeling overwhelmed. My thinking that I have too much to deal with leads to bartering. Yet I tell myself it's okay to sit on it for another day or two.

Then Leann calls.

"Hey Paul, would you mind if I took Lola on your weekend? Corrine and Jocko are gonna be in town with their kids. I really want to have some time with them. Is that okay?"

My gut tells me to tell her no. From the beginning, these friends of hers shunned me because of our age difference. It was the first time *anyone* considered me too old. Boy, did it hurt.

With reluctance, I agree, mainly because I don't want to be possessive of Lola. That wouldn't be fair to her. Leann's been making an effort to see Lola, so I say yes.

~~~

My assignment is to write out a list of the harm I caused, my reasons for causing it, the outcome, and how I would've felt had I been in that person's shoes. Being thorough in my journaling, I see how often I justified or rationalized my wrongdoings.

Midway through, I start to remember situations I blocked out. Recollections of people who harmed me as much as I did them, if not more. My brothers who resented, teased, and chided me for being the "spoiled rotten" youngest. My first love, who feared getting too serious and started dating her boss's son, then called me, crying, after he got her drunk and forced himself on her. My second love who, while on our way to terminate an unwanted pregnancy, confessed
~~~

the procedure was already paid for by one of the guys who might've been the one who got her pregnant, then kept my money. The punk band I quit because they just wanted to sit around and get stoned who afterward sent someone to break my hands. Why can't I make a list of those things?

My sponsor cautions against glorifying such creative defenses.

All rationalizations of the harm we cause must be set aside before compiling the names of those owed amends. Willingness to acknowledge our part in, and the repair of any wreckage created is crucial. If we ever hope to be assured the freedom of a spiritual awakening, this is the must-do work. We must be willing to diminish our self-centered behavior.

But there are two sides to every coin.

One side of me is resistant to change. Self-loathing is familiar. I'll look for ways to legitimize my negative self-talk. My past makes me as guilty as anyone I decry as harmful, callous, or wicked. Outside of murder or rape, I've been every bit an offender, perpetrator, or instigator.

The real me can't turn away, lest I'm doomed to repeat. This is, at the very least, partially who I've been. Now I'm a forty-year-old man who woke up one day on the wrong side of reality. Instead of lashing out as he's grown accustomed to, he's decided upon a new path—be kind and tolerant and forgiving. He'll be where he says he'll be and be there on time; do what he promises to do; be honest, productive, accountable, and responsible; learn how to take no for an answer, and how to not always have to get his way; learn how to internalize feedback as the potential for improvement instead of judgment and criticism to defy and resent. Just because he changes everything about himself, is he then owed a smooth, easy road?

The other side of me is finding that, by thinking of myself less, I'm learning to love myself more. My old fantasies of feeling owed happen less and less. When I used to hurt people in oblivious, careless ways, I would reason I didn't mean to. But I did. My road ahead is being paved with the mile markers of my past.

~~~

For the first time since the restraining order was dropped, I'm kid-free for an entire weekend. I attend meetings, work on my assignment, then go out. A co-worker, Steve, invites me to hear him play drums for Debora Iyall, a Cowlitz Native American activist and lead singer for the 80s punk band Romeo Void. Being kid-free just isn't for me anymore. I love having my daughter present in my life and feel blessed to be present in hers. There's nothing I'd rather be doing.

Monday afternoon, I pick up Lola at daycare. Few joys rival the pure bliss of your kid running across a room, yelling out your name, with open arms to greet you. I feel as if I've reached, and finally get to rest on, a plateau where everything has fallen into place.

Our drive home from Colleen's starts off the same as every other.

"How was your weekend with Mommy and her friends, honey?"

"Good."

Something in her tone beckons me to pry.

"Yeah? You tell Daddy about it?"

Lola goes on to give an unusually descriptive account of the weekend's events. Leann left her with Corrine's family, but then disappeared with Jocko. When Lola got worried and upset, everyone told her to relax and chill. Leann did not get back until late in the evening.
~~~

Picturing my four-year-old feeling left alone and frightened, without a way to get ahold of me, makes me grimace. She should feel safe in the care of her mother, whom I trusted to watch over her. My teeth feel like they've been welded together. Lola tells a graphic account of what happened next.

"Momma got back late. We went to bed. At first, I was sleeping with the other kids, but Momma wanted me close to her. When I woke up, Jocko was in bed with us."

"*What!*" My loud, angry tone startles Lola. I reset, then restate it nicely, with a humorous, calm sarcasm. Showing my escalating rage might scare the information coming from her mouth right back into her head.

"I mean . . . what, honey?"

"Yeah. Jocko was in bed with Momma and me," she says, as if it's normal.

Using a playful, joking tone, I pretend what she's telling me doesn't seem so very weird or wrong. My insides, however, churn. Downplaying this is a way to get as much truth out as a confused child can relay.

"What was he doing in bed with you guys? Where was Corrine?"

"I don't know," Lola answers, drawing out her words. Her eyes cross, looking up, as if she's seeing into her brain for an answer. "I don't know. But him and Mommy were laying right next to each other."

"Yeah?" I ask nonchalantly, putting on my left turn signal.

"And then he stuck his finger in my butt!"

She emphasizes the word *butt* the way innocent little kids do, like fart or poop.

"In your butt?" I'm especially conscious of my tone. I make myself sound entertained—like I'm hearing an improbable, incredible story. "Nooo. Come on. You're messing with me, right? Did he really?"

"Yes! And then Mommy woke up and pulled his finger from my butt."

Again, an emphasis on butt. I want to shed my skin. I'm imagining what really happened.

"Then what happened? Wait. Are you making this up?" I ask in a teasing voice. I'm hoping she feels at ease enough to disclose everything without holding back. Either that or admit to telling an imaginative story.

"When Mommy woke up, he stopped."

"What an interesting story, honey. How do you feel about it?"

"I don't know, Daddy. You're not mad at me?"

"Why would I be mad at you? You did the right thing. You told me what's going on. You did real good, honey."

The wide smile that comes over her face seems to dispel some internal angst. Whatever she's afraid of, I think I made it go away for the moment.

I do things as normally as possible once we're home. I wait about fifteen minutes for the ability to process this, then call my sponsor. Neither of us is equipped to deal with it. He suggests I revisit the conversation by asking her again for details.

My brain runs through the tidbits of information she has given and finds things that don't match up. This time I'll try asking what she remembers, but in a different way. I'm no expert at psychology, nor am I qualified to extract information. This is, however, my child. I've known her from the moment she was born. My unparalleled insight into how her mind works enables me to nail down some important details. Even though being deceptive is my go-to, I can't stomach the idea of having to use trickery to get the truth out of my own kid.

With three dress-up dolls as decoys, I sit by her on the couch, pretending what she told me in the car was forgotten because I was preoccupied with driving. With a defusing smile, I apologize, then ask her to tell me again. This time, she adds more insight about the fun she had with the other kids there.

As she recounts the part when her mom came back from wherever she disappeared to, Lola moves from the couch onto the living room floor. She starts making a physical gesture. Using body motions to provide a charades-enhanced version of her story, she does a pretty believable reenactment of two people having sex.

I hold back my feelings of disgust. My assumption is that Jocko had sex with Leann while Lola was sleeping in the same bed, and in doing so, inappropriately fondled her. I can't think of another way this played out. Nor can I, by any stretch of the imagination, believe Lola would make this up.

My sponsor is shocked when he hears my matter-of-fact update. I'm as surprised as he is that I'm cool headed. Neither of us knows if I'm in survival or denial mode. The worst thoughts in my head are ones of killing this fucking creep after chopping off his appendage. My sponsor suggests wasting no time getting ahold of Child Protective Services. We hang up. To be certain not to straggle, I start dialing.

The receptionist tells me to bring Lola to a hospital right away. She recommends one where they do specific tests for these kinds of things that involve kids. Scribbling directions on a pad, I'm barely able to focus on a word she says.

I tell Lola we're going on a little adventure, then prepare to make my next call.

~

I recite the Serenity Prayer. So far, every time I turn my will and my life over to God, things turn out better than they would have had I taken matters into my own hands. However, it's the "wisdom to know the difference" part of the Serenity Prayer that causes speculation on my part. Do I have wisdom yet? If I'm asking, the answer is probably no. *Which part of this am I supposed to accept and which part am I supposed to change?*

Through prayer I ask God to guide, if not intervene. It's a way of countering my angry, sickening, vengeful thoughts with the tools of the program. Only after running these checks and balances am I able to see, first and foremost, the need to be here for Lola. But I'm losing ground, fast.

~

I call Leann.

As I'm relaying Lola's story to her, I notice myself speaking in a voice I've never used. Firm, calm, and direct. Traits I'm not conditioned with. Leann seems disarmed by this. She's not being defensive. She sounds surprised by what I'm telling her. I can't tell if it's an act.

"Ooh, that fucker," she says, adding, "Little sneaky bastard."

Of all the various responses a person could have to what I just told her, she chooses to place blame elsewhere. How convenient. This must be what feeling disheartened is like. My chin quivers. I don't want to know the future of where all of this is going.

Many questions are still unanswered. I'm careful of my wording so as not to come across as accusatory. Leann probably knows she must portray innocence. This situation is light years beyond my comprehension.

I start by asking her to go through her timeline of events so I can match it up to Lola's. Leann tries to remember but can't. My pace around the kitchen floor quickens. I'm straining to find a way to outsmart her. She can't explain where she was all day.

"This happened on your watch. Being able to account for your whereabouts is crucial. Not for my sake, of course, but in case you get asked."

Taking this unauthoritative stance gets her to be a little more open. I detect genuine worry mixed with defensiveness. For the most part, she expresses concern for Lola's well-being. We both agree that our child couldn't make up something this serious.

"I already called CPS. They suggested I bring Lola to a hospital to be checked out ASAP."

"Good idea. I'm coming with you," she demands.

Weighing whether or not I can use this to my benefit, I pause.

"Fine. Can you be ready to leave in twenty minutes?"

"Yes. I can be ready, but I'll need a ride."

"Okay. Where am I picking you up from?"

She hesitates, which feels dramatic considering the urgency of the situation.

"Do you know where Colleen lives?"

"Yeah. Wait, why?"

My intuition relays a guess before she explains. It's right. For a month now, Leann's been living with Colleen.

Moving the phone away from my ear, I bring it level with my chest, then glare at it while my other hand covers my mouth. Never underestimate the resourcefulness of how the endless, mindless behavior of an addict can shatter anyone's resolve. Left with no alternative but to decathect from my wishful dreams of a healthy co-parenting relationship, I agree to let her come along. My choice is justified. Now she'll have to deal head-on with the consequences of her neglect.

In a monotone voice, I tell Leann we're on our way. Raw emotions splash among the hallways of my brain. Aerated by feelings of bitterness and betrayal, my swirling thoughts are forced to mix like taffy and come up with . . . something. Before I can plot revenge, or wallow in victim mode, I must pull back to face my priorities. I have a daughter to defend.

Chasten my soul.

My head bobs. One moment, I'm punishing myself for having taken advantage of women who were simply trying to get through their day but got tangled up with me. The next, I'm having to protect my little girl from women; a world of contemptible, callous ones, including her own mother. It's nice to think of myself as the bigger person, but I know better.

Is this payback? Do I expect the human condition to have changed just because I have? Yes, I do. But it doesn't. And I now know it won't. The difference today is, I feel every last fucking bit of it.

While Lola gets ready, I gaze out my kitchen window, reflecting on possible outcomes. It's hard not to feel injured. Colleen is providing Leann with a safe haven. I could take it personally, but I doubt their actions are centered around me. Similarly, I never saw my past actions as anything but justified. I used to think I had no choice other than to insulate myself from the cold, cruel world by jabbing, then withdrawing.

Because of how I've lived, a chosen action would have to be pretty fucked up for me to find it repulsive. Molestation and sexualization of children are among those. Male or female, I see the perpetrators as having a compulsive, heartless, immoral illness with no known cure. An accomplice is just as guilty in my book. Now my child is wounded.

I want to cry. For my little girl. For my life. For humanity. For my own stupidity.

But I cannot show emotion. Not right now.

35

Wicked Game

We arrive at Colleen's home. I leave the van running to expedite our departure. Leann has me wait in the foyer. Lola goes in with her as Leann finishes getting ready. I yell a reminder to hurry.

Colleen comes out from behind the entryway door. Her entrance appears preplanned. She leans back against the door, closing it behind her.

"Can I talk to you outside for a minute?"

"Sure. What's up?"

"It's what you are about to do here, Paul. I know what you're really up to."

"Yeah? And what is that, Colleen?"

"You plan on stripping custody away from Lola's mom."

Ahh, her choice of words.

Some women are adept at snipping away at heartstrings—in the name of a child's best interest. I call bullshit. They do it to make themselves look superior, heroic. It's done as a secret-sisterhood handshake, where the upholding of estrogenic camaraderie supersedes child safety. Some do it with scorned fury to make men look clueless and detached, incapable of child-rearing. Colleen's stonewalling is not being done with my child's best interest in mind. *Nobody is* taking *anything, especially custody.*

Spirited conflict rarely occurs without some inclusion of unresolved issues from prior feelings or past interactions. Through this filter, anything Colleen has to say is seen as an insult to my sensibilities. Heavily weighted with skewed perceptions and animosity, I reposition my feet in a wide stance directly in front of her.

I let out an ugly laugh.

I'm seething with a pent-up readiness to engage in battle with all womanity. Over Colleen's contempt. Over her sense of entitlement, as though she's bestowed supernatural birthrights to demean, abuse, or neglect children. Over her cantankerous, pompous apathy toward my daughter's alleged molestation. Over her insinuating comment, I prepare to defend myself with a trench coat of verbiage. Whatever I believe to be fact becomes pure, unquestionable truth for my battle cry. I open my mouth like an archer pulling back the bowstring.

"No, that's not true," I answer in a measured tone. "Somebody inappropriately touched my daughter on Leann's watch. I'm doing the right thing. The thing Child Protective Services suggested to get to the bottom of this."

"Well, you know that, as a childcare provider with a master's degree in psychology, I am also a mandatory reporter. In fact, at my business, I have all the paperwork you'll need to fill out and send in."

"Send in?" I ask, pretending to have misheard. I take two steps back to be certain she feels the ice in my stare.

"Yes. I could walk you through the steps necessary to file a report on what *you* think happened."

The electrical pulses in my brain go haywire. A flood of adrenaline thrusts both fight and flight through my bloodstream simultaneously. The ensuing tug-of-war causes paralysis.

Before hyped-up rage clouds my judgment, my program-infused survivalist spade digs for an alternative. I need logic to counter the thoughts running amok. Meanwhile, I open my mind to hearing only as much information out of her as being courteous will force me to bear.

"So, are you saying this is something *I* made up?"

"Not necessarily you."

"Who then?"

Colleen averts her eyes. Her forehead scrunches.

"Lola?" I ask, lifting one eyebrow.

"Exactly. I don't know why you can't accept that I deal with these things all the time. Lola's got a wild imagination. Most kids, at this point in development, make up all kinds of stories."

My head screams, *Go fucking kill yourself.*

"So do adults."

I take a sharp, focused breath in. Holding it in long enough to regain control, I start to hear hissing in my ears. I'm doubtful I can sidestep doing something outrageous that I'll owe amends for later. Meanwhile, Colleen continues her condescending, matter-of-fact explanation as if I'm actually buying it.

"You see, Paul, this kind of thing is more common than you think. If you cared for kids professionally as I do, for as long as I have, you would know this as well as I do. I am on your side. We've got to report what was said, that's correct, just in case there's a minute chance something questionable actually happened. If you want, I can put all the paperwork together, then you can come down to sign it on, say, next Tuesday. Would that work for you?"

"No. No. No."

My accelerating blood pressure pounds in my eardrums. My throat is parched. My voice sounds raw. "No, what, Paul? This is a common misunderstanding parents make all the time. Reporting's really no big deal. It's simply a formality."

"A formality? Are you calling my daughter a liar?"

"No, I explained—"

"Do you really think nothing happened? That this was all made up?" My voice rises twenty decibels.

"I'm saying you're making a bigger deal out of this than it needs to be. You've gotta relax and realize this is a FOUR. YEAR. OLD we're talking about here. Telling stories is what four-year-olds do!"

"You're going to use that excuse again? You used it already when I told you Lola said you and Leann were talking shit about me in front of her. I believe her, not you."

"You're not hearing me. I'm here to help." Her tone softens again. "Either tomorrow or Tuesday we can—"

"Your *job* is to protect children. I can't believe you'd want to put this off. Why, Colleen? Why? So you can protect Leann? Because she's the spitting image of your daughter who couldn't handle her liquor?

You think you're going to somehow save her or get back at your ex by taking Leann's side with this?"

"I'm not taking sides. But I do think—"

"It doesn't matter what you think! You are not preventing me from getting Lola checked by doctors. This is what Child Services made clear I should do. I trust them, not you. They don't have a dog in the fight, but you do. How dare you try to stop me! You'd like me to wait a few days, wouldn't you? Just long enough to make me look bad. Long enough for you to prove I'm not my daughter's advocate. Why? I know why—so you can protect your new roommate. Shame on you, Colleen, for not doing what's best for a child."

I bulldoze my way past Colleen to get Lola so we can leave. I look around for what I'm going to break first—a reactionary urge I'm never able to suppress for long. I yell to Leann she has one minute or I'm going without her. No more dillydallying. Her ploy to sic the dog on me has failed.

Now Leann must face the consequences of her neglect—the real reason I want her to come along.

Colleen runs in right behind me, telling me to get out. Her cell phone readied and in hand, she threatens to call 911.

"Please call the cops," I beg. Not being ballsy or confident, just knowing I'd be gone by the time they arrived.

Arms waving, pointing at the door, Colleen maneuvers herself around me. She puts her arms out to corral me like a kid, forcing me out without using force. Her aggression comes close to triggering my explosive personality disorder. Not today. Not this time. Deep down I know the cost: Lola. Before there's destruction of property or worse, I'm out of there.

Leann follows at my heels. The three of us get into the van. Checking all around for cops, I scout an exit to make my getaway. Leann is still buckling Lola in as the tires squeal. The van doesn't accelerate fast enough. I can't bring myself to look at Colleen's dopey face as we pass her by.

Blocks away, I calm myself down for Lola's sake. Leann buckles herself in on the bench seat next to Lola. I joke with Lola to make this look like a normal event. Leann bombards Lola with questions about what happened.

"Leann!" I say to get her attention. "Now is not the time."

Lola should be made to feel she's done the right thing by reporting. It's how I raised her. Ever since she could speak full sentences, I've taught her about protecting her privates. The reasons when, how, and why to report.

~

Traffic into Portland from Beaverton is a slow crawl. Sitting on the freeway, it dawns on me that I left home without the address. When we finally get downtown, I pull up alongside a motorcycle cop. Leann rolls down her window to ask for directions.

The officer is knowledgeable. He informs us that the clinic will be closed before we reach it. Assuming why we're wanting to have our daughter seen, he has us follow him. With the aid of flashing red lights, we're led to a different hospital.

We're not waiting long in the ER before being escorted to a wing providing professional services for these exact types of situations. In fact, this clinic is renowned for helping victims and their families deal with what we're going through. I'm reflecting on ways this nightmare could get worse when the staff comes to take Lola back to examine her. They ask that "just the mom" be alone in the room with her. I'm opposed (with good reason), but don't argue the point. Now is not the time.

Within minutes, Leann comes out, unable to bear having to watch an entire staff thoroughly scrutinize our baby any longer. Leann wants to leave, but she's not getting off the hook this easily. Whether or not she's guilty of having a part in what happened, I insist she stay through this. Tough as it must've been to watch the doctors do their fact gathering, none of us would have been in this position had she put Lola first.

The team invites us to join them in a private room. One offers bottled water. Another asks us to sit down.

"I prefer to stand," I say.

"We could not find detectable proof of penetration," a woman says. Her arms are stiff beside her body. She takes a breath in as if to say something but doesn't.

I sigh. I'd like to believe this is done. Maybe Lola *was* just using her great imagination. That would be a relief.

"You need to follow up on this right away," the other clinician states. To be certain we're clear on his instruction, he steps in front of us to gain direct eye contact. I catch the other clinician, the woman, giving Leann an intense look. When Leann notices, the woman averts her eyes, looking down at the lab papers. She starts to read.

"Lola should be seen first thing in the morning so our team can pursue further fact-finding. We'd like her to begin what's called *play therapy*. This is done by psychologists and therapists who are experts at using props to extract information children have a hard time putting into words."

Leann rises from her seat, breaking the hand-on-shoulder contact one clinician has on her.

"I think we're good here."

I do a double take at her, like she's being inconsiderate, evasive. The staff looks at each other, slightly puzzled, slightly suspect. Like her response is unexpected.

"I'm good with coming back. When and where?" I announce before sitting. It just became important for me to define clear independence from the other parent. I remain seated, posture strong, awaiting details.

Leann folds her arms. Her skin tone is like a stain of spilled wine. My gut tells me she's hiding something—part of her story is being left out intentionally. But what?

I'd rather not think about it. I don't want to let it go, either. Her boyfriend shows up to take her home. Will she be honest with *him* as to why she's here?

I write the appointment down. This means I'll have to call in sick to work. This is still a new job, and the economy is tanking. My employer's been understanding so far, but how can I be a responsible employee and parent simultaneously?

36

Never There

I try for a third time to reach Leann as Lola and I finish breakfast. She isn't answering. She'll miss what could be one of the most important appointments of Lola's life. Go figure. Good thing I didn't bother mentioning to Lola that her mom might come along. Absent. Again.

Though the drive into Portland is fraught with traffic, I'm not my usual stressed, angsty commuter self. The driver's seat is tilted back and Lola and I are singing along to songs on the radio. To make her laugh, I purposefully throw in the wrong lyrics, then cover for it by saying, "Oops, wrong verse."

Our time together is precious. Every few minutes, I sneak a peek at her. The sparkle of curiosity in her eyes is returning. She's no longer lost in a distant stare. Singing loud, her voice beams with joy. I day-dream she'll star in a Broadway play some day.

Taking in our surroundings at the clinic, I notice how serious the kids and parents are. It's obvious they're perturbed by our goofing around. This bothers me. Why can't they be more jovial for their kids' sakes instead of making something downright disgusting feel even more horrible for the kid who went through it? It's in the kids' demeanor. Where abundant life energy should radiate, there's a void.

After check-in, Lola runs to the designated play area. A host of enticing toys is set out. Toys neither of us have ever seen in stores. Meanwhile, I'm evaluating what this place is. What kind of psychological probing are these experts about to embark on with Lola? Has the investigation already begun, based on which toy she gravitates to?

The counselor calls Lola's name. She invites her to come back, and to bring the toy she's playing with. I give Lola an extra-long squeeze and kiss on the forehead to reassure my little bean all will be fine before the staffer escorts her away. We half wave as they go in, hand in hand. She's so curious and excited that she doesn't even look back. As I fill with pride, three workers appear out of nowhere. One stands on each side and in front of me.

"Would you mind following us this way, Mr. Summers?"

"Me? How long it will take? Someone just took my daughter back. I need to be out here when she's done, or she might get freaked out."

"You don't need to worry. We have everything handled. She'll be with psychologists for a while. You'll have plenty of time."

As they bring me back, I think about work. We need to wrap this up before too long so I can go in. I didn't tell my boss I'd be out all day. I left it open so as not to take advantage.

I tag along behind the female, followed by two males. Nothing has been made clear as to what role or title any of them have. They're wearing different-colored hospital scrubs. Counselors? Nurses? Interns? Doctors? Should I have asked?

How abrupt and nerve-racking this is. Remembering why we're here calms me. A responsible, loving parent, I'm here to help Lola relay the occurrence she encountered. Real or imagined, I'm following through for her sake.

The four of us wait in a hallway for a room. Not a word is spoken. No one even looks at each other.

A couple comes out of one of the rooms. Both are teary-eyed and guarded. They walk past us at a fast pace. A staff member then comes out and gives us the go-ahead to enter some sort of interrogation room. A sparse setup—one table, three chairs, acoustic panel walls, and a two-way mirror—gives off icy energy. I know the mirror is two-way because someone left a light on in the observation room, illuminating it enough to silhouette a body behind a video camera anchored on a tripod. The light stays on as the inquiry begins.

The two men sit across from each other. They take turns asking me questions, playing good cop/bad cop. With nothing to hide and everything to be proud of, I field their long list of similar yet varied investigative inquiries. Most have nothing to do with raising my daughter. I'm not savvy enough in psychology to figure out what subconscious tidbits they're trying to extract.

I'm more honest than they need me to be, including disclosing details of when I spanked Lola because she wouldn't stop asking when her mom and I were getting back together. A temporary loss of control I regret to my marrow. Divulging too much is risky. However, it's not as risky as being deceptive. Any secret withheld turns into a niche for deceit, denial, and destructive thoughts to gain a foothold. A risk I'm not willing to toy with.

I'm no longer slouched as I inform them I'm a recovering drug addict. My arms stretch out over the table as I explain. "I believe my daughter is in this predicament because her mom continues to use drugs."

I go on clarifying with passion while trying to minimize any agitation in my tone.

"Few parents would do as much as I have to protect their kid from this. I tried getting an Emergency Order of Protective Custody but was denied by the judge because I couldn't provide proof the mom was endangering our child's well-being. It wasn't possible to provide proof because I work full time, attend meetings, and parent the rest of the time. My focus is my kid, not her mom."

I don't stop there. Time to relay *my* experience—the story no one has asked to hear. This recorded deposition might be the only opportunity I'll ever have to share *my* truth. A rare chance to inform the powers that be everything I see as sinkholes in their existing protocols.

"So far, all that's happened is CPS sent a caseworker to do a wellness check on me at my residence. As far as I know, Neil, the caseworker, has yet to observe the conditions Lola's exposed to when she's with her mom.

"I want the state to take my word for it when I say my daughter is in danger. At the very least, provide the same level of active interest given as when the state took her mom's word, without proof, that I was a threat to their safety."

I don't like being confrontational, but I have to let this out. One reason I'm here at this "clinic" is because my child has been victimized by the state's ineptitude. Yet I'm here, enduring this intrusive interrogation. I'm here, feeling forlorn. I'm here, standing up for my little girl.

After a long silence, I'm given a sincere acknowledgment of my frustration. The staff then conclude their inquiry. They seem satisfied with the results of their questioning, especially my opinions on parenting and the circumstances surrounding the alleged abuse.

My choice to be brutally honest is similar to old behavior, but different. Being candid, expressing feelings without expectation, and knowing I'm worthy of sharing them, are firsts for me. I'm grateful for the suggestion of practicing honesty. The program has given this to me. It's not only saving my life, but possibly my daughter's as well.

As we're wrapping up, the bad-cop guy lets loose a wide, comforting smile. He admits being relieved I showed no fear of his approach. "It's rare I get a parent in that chair who isn't covering up something. I always get to the bottom of it."

I half laugh, trying to imagine how impossible this would've been if I were still using. These are qualified experts who do this dance daily. A dope fiend avoids these types of interactions at all costs, which explains a certain someone's absence. Nevertheless, no determination has been made by the state as to who is unfit to parent.

As the conversation slides into small talk, the woman who brought Lola back earlier walks her into the interrogation room to reunite us. We bonk heads running toward each other. The woman comments, "The special bond between you two is obvious. An emotionless, blind person could pick up on just how close you are."

Before we can leave, a staff member takes me aside. They believe inappropriate touching was involved, but there's no evidence to conclude penetration of any sort occurred.

"The state would like to pursue bringing the perpetrator in to face charges. Would you be on board with that?"

"Of course."

"Good," she says. "We've reached out to your caseworker. Be expecting a call soon to follow up."

Lola and I are free to go. We share the same feeling of never wanting to return. I'm guessing we're done with this situation. The police will handle it from here. Maybe someday in the future justice will be served.

We're not two feet outside the door when my phone rings.

37

Lightning Crashes

"Hi Paul. Neil with CPS. We have an extremely urgent matter to speak with you and Leann about. We need you to come to our Washington County headquarters by two today."

"I'd have to call work. Is this about what happened to Lola? Because I'm just now leaving the play therapy place."

"I cannot speak regarding any of this over the phone. It is, however, imperative you come in *today*. And you need to make sure Lola's mom is present."

"Okay, I'll be there, but I don't have any idea where Leann is. She's not answering her phone. Also, I don't think I can find someone to watch Lola. It's too short of notice."

"You can bring Lola. It'll be better that she's with you, anyway. Do you have another number for Leann?"

I provide Neil with everything I have, six different numbers in less than ten months. Next, I call my work to notify them I won't be in. My dispatcher is not happy. He already routed me for the day's deliveries. Multiple levels of concern interfere with clear thinking.

Worried about presenting an upbeat façade for Lola, I glance at her in the rearview mirror. Her innocent face is comforting. To her, today is a bonus day, a day of having Daddy all to herself.

We arrive at the CPS office early. Neil directs us to wait in a large room. The floor is filled with toys. So many fun things for Lola to play with. One section is for boys, one for girls. There's a couch and two chairs for adults.

Lola gets lost in her own little world right away. I observe her—how she's drawn to Barbies, stuffed animals, and mini plastic kitchen appliances, especially make-believe tea party utensils. Toys I can't afford.

As with the play therapy place, I notice someone standing behind a two-way mirror holding a large camera. *What are they planning to capture?*

A cold draft moves past where I sit alone on the right side of the couch.

Leann shows up. Her skin is splotchy. She appears shaken, disheveled. Her eyes dart from one place to the next; anywhere but to connect with mine. She, too, is bewildered. She gives Lola a quick kiss on the top of her head, then sits on the sofa. A cushion separates us. Neil comes into the room and sits facing us on a squeaky wooden chair.

"Do you guys know why we called you here?" he begins.

"I'm guessing it has something to do with what happened this past weekend," I answer.

"Like I told Paul last night, I was asleep," Leann offers. Her tone is defensive. "I'm not sure why Lola made up this story about what happened."

Lola, just ten feet away, looks over. She listens while pretending to be playing, making soft, conversational voices between the dolls in her hands. I'd rather be sitting by her, playing as well.

Neil says to Leann, "Well, according to our experts, who I trust, something *did* happen while you had supervision of your daughter. This puts the state in an unfortunate position."

"Ahh," Leann grumbles.

"We have been asking you for a urine sample due to allegations of substance abuse and putting Lola in an unsafe environment while under your care," Neil says.

"She is not unsafe when she is with me! I love her. I am a good mother. We have fun together."

"Fun, for Lola, is not what occurred while under your care on the night in question," Neil continues. "Through play therapy examination, our experts were able to extract that there was, during this incident, neglect as well as a lack of necessary protection and guardianship. Based on their findings, the state has determined that your daughter is not safe when she is under your supervision."

Leann leaps up. "You! You did this!" she shouts, pointing at me. "You're trying to take my daughter away from me. You made all this up so you could get custody."

Even though I think I know what this means, I stay silent. As I ponder what to do next, I look up. Leann is perched over me, shaking her finger in my face. Not to argue or have a discussion, but to accuse.

Deniability gushes from the person who should've stopped at nothing to make sure her baby was protected.

She goes to sit back down, then stands right back up. She paces back and forth like a prize fighter waiting for the bell to sound inside the ring. I'm in search of some compassionate middle ground—or a way to skirt around having to defend myself. This is heartbreaking. From the moment she arrived, I'm seeing her for what she really is . . . maybe for the first time since we met at work six years ago.

Neil speaks to Leann in an even tone. "If you offer to take a urine test right now, you could show the state that you're not using drugs, then—"

"Ah, see, I don't always have her in my care. What I do with my free time is *my* business," Leann interjects. "You guys are just trying to trap me into giving some proof that don't mean shit. I'm a good mom. I love my daughter. We have fun."

I notice the broken-record statements. It's as if she's trying to convince not only Neil but herself.

"Well, the state has no choice but to temporarily grant full custody to the father. It has been determined that you are using drugs."

"You don't know that!" Leann stomps her foot.

"Well, in a way, we do. I've asked you repeatedly for months to provide a urine sample. No reasonable parent would continue putting off something this important. You've left us no choice. The safety of one of the citizens of this state needs to be protected, thus the legal ruling we are making. Unless you're willing to be tested right now."

Leann assumes an aggressive stance, legs apart, planting her right foot on the floor between my legs. Her knee leans into the couch, her outstretched fingers inches from my cheeks. "You did this! This is all you."

She raises her arm so fast I flinch, then cups her hand behind her ear. "What? Huh?" she says, sounding like a dimwit.

"Say something. Just because you're clean for a little while, you think that makes you a better parent than me. Huh, Paul? Look at me!"

I look up. Her lips are pursed, flinging moistureless spit in every direction, her pupils dilated. The lens reflect a ghostlike vacancy. I can't bear peering into them. What I see is hauntingly dark. I lower my chin.

"Why?" she asks in a soft voice so I'll make eye contact. "Why do you want to take her away from me?" Leann turns and looks at Lola, points to her, then pouts. "This is going to hurt *her*. Why would you do this?"

When tears don't come, her tirade continues. "You're the one who's a fraud here." Her voice turns demonic and gravelly. She faces Neil and demands, "Why the fuck won't you ask *him* to take a pee test? Huh?"

"I'd be happy to."

"You see, Leann? Paul has no problem providing a urine sample. That tells us a lot about him. And about you," Neil says.

"Why don't you take a fuckin' hair follicle test from him, then? Anybody can get clean long enough to pass a stupid urine test." Leann huffs between words. She looks at me. "I don't believe you've been clean all this time." Then she says to Neil, "Test his hair to see if he's lying!"

Mid-sentence, Leann swipes at my face. I don't think to block her hand. My defensive guards are down. I consider this a protected environment. One shouldn't have to shield against a physical attack here.

Leann snatches at my goatee hair. I've been growing it out since the day she left because I wanted a visual reminder of my broken marriage. I made a vow not to trim it until our divorce is finalized. It's about five inches long and resembles a fluffy bunny tail. She grabs a handful. The pain of the strands being ripped from the follicles beneath my skin is sharp enough to scream.

If our genders were reversed, had I come at her with this magnitude, I would've been thrown face down to the floor, a knee forced into my spine and ribcage, an open palm at the back of my neck bulldozing my face roughly into the carpet. I'd be manually restrained and then placed in handcuffs.

But our genders are not reversed. Not so much as a finger is raised to intervene. I stay put, immobilized with astonishment. Am I supposed to sit here and take this abuse? Why? Because I was born male? Is this fair, equal, and just?

Leann holds my chin hairs right up to my crisscrossing deer-in-the-headlights eyeballs, like a proverbial ninja showing her victim the heart she's ripped out before the loss of blood pumping from the missing organ ends his life. She sprinkles my red, black, and gray chin curls over the top of my balding head; her thumb rolling them off over her long, shaky fingertips.

Through watery eyes, I look to see Neil's reaction. I don't see him anywhere. Maybe he left to summon security guards. I'm a numb sort of docile. Knowing there's a camera on us helps, but anger is burgeoning inside me. I hold out my arm at a forty-five-degree angle to create some space between us. Leann backs away to a distance that is more tolerable but continues to let off steam by incessantly screaming expletives.

Lola stops playing. She's watching us, yet her gaze is off somewhere distant. It may have joined her thoughts far away—some place safer, loving, with less drama.

Leann resumes hovering over me. I scoot to the edge of the cushion to better defend myself. Her finger quivers just inches from my face. Her gait is intentional, menacing. Back and forth, toward and away. Her mouth spews hateful promises of retribution.

Lola's baby blues roam around the room until they reconnect with mine. An unspoken contemplation of indifference between us mutates into solidarity. I no longer hear Leann. Only Lola's mind. Her stare, uncertain with a pinch of hopelessness, lowers for just a split second. Then she springs up and runs to me. My baby jumps into my lap like a little wallaby.

Witnessing this, Leann turns away, perhaps unable to handle visual proof of the unbreakable bond she's tried to destroy. Under her breath she mumbles, "Isn't this just fucking great?"

I put one arm around Lola. The other is held in the air for protection just in case Leann succumbs to another wave of hostile urges. Seeing the two of us sitting defenseless, she turns away. Her arms start to shake. She turns back toward us. A frenzied rage has come over her face. Before she can start in again, Neil walks back in. Not with security guards, but with paperwork to sign.

Leann momentarily restrains herself. Lola gives me a squeeze with all her might. I reciprocate to let her know she's safe, but it doesn't quite feel like this storm has passed.

Neil instructs Leann to "come sit" where he has set some papers on a desk. The two go over the details of what would need to happen for her to regain custodial rights. For the time being, she's only allowed supervised visits. Until she proves she's off drugs, the state-mandated protective custody order stands—the order I asked for months ago that had been denied. The order granted only because a man attempted to molest my daughter while having sex with her mom in the same bed. Who knows what else happened to Lola during the months and months I waited for the state to hear my plea? A plea they never listened to.

How would this have played out if my genitalia were different?

"Daddy. I need to go potty," Lola says, tugging my arm.

Neil tells me our part is done. We exit the cold, dimly lit, life-altering room once and forever more. After a restroom break, we head outside to leave.

Right behind us, too close for comfort, comes Leann. Her ranting resumes. She screams to get my attention. I cradle Lola. She edges her little body further into the safety of my arms. Her eyes fixate on my face, awaiting my reaction.

I ask Neil, who has followed Leann out, to please tell her to stop. He intervenes. He tells her she needs to take it down a notch, but his soft, feminine voice doesn't faze her. She comes at me all over again. Taunting, pointing, expelling. She zigzags back and forth in my path. Every possible derogatory, instigative, bad-memory-inducing remark she can yank from our past gets thrown at me to see what might stick—any and every button or trigger she can recall just to get my explosive disorder to unfold, unlock, and unleash.

Once our superior self-will is enacted, an addict refuses to give up. It doesn't matter how convincingly we're defeated. If there's anything Leann can do to strip Lola from my arms, even if it means our child becomes a ward of the state, she's going to try it right here, right now.

Neil gets between us, his tone more stern. He pulls Leann aside and they exchange words. I quicken my pace to get beside my van in case she gets weird again. This way I won't have too much distance to travel to take Lola to safety.

"Paul. Would you mind if I gave Lola a hug before you guys go?"

I turn to assess Leann's level of sincerity. With eyes pitched upward as her head tips down, she holds out her arms. Lola looks at me, clearly expecting me to make an accurate evaluation in the trustworthiness of her mother's gesture. With a firm grasp under her armpits, I raise Lola up, out, and over into her mom's grabbing hands.

"Honey. I love you. Mommy's going to miss you. I'll see you soon though, okay?"

"Okay, Mommy."

"Just one more hug before my baby is torn from Mommy's loving arms."

"Good God. Really!" I bark, with a rolling of my eyes. *Enough already.*

The drama. The avoidance of accountability. The seething hatred and spewed disdain. For a moment, I thought she'd shut it off. But this verbal jab signals the return of Mrs. Hyde.

I've had enough of her unpredictable behavior. My leg fidgets. My foot inches in, closer. I smile to play nice, but I can't downplay how uneasy this makes me. I never *ever* wanted my daughter to be separated from her birth mother. I open my arms to take Lola back.

Leann will, from this day forward, collect the results of her choices. A symptom of being powerless over drug use, denial blinds us from seeing what's being sacrificed by choosing to get high. Both of us had high hopes of being great parents, and maybe we were for a while, but we fell short. One of us is choosing to change how the story ends.

Suddenly, like a baseball pitcher on the mound, bottom of the ninth inning, one strike away from winning the series, adjusting his jersey while taking a deep breath and looking up at the tens of thousands of people in the stands, everything becomes real. This is not a feeling to suppress. It is the moment to take it all in.

This is not how I wanted things to turn out. I never started getting high to end up a drug addict. I never wanted a baby, expecting to neglect her needs; never got married anticipating a day would come where I'd say to my daughter's mother, "Your time is up, hand my kid back to me."

Yet, this all happened.

Of affording Leann too much wishful thinking and enabling, I am guilty. I purposefully chose not to trick her, not to go in bully-style, guns blazing, forcing her to change or bow to my will—no matter how self-righteous I felt, or how often I secretly wanted to. I knew deep down doing so would take away the empowerment she'll gain by looking at and owning her part.

She has to do this on her own. Or not. I've turned matters over to a Higher Power to intervene, praying for God to do for this family what I could not do myself: move it toward a better outcome.

"Are you okay?" Neil asks.

I flinch. I'd forgotten he was beside me. He's stayed close to make sure Leann doesn't take her irrational behavior to a physical level. I'm bawling, which I *never* do in front of strangers. A thought swings into my head like a wrecking ball: I should call this off, it's too painful for all parties.

I have a shitty suspicion that even this tragic incident lacks enough impact to encourage Leann to get better. She'll carry it as her torch to go out and get worse. I hate the likelihood that this could break her, but it has that potential.

"This is really tearing me up inside," I confess, no longer caring to hide my sadness. "No one knows how hard this is for me."

Neil gives me a hug. I take it as an affirmation that I'm doing the right thing. I'd appreciate his gesture more if I weren't so scrambled. I'm in shock.

Leann hands Lola back. At some level, she must know by the tears I'm shedding that this wasn't about winning or revenge. Although it probably doesn't register beyond her not getting what she wants. She's too high.

Looking into Lola's too-young-to-understand face brings a realization of my purpose. I'm committed and accountable to her. Now capable of following through, my purpose will be nurtured to fruition. I'm protecting our child. This day is teaching me firsthand, parenting requires making very, very hard choices.

Neil asks Leann to come back inside with him.

Buckling Lola in as they head off, I keep an eye on them, just in case. Once I slide the van door closed, there's no looking back.

The last tears dry and harden on my cheeks as I drive to *our* home. The tension in my muscles ease, but I'm empty inside. I have full responsibility and liability now. At any other time, this would've scared the shit out of me. I would've put on all the proper people-pleasing faces, jumped through all the perfect-parent hoops to get onlookers to believe, then driven off the road.

Today, none of those masks interest me. Just because I've fucked up in the past is no clear indication I will today, or in the future. It is truly never too late to restart your life. If I can reinvent myself, anyone can.

Today, I'm a dad. I am my kid's dad. I have a girl to raise into a woman.

38

Somebody I Used to Know

I have less than twenty-four hours to make drastic changes, the most important of which is finding a new full-time daycare. My options are slim; time available to run from place to place slim; time to evaluate them, slimmer. No way in hell am I taking Lola back to Colleen's, so I pray. Somehow praying introduces ideas all my overthinking under pressure can't come up with.

I ask for help from my new family—parents in recovery. A woman raising two daughters on her own comes to mind. Lola plays with her oldest at a larger meeting we attend. She recommends her friend Cynthia, who runs a daycare from her double-wide trailer home. I'm hesitant because it sounds too ghetto, too white trash.

Reality check. An examination of the options on the table is needed. My "smarter-better-than-thou" mindset has already driven me to addiction, potential divorce, and near childlessness. Procrastination in replacing Colleen was my choice. As a consequence, I'm forced to let go of my idealistic preferences. None match with reality, so I give Cynthia a call.

Next, I have to officially terminate my arrangement with Colleen. I don't want the conflict, afraid I'll lose my cool. I'll do just about anything to avoid a face-to-face with her. So instead of doing so, I just stop taking Lola there.

Days later, I get a message from Colleen's new assistant asking why Lola hasn't shown up. *Why on God's earth would I bring my child into an unsafe, biased, man-hating environment?* The logic is perfect in my mind. Then again, it always is.

The calls go on for days. Isn't not answering a hint? They finally stop.

Two weeks later, a bill arrives. Not only is Colleen charging for the remainder of the month, she's included an invoice for the upcoming month. I'm obligated to pay, pending her receipt of an official letter from me stating my decision to conclude services.

She has a case. The terms are stated in our contract. I'm burdened with preparing a form, then signing and sending it via registered mail. I cross my t's and jump through the hoops. The official letter gets refused. I go through every step a second time and send it again. Perseverance. No response.

With Lola staying the night with her grandparents, Matt and I get together to go over my amends. I need to be ready and willing to reach out to each person on my list, provided I don't push it too hard, injure them, or someone close to them. We prioritize the names together. As part of an ongoing process, we will talk about each amends, pray for that person, then discuss how to make each specific amends. For those we deem too painful to reach out to at this time, we discuss making a Living Amends. This is when the amends are made daily by living in healthier ways than I did in the past. For the others, the amends are not going to be done via speed-dial robo-apologizing.

"Hey, it's me, Paul. Remember me? The ____ (fill in the blank with cheating, lying, mind-fucking, thieving, promise-breaking, violent, raging, verbally assaulting, game-playing, reputation-compromising, bullying, abusing, public shaming, humiliating, abandoning, heartless, using, betraying, blaming) guy who convinced you everything was your fault? Hi! Just wanted to pop into your life real quick, tear that forgotten scab open wide, pour some isopropyl alcohol on the wound then, as you're writhing in pain, I'll tell you with all sincerity, 'I'm sorry, so sorry.'"

No.

The people I've hurt, the ones my gravitational pull brought close, heard those words spoken more than most. This isn't about apologizing to them . . . again. Nor is it about convincing them how much I've changed. In most cases, hearing of or witnessing my changes will not suffice. It's not their first rodeo.

It's about expressing the reasons why I'm seeing the wrong in making those choices today. I've never stopped feeling bad about the ways I've harmed. Saying sorry won't change that, nor will it make anyone feel better. Putting an end to the behaviors that hurt them (and myself), through what's called a Living Amends, might.

It's worth a shot. To the best of my ability, with an understanding that I won't be perfect at it, I'm willing to try. And being willing to do whatever it takes to make my wrongs right, no matter how uncomfortable it gets, is how I'm committing to living differently.

This will help me learn the wisdom part of the Serenity Prayer, because part of why I got loaded was to bury the guilt, pain, and shame I caused people who loved me. Today I have a taste of what it's like to be a dependable, honorable, trustworthy, generous, decent human being. Although having integrity isn't easy for me, my worst day living by these principles is far better than my best day compromising my dignity for inebriation. Some choices I made were learned. Some were seen as my only option. By identifying what's broken, I can figure out what to fix.

Although it's suggested we place our own name at the top of our amends list, I put mine underneath Lola's. I won't place myself first. Not yet.

Next on my list are my mom and dad, then my brother and his wife. Knowing they've been anticipating the day I ask forgiveness fills me with unspeakable joy instead of the feeling of an unbearable burden. They've been able to see the growth firsthand. Those who haven't heard from me in years might be more skeptical.

"It's not about the outcome, it's about being willing," my sponsor reminds me.

As I internalize, then practice being willing, my attitude changes. One of hope replaces one of despair. I'm a little slow, but I'm beginning to understand the synergistic concept: If those I harmed could forgive me for all the crap I pulled, I could learn to forgive the ones who have harmed me. People like Lola's mom.

If I turn my back on the hope that she could one day get off drugs, I'll be turning my back on the very program that is helping me do the same—thus denying myself being served a full portion of growth.

This doesn't mean I'm willing to be a doormat, enabler, or fool. Not at all. Through acceptance, tolerance, and understanding, I just might discover I enjoy peace instead of a perpetual embodiment of bitterness. Perhaps then I can roll out of the mucky quagmire ruts and forge ahead on the path I was meant to tread. Perhaps one day Lola will find it hard to believe what kind of person I was in the past.

~

Peace and serenity. The goals of recovery. Each day I'm clean, I find it harder to understand why I chose undermining over the enhancement and development of self and relationships. Or why I often wait until the pain becomes too great. The burden, too great. Each day I'm clean, I have a better chance of seeing that I do have a choice. On this day, I choose to stop adding to the pile. To keep my side of the street clean. To demonstrate, by example, how people can and do change.

The last part of my assignment was to ask ten people how they pray. Most suggest that I seek meaning and direction, then be open to what comes. Their answers get incorporated into my own prayer. This way, it's not some copy-and-paste prayer.

To me, prayer is private. It's the ultimate, intimate conversation with God. By choosing to pray, I'm opening my ears for words, my eyes for what others call the neon signs, my mind for new thoughts. I'm not expected to pray or meditate a specific way, nor is this an expectation set by referencing how I've chosen to. It's one of an unlimited number of ways to achieve conscious contact. Each of us has an individual right to believe in any Power we choose.

To reinforce my recovery and make sure I don't revert back to my own thoughts as my compass, each day begins with reading recovery literature, after which I pray for knowledge of His will, the willingness to listen for and hear His will, and then the courage, power, and strength to carry it out.

Before bed, I thank the God of my understanding for another day clean, another day sober, for my family by my side, and for any other blessings I recognize. I call the grandparents' house to say good night to Lola. While Carol's on the phone, I let her know my parents are in town and that they'll be with me when I pick up Lola. She thanks me for the good news. Through all that's gone down over the past year, the two sets of grandparents have maintained their friendship.

I hesitate to ask Carol about Leann. I haven't heard from her since the CPS incident, even though I made it clear she's always welcome to call or stop by to see Lola. It's been weeks. I'm curious if Leann has withdrawn *all* contact—a game many addicts play to get their way.

I'd rather not question Lola for details about time with her mom. That's theirs to cherish. I don't want her to ever feel she's being used as an informant. From a parental standpoint, though, I need to ask.

According to Carol, Leann's been over when Lola stays the night. Carol continues to tell me that all of this has been a rough go for her and Patrick. He doesn't approve of Leann's mental state. Whenever he conveys his suspicions to her, it turns into a screaming argument in their home. They have no way to prove what it is they think they observe. If they accuse her of being on something, Leann storms off for the night, leaving them to watch Lola.

Carol is just getting started.

"I have failed as a parent," she says.

To hear such a strong woman broken by her own kin is unsettling. Carol's a few sheets to the wind, but I can tell she's speaking from the heart. Years of playing bars have given me this nonscientific ability. I can spot the difference between when a person spews "poor me" inebriated elation and when they're being transparent with feelings they've kept guarded when they're sober.

Hearing Carol lament, I'm beginning to understand the plight of the hardworking, responsible, devoted parent. I'm a novice at unconditional love. In fact, I used to see compassion as the self-centered "look at me" deed of a martyr. Now I'm seeing it as an expression of pure love. Something I don't yet know I'm capable of. I choke up a little. This is my chance to let them know how I feel.

"I've been meaning to tell you something, Carol. Lola and I are blessed to have you and Patrick. I couldn't do this without your help. You guys have been rock solid through all this, without exception or condition. We may not always agree, but if anything were to happen to me, you're the only people around here I can entrust Lola to. The only stability she's ever known comes from you guys. To me, your bond with her is inseparable."

"Thank you, Paul."

Crediting my in-laws without expectation is a step toward adulthood. Giving praise shows the makings of humility. Treating someone with respect is a sign of self-respect. This marks a definable measure of growth and stills my spirit. Now I have proof that it *is* within me to give compassion—to reach deep within for something inside that can serve others. It doesn't need to be material or financial to be sincere.

~

I'll never know what it means to have grandparents. I can't fathom their bond with my child. The one time I saw my grandpa, I was three. Besides pictures, my only memory of him is of his chronic burping. He died of stomach cancer.

I met Grandma Lily through a screen door during a family vacation in New York. I was ten. She still lived with the milkman she left Grandpa for. They were on welfare. She was too drunk to come outside and greet us. It was midafternoon. Lily died of alcoholic dementia.

My dad never let go of resenting his mother for abandoning him and his sister. I can count the number of times he spoke her name on one hand. He lived by a simple code: you never turn your back on family. Which explains why he resents Lola's mom. His feelings are steeped in experience.

My father admitted to me one day that he once tried leaving our family. He'd packed his things and started driving toward Laguna Beach, California. In less than an hour he pulled over, unable to continue because of nonstop crying. He pictured us boys, how fucked up we'd be, feeling abandoned for the rest of our lives. His experience bears firsthand knowledge of what it is to bear those feelings. Just as Lola does.

39

Birthday

It's June 26. Today I celebrate accumulating one complete year clean. Three hundred and sixty-five days, nights, weekends, and holidays, one day at a time.

My parents are with me when I pick up Lola from Carol's. Seeing them, Lola isn't sure who to run to or hug first.

Patrick and Carol congratulate me. I'm honored. Trying to be funny, and bragging a bit maybe, I remind them of the drug kit I gave them when I had less than a month clean. I was desperate to get clean. It was one of many spontaneous ideas that seemed to have come from outside myself.

"Remember when I said to you if you ever suspect I'm loaded, you have my permission to make me pee in it, and if I refuse, you are not to let me leave with Lola?"

"We know you've got this, Paul. We threw that kit away a long time ago."

Even then, I was thinking up ways of holding myself accountable (even though I stole it from the temp agency bathroom).

My dad can tell I'm getting antsy. I don't want to be late. My plan was to drop my parents off here so the four grandparents could get caught up. Then, to my surprise, my parents ask if they can join me.

"I'd be honored," I reply, without thinking.

My stomach churns. Although I've come a long way working on oversensitivity, I haven't let go of when my parents called addicts disgusting, fucked-up people. I'm a little concerned about how they'll relate to a room full of us. Before I can reverse my decision, Patrick and Carol agree to watch Lola a while longer.

We arrive early. There's time to introduce my parents to people I look up to. Everyone seems receptive to them being here. Most addicts know the closer you are to us in our active addiction, the more direct harm you experience. My parents sit beside me on the hard plastic chairs.

My thoughts wander. I'm taken back to the first birthday celebration meeting I attended. It was for an addict named Linnea. She was collecting her one-year tag that afternoon. It was her second time reaching the milestone. It had taken her three years to get back to accumulating that much continuous clean time again.

I admired how her parents and nineteen-year-old daughter were sitting beside her for support. Linnea's mom shared first.

"My husband and I are happy for you, Linnea. But," she said, looking around, "can I be honest here? We're a little uneasy."

Most of us responded positively, goading her on. Linnea, stiff as a statue, listened.

"Last time, the first time we were here to celebrate our daughter being off drugs for a year, made us so upset. It hurt more than anything when she didn't show up. This thing you guys call a *disease* is baffling to us. I don't get how you people carry on supporting each other through relapses and failures without giving up. We just don't understand. We're tired of hoping for the best."

Hearing that, every head in the room nodded.

I pictured how much shit I've slung at my most faithful supporters—my family. How it oscillated. I wondered if I'll ever allow myself to feel the pain I've caused or if it would be too much to bear. If I did, would I go right back out to use? Would my bottom have a trap door?

Linnea's friend shared next. She went on to tell the tale of what happened that night years ago.

"We'd gone to Goodwill to purchase a nice outfit and matching purse for the birthday celebration. On our way to the meeting, Linnea was transferring items from her old purse into her new one. We were blasting the music, dancing in the car. Linnea was so excited to hold up her hand and finally claim a whole year clean.

"Then she's like, 'What the fuck is this?', and I'm like, 'What's what?'

"Inside the purse was a baggie of crystal meth. Linnea started seriously wigging out. Being on probation, she had distanced herself from drugs the whole time. I yelled over and over at her to dump it.

"But she just couldn't resist the temptation. She was mesmerized by it being in the purse she bought. It was like a switch went off. I remember her saying something crazy like, 'God must've put it there.'

"She just started chopping it up. You know how it goes. It's like, automatic. Nothing could stop it. I ended up joining her that night. We both lost our clean date.

"That shit fucked me up for a long time. I was fortunate to find my way right back. I am so relieved to be here tonight with you, Linnea. I love you."

Linnea's daughter, Kayla, spoke next. She had a hard time articulating her feelings through angry sobs. Addressing her mother, she said, "I just want to know why. Because it makes no sense, Mom, how you chose dope over me so many times."

She turned to face the room, its resonant vibrations now deadened. Each of us felt the guilt of our past. "If any of you can explain to me why, please do."

Many eyes dropped anchor in shame or in search of healing words on the concrete basement floor. I squinted through the salty meniscus covering my sight. I thought about Lola. *Is this my daughter's future? Will she have to say these things about me in coming years? About her mom?*

Kayla went on to recount some of her memories of being the daughter of a drug addict. How often she'd be waiting outside in the rain to be picked up from school or a friend's home. No call, no show. How, over time, she figured that if Mom hadn't showed after a certain amount of time, it meant Mom wouldn't be around for days. Then Mom would show up like nothing happened, usually with some man in tow who treated her like he owned her. How disgusted it made her, knowing her mom would then be indulging in nefarious activities, locked in her bedroom for days on end.

Last, Kayla spoke about her own struggle with alcohol and cocaine.

Tragic and heartbreaking is this disease. It runs in, through, and over families.

Kayla's testimony was my blaring midday air-raid siren. I lowered my head, cradling it in my outstretched forefinger and thumb. I told myself that if I ever mistreated Lola like that, I didn't deserve her.

Today, as I relive that memory, I know the only way I won't ever hear my kid saying those things about me is by staying clean.

~

Tonight, I've come to collect my first, and hopefully only, One Year key tag. The program hands these out, not as a reward for staying clean, but to show someone new that recovery is possible. Being clean is its own reward.

When the meeting secretary asks, "Is there anyone here celebrating one year?" I stand up, proud, and raise my arms, pointing upward, crediting my Higher Power.

"I'm Paul. I am an addict."

I accept my key tag, hug the secretary, then sit down. My fellow recovery brothers and sisters applaud, as do my parents. I've made them proud of me, which hasn't happened for ten years. Not since I got them comp tickets to watch my band open for Al Green at the Joint in the Hard Rock Hotel in Vegas. Or maybe it was when I put out my CD, *Brag's a Good Dog,* showing them once and for all that music wasn't a hobby.

My parents hold back from showing emotion, but I see it on their faces. Watching this, I'm honored to have them here at this pivotal moment. The person chairing asks, "Are there any burning desires?"

Silence.

The anxiety I started having over the possibility of them saying anything gets released in one long, drawn-out exhale. Then, realizing the meeting is about to close, my mom pops up out of her seat.

"Can I say something?"

Most heads nod. For me, this just got *uncomfortable*. It's out of the ordinary, out of character for my mom.

"I'm the mom of Paul over here. He's our son."

I feel my skin flush. A panic of anticipation. Mom's always been the quiet one. I can see my dad performing some attention-getting stunt, but never Mom.

"Absolutely. You are more than welcome to say something. We're glad you're here," the chairperson says, extending hospitably.

"Thank you. My husband and I . . ." As if on cue, my dad springs up.

My mouth drops.

"My husband and I just want to let each one of you know how pleased we are with all of you in how you guys are doing something about your problem. It's been an awakening sitting here, listening to your stories. But most of all, we want to personally thank you for saving our son's life."

I fight back hiccupping sobs. My heart melts with all the love burning in the center of my chest. My mom continues. "Would it be okay? Well, damnit. I don't care if it's okay. We're going to go around and hug each and every last one of you."

There's an outburst of laughter mixed with handclaps. I don't think anyone here has ever seen or done anything like this. I haven't. My mom turns to my dad. His jaw is down to his clavicle.

"Well? Are you going to join me?" she asks.

Awestruck, his head bobs in short, rapid nods of obedience.

My parents go from person to person, hugging every addict in the room. Some squint in my direction, pleased, while hugging my mom. A few comment on what a great hugger she is.

This is one of those rare, undeniable instances. Gifts of recovery. A moment to forever cherish.

40

One Day At A Time

A month ago, I was asked to chair the Saturday night podium meeting in commemoration of my milestone. I've come to give back by speaking about what a big deal this accomplishment is and to share about what went into this hard-earned triumph. My parents and daughter are here to support the man and father I've stepped up to become.

I open with the Serenity Prayer. Then, following meeting guidelines, I invite people up to the podium to read literature. Between readings, I hover close by. While someone is reading, I take a sip of soda, then accidentally spill it all over a table of brochures and books. Chairing shouldn't be this awkward for me.

The heat rising off the attendees has created a savannah-like microclimate inside the hall. My mom fans her face, then Lola's, who sits on my dad's thigh, coloring. Two home group members get up and go from sill to sill, opening the double-hung windows to let fresh air in. Their distraction draws my attention outside, where I take a long look before I'm up to speak.

In the stuffy, packed room, I stand in silence.

This time of year—the placement of the sun, the warmth of the day, the kaleidoscope of early summer colors on leaves of trees, bushes, and flower pedals, the abundance of fragrance, the pollen, and Willamette Valley allergens, the addicts gathering—bears resemblance to just how things were a year ago . . . yet none of it is the same. On that fateful day, I approached this very podium in tears. Broken and hopeless.

Reflecting on the distance I've traveled during my recovery journey, my thoughts float by like dust specks swimming in nonsensical patterns through filtered sunlight. Though my eyes are open, all I see are memories. Overdoses, pain, and manic survival. Ravaged family members dragged to the brink who would've seceded from bloodlines, if that were possible. Distraught lovers and failed friendships. Explosive physical and verbal excesses. Demolition of property and dreams. Burned bridges and extended olive branches. White flags and dissolution of vows. And finally, mostly, the paucity of parenting. All being felt at once.

I shake my head to refocus. Looking at those gathered, I give a nod of acknowledgment to my daughter, parents, and sponsor and take one last pause to absorb the sweet spot of this moment. To savor its modesty. An everlasting split second in which no egocentric judgment or expectation of accolades is allowed. When gains and losses equal zero.

In this silence, I pray for God to speak. For His words to come through my mouth into the back pocket of every person here. That the words remain there until reached for, in a moment of desperation, when the person hearing them is in dire straits—debating between the next hit or the next right decision. That these words guide and help them find their own pathway to the truth.

It is suggested that we offer our experience, strength, and hope.

I start off by sharing my experience, the story of the way I've lived. This is how I'll relate to anyone in the room afflicted with this disease. It is tantamount that newcomers get the sense we are cut from the same fabric so they know they are in the right place. As I share, I'm careful not to go into vivid details because doing so would be glorifying the past.

My strength is shared by relaying the personal improvement I've made through following a program. That by opening up to and allowing my Higher Power to change me, a seed was nourished. By admitting I was broken, I found healing. How, in surrendering to my weaknesses, I'm finding empowerment. How, in seeing the steps as a manual for transformation, I'm less resistant to change. How, through swapping out those old drug goggles, it has become possible to spot behavioral patterns. Since the four people I owe the greatest amends to are here, I devote extra time to this.

"If I harm someone from here on out, I'll have to make amends to them at some point. It's a damn good deterrent to lashing out. Repairing my past is helping me to be a better person in the present. For example, at least two ex-girlfriends made it abundantly clear they want nothing to do with my having any contact with them whatsoever. It's been twenty years, yet they still see me as a manipulative monster. That's how much of a dickhead I was. Making an effort to relieve them of the burden my actions left imprinted in their hearts could be seen as another selfish pursuit to get what I want. Even with the best of intentions, I may never be able to repair the harm. Making amends is about being willing to accept and respect the wishes of those whom we harmed as a consequence of our actions. My part is to be willing to try, then let it go and leave it up to God.

"Some days, it feels like everything I do is under a microscope. But I'm learning to give myself a break. I fall short sometimes, then do things on other days that are mind-blowing compared to the life I led before recovery, although making those comparisons isn't the healthiest measuring stick.

Catching myself rambling, it dawns on me. The newcomers here won't be moved by slogans or restated program literature alone. They need to hear a message they can relate to.

"An opportunity arises almost daily for me to remind myself that the goal is to seek progress, not perfection. It seems like I never know when to put down the bat and stop beating myself up. It's normal for me to suck at these things. But that doesn't mean to stop trying. For today, I'm learning how to set boundaries as well as other things. You know, like how to reveal feelings without fear, or to make, then keep, plans.

"My hope is expressed in telling my story, in showing the ways I'm learning to trust the evidence given by the presence of my Higher Power instead of the fear and the recklessness of following my will.

"By doing so, I get to practice placing trust in God—having faith I'll be okay doing these things. Oh, and I'm learning how to be okay with who I am by accepting the things I do and the unique qualities I possess. Lastly, I'm learning to invite and include God in every fiber of my life.

"Today, I'm optimistic. Old ways of living can be eradicated. I don't ever have to use again, even if I want to. I was taught that here, then shown how it works."

I look over at my folks as I close out my sharing, then I look at the rest of the room. They applaud and congratulate me after I vacate the podium.

Lola stretches out her arms to embrace the parent she's proud to call Dad. It's odd. I don't recall ever being this content during my active addiction . . . which means my disease is looking for a way to steal this moment. It is what it is. I give it a devious smile, knowing I have the tools to procure my power over this disease right back.

41

Do They Know It's Christmas?

Parenting is hard enough. I'm struggling to get by with what I make. The price of after-school care leaves nothing for a rainy day. The office staff at Lola's school helps me with filing for government assistance to see if I qualify for reduced-price meals. Because of the overtime I'm required to work, my monthly income is twenty-seven dollars above the poverty level, which means help is denied.

I could use some financial support. A single parent working full time has neither the availability nor resources to track down their child's Disneyland dad or Magic Mountain mom. Bringing the absent parent's imposed financial accountability to fruition is where the courts come in.

I ask my boss for a cost-of-living raise. He offers to lay me off. I give it serious thought, then pray.

Pride wants what it wants with only shortsighted immediacy. Mine doesn't want to look at the years it ran my life into desolation. Nor does it want me to see how depending on the system will, over time, hinder my growth.

Toughing it out is called for. How else will I learn integrity, other than by being honest, no matter how much strain it puts on my finances? As tempting as collecting a paycheck while staying home appears, I know better. Complacency lurks among idle hours.

I'm holding on to my job with everything I have. As Christmas approaches, melancholy comes—along with a reprisal. But as the sole parental influence on Lola's holiday state of mind, I have to stuff down my disadvantageous reality. I'm broke. Credit card spending isn't an option. I have a five-year-old to furnish *'Tis the Season* jolly for.

Necessity makes me part mother now. I tap into female energy to get inventive. Using construction paper, I create a fireplace backdrop for Santa to come down the chimney. Lola and I make cards, ornaments, stringers. We bake cookies.

I turn getting a tree into an adventure. We drive into the country to a place where you cut your own tree. There are reindeer and hot chocolate. Magical memories made for under twenty dollars.

On Christmas Eve day, Leann calls, wanting to spend the night so she can be with Lola on Christmas morning. It's the first time in weeks we've heard from her. I agree to pick her up at the light-rail station at 7:00 pm.

By 7:30 pm, I'm exhausted from taking Lola on short walks around the station. The rain is pouring. Sitting in the van with the heater on, I send a text on my pay-as-you-go phone. I don't know if I should drive back home or not.

I'm indecisive until 8:45 pm, when Leann arrives. She gets in and sits in the back seat with Lola. They carry on as if nothing is a problem. Lola's happy. I wish I had my child's ability to forgive.

"You could at least say you're sorry for being late," I blurt, interrupting their fun. Both stop talking. Lola's face seems to suggest she's proud of me for speaking up for us.

"Sorry," Leann says.

They play together in Lola's room. Fifteen minutes later, Leann runs to the bathroom. Through the bathroom door, I hear Leann choking back, then releasing vomit. She comes out, then beelines it back into Lola's room, closing the door behind her. Fifteen minutes later, this repeats.

I stop her when she comes out to see if she's okay. Within seconds, I spot it. She's dope sick—she's likely taken too much of something. I know better than to confront her. Not here, not now. For the next two hours, she's wilting near the toilet.

On Christmas morning, Lola's eyes light up at the sparse gifts under the tree with *From Santa* inscribed with penmanship that looks nothing like mine on them. The milk she left out on our table is gone, the cookies half-eaten. Only gnawed remains are left of the carrots for Rudolph and company.

Lola is loud and gleeful as she opens her presents. Leann is asleep on the futon through all of it. After breakfast, Lola shows off her gently used toys to her friends downstairs. Tuckered out from playing, she comes upstairs for lunch.

"Daddy, why does Momma come here to sleep all day?"

"Maybe you should wake her up, honey."

It's 1:30 in the afternoon. Leann is too hungover—beset by withdrawals—to function. She plows through disoriented actions with a goal I remember all too well: get up, get out, get loaded. Lola looks sad. Leann tells her she loves her but has to go.

To avoid a confrontation in front of our daughter, I wait fifteen minutes, then call Leann.

"Hey, Paul. I'm really busy. What's up?"

"I need to make this clear. I don't want an argument, or denial, because I know. Don't ever come over loaded or dope sick again, or you won't be welcome back. Do you understand?"

"Sure. Can I stop by tomorrow?"

"No. Not after that stunt you just pulled. No."

Without any real expectation of collecting child support, I want to see what will happen if I try. The amount of support owed is written in the divorce papers finalized months ago. It's a requirement by state law. Having never received a dime, I call the county office asking for my daughter's case to be set into motion.

As far as I know, Leann is living however she wants. Oregon state law does not allow a parent to terminate rights to their kid. If so, I would've offered Leann the option as an alternative to paying the mounting back child support. The system continues to fail my daughter left and right.

Through my advocacy plight, I find a disproportionate number of men who had their driver's licenses revoked, were fined, or ended up in jail because of failure to pay support for their kids, who, in many cases, they were denied access to. Why isn't my daughter's mom being penalized to the same degree? Leann gets food stamps, a bus pass, and college tuition—welfare benefits I've been denied.

Months pass before I push for answers. I am given a pitiless list of excuses for why my daughter isn't worthy of the district attorney's involvement in attaining her other parent's financial support. The Oregon office promises me repeatedly they'll get the judge to be stern. Hearing after hearing, support gets kicked like a dented can down the road.

I'm so busy taking care of the daily business of raising a kid, it'd be easier not to involve myself. So, I pray.

Then I read a short story about standing up for things you believe in. Because the story sort of fell in my lap right after I prayed, I trust it applies. I check my motives to see if anything is unbalanced. Am I holding a resentment? What's my incentive? Manipulation?

My answers feel self-determined, so I drop the idea. But the next day, a letter from Child Support Services arrives. The state is asking if I have new information to offer at an upcoming court appearance.

My sponsor tells me to talk to other mothers in the program who have experience in the arena of attaining support. I'm given a good schooling. Tugging heartstrings, an approach most men don't think of, is the most common response. One insists I mention Lola's tattered clothing. I disagree, fearful it will make my parenting appear inefficient.

Still, I don't feel right about forcing matters. I need to be certain I don't carry any secret expectations of "fixing" Leann. Threatening jail time or pressuring her to handle her responsibilities—none of these are within my control. What's most important is Lola. Who is her advocate, if not me?

The day of the hearing, I go in late to work to be on time for my kid.

Leann looks aghast when I walk into the courtroom. It's been months since we've seen each other. Since Christmas. Her absence has been rough on Lola. About six weeks after the last time her mom withdrew all contact, Lola was diagnosed with type 1 diabetes.

The legal aid representing the county approaches me. She tries persuading me to remain seated when Lola's case gets called. "The process will go favorably if you let us handle communication with the judge."

"I didn't drive across town to be silent. Maybe I'm being naïve," I state, making direct eye contact, "but I expect to contribute to the conversation today."

She rolls her eyes.

From the back of the crowded seating area where I sit, I wait, watching meticulously how the judge rules on each case. Leann looks over her shoulder more than once. My presence has her flustered.

Once our case is called, the judge asks if there's anyone here on behalf of Lola. I raise my hand. For some reason, I'm not called up to the front like every woman seeking support has been. I'm forced to address her honor across the entire courtroom.

"Make it quick, sir. What do you have to say?"

"Thank you, your honor. I'm here to advocate for my daughter who has yet to receive any support from her other parent. I would like to know when the state is going to hold her accountable for nonpayment."

The judge's demeanor, held stoic for the ninety or so minutes I've been here, changes in an instant. She glares at me with disdain.

"Sir! You cannot come in here and expect the state to bend to your wishes. We have been collaborating with Mrs. Summers to find a solution that works for her to pay her debt. You don't expect her to come up with the money out of thin air, do you?"

Amidst female laughter, my curiosity peaks. Why aren't the women here seeking support seeing how we are one and the same?

When a man doesn't step up for his kid, he's a loser. When he does, what is he? Let's see. By disparaging a male, this system is failing a female.

I won't have it.

"Okay, your honor. I have here," I hold up a manila file, "a folder *full* of letters from the district attorney denoting times the other parent was served." I take out the notices one by one. "Again and again, there have been orders to pay child support. Each time, according to these letters, when she has shown up for the hearing, the expectation is put on her again, and again it goes without being enforced."

"What exactly are you asking, mister?"

"Enforce what you say you're going to enforce." My tone slips, sounding more daring and combative than resolution-seeking.

"And what good would it do to put her in jail? Do you really think this will solve *your* problem? *You'll* never get a dime out of her if she can't work."

Did you say the same thing to every mom here seeking support from a deadbeat father? No! Why not? Don't you know statistically men are more likely to be incarcerated, pay higher child support compared to women, and receive less visitation regarding their biological children?

If only I had the balls to say this out loud.

"But she'll never bother to find work if she's not held accountable . . ."

Gasps fill the courtroom.

"Your honor, my little girl gets made fun of at school because her pants are too high off her feet. There are holes in her shoes. I can't afford new ones; she's growing so fast. She was just diagnosed with type 1 diabetes. The cost of insulin alone each month is more than the prearranged support amount. *Our* little girl has never seen a dime. I believe her mother isn't working because she has substance abuse issues. Maybe jail would help her. I don't know. I'd do anything for my daughter."

"I disagree with you, sir. However, I will do this." The judge turns to Leann. "Mrs. Summers, this court is ordering you to pay one hundred dollars by the end of the month, or Washington County will issue a warrant for your arrest. Is that clear?:

"Yes."

"Any reason why you would not be able to make that payment in this time frame?"

"No."

"Next case!"

Sometimes, even knowing I've done the right thing offers little relief.

As a man raising his daughter single-handedly, I'm a minority. This is no task for the faint of heart. It is, however, one of purpose. The more tired life makes me, the higher level of it I'm living and engaging in. Until the day comes when I know at my core I'm doing it for me, for all the healthy right reasons, I'm doing it for her.

Postscript: Who Can This Help?

As the loved one of an addict, you are as powerless, if not more, over the disease of addiction as the addict is. Please reach out for help for yourself to better understand the potential toll. Anonymous meetings provide a welcoming environment where you can listen. Helping someone is at times harder than being the person afflicted. They, at least, have a choice.

In order to walk the fine line between enabling and rescuing, do neither. Inaction is the most effective technique. Yet, because it seems like nothing is being done, it's a challenging strategy to implement. This is the hardest place for anyone who loves an addict to stay, and to stay sane. It feels like you're not doing enough because nothing's being resolved soon enough. But here's what you must hear: fixing is enabling. Rescuing diminishes one's self-respect. Neither work.

For every addict who acts on the premise they need to find recovery, there are scores who "visit" the programs available. Either to buy time, avoid prosecution, save face by pretending they have good intentions, or to lower their tolerance. Addicts will do anything to keep the consumption going. Likewise, when any person has the courage to turn away from the misery of active addiction, they are doing so with immense courage.

This disease encourages a type of Russian roulette excitement. It's not necessarily a junkie or a skid row bum who destroys everything around themselves. This disease does not discriminate. There are times I've wanted to protect myself from the pain of losing someone to this disease by insulating my heart with a buffer zone.

But I am those people.

Their misery, their drug-drowned decision-making, uplifts my cause to continue traversing the path I'm on. By their going out and doing the research, then reporting back by raising their hand at a meeting, they are helping me stay clean. I get to help another human, just as I was helped, by sharing what I've learned. Hate the disease, not the person afflicted.

Who can this help? This is the question.

Mykeal is one of countless people I've lost to addiction. His wife got away from the storm, which, as opposed to having to watch him die, was wise. There's nothing she could've done. At one point he accumulated a year sober but went back out and used. He left behind a little boy. I'll miss the spontaneous magic we created through making music together. It was hard enough losing friends while in active addiction. Now that I'm clean and sober, each loss is a tragedy that I know could've been avoided. Each loss hurts.

I've worked with family members of addicts along the way. Often, I am the first to explain to them how they are not to blame, no matter what—regardless of what the addict or alcoholic whose brain is clouded by denial and rationalization, tells them. It will be phenomenal if this book can save even a single life. If it can help the family and community attached to that person's behaviors, then more sense will be made as to why God saw my life fit to save.

I know with absolute certainty I would not have any of this without placing first the relationship I have with the God of my understanding. My way of life and thinking had to be changed from the inside out by letting an outside Power of my choosing in.

Finally, I'm blessed with opportunities to interact with addict parents. When they first get clean, the hardest thing for them to deal with is the painful guilt they feel the moment the numbing has been removed. Once that crutch is stripped away, reality sets in. There is an awakening that comes when we admit our powerlessness, accept who we have been, and allow what we can be. I'm proof.

Just ask my daughter.

Acknowledgments

My ultimate gratitude goes to God, the Higher Power of my understanding. Thank you for guiding me through the words and actions of others, giving me the courage to carry out your will, and trusting me to share the gift of hope and faith.

To my parents, Paul Sr. and Margaret. Not a day goes by without a memory of you both. It's debatable whether your parenting had something to do with how I ran amok, yet it absolutely has everything to do with the strength and courage necessary to tell this story. Thank you, Mom and Dad.

To my daughter, Lola. Thank you honey, for saving my life. However unwilling you might have been, you were there by my side through a few years of active addiction and many more of finding my way.

To my wife today, Jennifer. Thank you for your strength and devotion. Thanks for allowing space to breathe as an author and for believing in my ability to tend to our family while I do so. It is for my stepkids, Zoe and Evan. Thank you for sharing your time with my need to craft this book. For my kids, thank you for being patient with me and having faith that I'll always prioritize being the dad you need. To my stepkids, thanks for trusting me to be the male parent you never had.

To my Uncle John for showing me how a person can get sober. Thank you. I've often speculated that in your last breaths you knew you had won and went peacefully. Maybe all those forty-two years of staying sober *no matter what* was your final thought. This disease wanted to deprive you of all the joys of raising your little girl and of having a heart of art and love. I can hear you in your Italian New Yorker accent: "Don't thank me, Pauly, thank the program."

To my Auntie M who, in addition to unconditional support, showed me how you can set a boundary that just might help teach a loved one a healthy lesson.

To my ex-wife, thank you for finding me worthy of making a child with. The day you left with her was, in hindsight, the best day of my life. The only thing that saddens me as much as knowing I can't heal the pain of abandonment that will always waterlog Lola's marrow, is that you'll never know the earned blessings of parenthood. Yes, I am grateful to you for bringing the worst uncertainty into my life, for the challenge you gave me arrested my addiction. I only wish I could've done the same for you.

To the recovery community, both in meetings and on social media. Thank you for sharing your inner psyche with anyone who might be prepared to hear it and for having faith in our community that any one of us may create tools which will morph into solutions.

Lastly, to let the following know my gratitude for our meaningful connection: The Summers, Rood, Mckeen, Huff, Anderson, Griebel, Fouts, Gulbrantson, Duarte, Schwartz, Minster, Cameron, Zafuto, Hudak, Wadhams, Kramer, Chandler, Haviv, Mullen, Greco, Diemer, Brady, Whalen, Jones, Wells, Damron, Locatelli, Fredianelli, Vesella, Sakamoto, Ronca, Byzanski, Melancon, Hourcadette, Parkhurst, Sullivan, Guthrie, and the Taylor families.

To friends Wade, Danny, Ruckus, Sandy, Nick, Tony, Carol, Scott, John, Toy, Robyn, Iris, Jerry, Adam, Bones, Doug, Robin, Lisa, Jackie, Tina, Baxter, David, Gary Ham, the Acoustic Asylum and Consolidated Supply peeps, L.V.H.C., Las Vegas Punk Rock Museum and the strangers on the road who gave up a couch.

To literary mentors Cristin Iris, Nancy Karmiller, Kate Ristau, Candace Johnson, Jennifer Springsteen, Hermann Hess, and Anne Lamott, but mostly Linda Stirling, my publisher, for turning my mess into this message.

To musical/spiritual influencers R. Carlos Nakai, The Beatles, Led Zeppelin, Prince, Peter Frampton, Elton John, Jimi Hendrix, The Doors, Grateful Dead, Dead Kennedys, Black Flag, X, The Cramps, Tycho, Les Brown, Mel Robbins, Jim Rohn, Louise Hay, and Bob Dylan.

To recovery guides Matt J, Eric E, Jim B, Scott C, Tony W, Patrick B, Stacy R, Julie and Brian M, Paul J, Mary O, Gilbert S, Debbie G, Matt H, Misty T, Alex P, Bryce D, Jeanette L, Lori M, and Laurie M, Jimmy K, Bill W, and many more.

To my peers given up to addiction: Todd Sampson, Mykael Lundstedt, Harland Crowe, Jimi Hicks, Ted Goodman, Matt Rollo, Brian Bonds, Billy Thornton, Joey Corbin, Tom Lowy, Tim Wright, Rick Huff, (Screamin') Robin Freeman, Burt Turner, Hal Clark, and the Grecos.

To the families of addicts, thank you for reaching out. For those of you who've read a ton of books and watched hundreds of interventions and rehab stories and still don't understand the addict, thank you for being open to hearing from the horse's mouth. This book is written for you—those of you hunkered down in the trenches, been exposed to and often blamed for the atrocities of substance abuse; those who cope with the loss and insanity; those who grapple with unwarranted guilt; those who feel hopeless watching a loved one embrace a path akin to suicide. Death by overdose is not the same as suicide. It is avoidable. War, murder, tragic accidents—each can be dealt with as a human condition. But extracting a loved one from the disease described in this memoir is an exercise in futility. The loved one must find their own life worth saving.

Finally, this is for the addict. Though the drugs used, or degree to which we used and hurt those around us vary, you and I are one in the same. We suffer from distorted self-determination—unorthodox ways of dealing with our problems and ourselves. Not a day goes by that I don't pray for you.

Printed in Great Britain
by Amazon